The Secrets of Business Mastery

The Secrets of Business Mastery

Build Wealth, Freedom and Market Domination for your Service Business in 12 Months or Less

MIKE AGUGLIARO

NEW YORK

NASHVILLE • MELBOURNE • VANCOUVER

THE SECRETS OF BUSINESS MASTERY
Build Wealth, Freedom and Market Domination for your Service Business in 12 Months or Less

Published in New York, New York, by Morgan James Publishing. Morgan James is a trademark of Morgan James, LLC. www.MorganJamesPublishing.com

The Morgan James Speakers Group can bring authors to your live event. For more information or to book an event visit The Morgan James Speakers Group at www.TheMorganJamesSpeakersGroup.com.

ISBN 9781683503255 paperback
ISBN 9781683503262 eBook
Library of Congress Control Number: 2016917895

Cover and Interior Design by:
Chris Treccani
www.3dogcreative.net

In an effort to support local communities, raise awareness and funds, Morgan James Publishing donates a percentage of all book sales for the life of each book to Habitat for Humanity Peninsula and Greater Williamsburg.

Get involved today! Visit
www.MorganJamesBuilds.com

DEDICATION

To my Goddess, soul mate, and amazing wife, Jennifer. Every time I look into your eyes, I see us as kids. Every hug is as special as the first one. Thank you for your endless support. You show me so much love. Alongside every warrior man is a strong, supportive woman. You are my purpose, my inspiration, and my heartbeat. I love you with all my heart.

To my two wonderful kids, Michael and Katelyn, for showing me love and patience while I go away to learn, listen to books on CD while we drive, and be my silly self. You are both so gifted at what you both do and Dad is so proud. There are no words that can even get close to the love I have for you both. Every moment I have with each of you is a gift.

CONTENTS

ACKNOWLEDGMENTS

Thank you to my business partner, Rob, for being a best friend, business partner, and for allowing me to be who I am in business—the crazy driver. You have always had my back. The stories we have created and the stories we create every day are so special. Love the feeling that we are just getting started in the next levels of business magic.

Thank you to my parents, John and Lois Agugliaro, for showing me endless support and love under all situations with no judgments. You have both helped any time I needed it.

Thank you to Sensei Eddie Wnorowski for being a great friend and dedicated student. You have made me a better instructor.

Thank you to my great friends, Sameer and Joe ("Big Papa"), who have been there for endless feedback and ideas, and rooting for me in anything I am doing.

Thank you to Morgan James Publishing, especially Author Relations Manager Megan Malone and Acquiring Editor Karen Anderson.

FOREWORD

It is a pleasure for me to write this foreword for my friend Mike Agugliaro's book, *The Secrets of Business Mastery*.

This is one of few books that you can actually refer to as a "bible" of business success. You can open it and start reading it anywhere. You will immediately start to get ideas to increase your sales and profitability.

Mike explains throughout the book the importance of three key business principles (and many, many more!)

The first is *clarity*. You learn how to become completely clear in every part of your business—in your products and services, in your marketing and sales, and in every essential business activity. Clarity is probably 95% of success over the long term.

The second principle that underlies this book is *focus*. You learn to get organized, to set priorities on your expenditures of time and energy, and to keep on track without getting distracted from your highest paying business activities.

The third principle you learn is *concentration*. It has been said that concentration does not guarantee your success, but lack of concentration guarantees that you will fail.

In this book, you learn the all-importance of "task completion." You don't get paid just for working, but for completing your most important tasks on schedule. THIS is the key to your reputation as one of the best in your business.

Finally, there is *action*. As you read these great ideas, resolve to put them into action immediately. One good method or technique aggressively applied is more than 1000 that just sit there on the shelf.

Welcome to *The Secrets of Business Mastery*. You are embarking on a journey of greater business success than you ever thought possible.

Brian Tracy
Solana Beach, December 2016

HOW TO GET THE
MOST OUT OF THIS BOOK

You're reading this book because you want to grow your business. But reading is only part of the process. I want you to be inspired and fully engaged throughout the process of business growth so I've listed several steps for you below. Think of it as a curriculum to grow your business. Be sure to complete every step because they all work together.

1. **Read this book.** Actively read this book with a pen in hand and a pad of paper and sticky notes nearby. Underline key points; add a star or exclamation point in the margin when you want something to stand out to you. On the pad of paper, make a list of the actions you'll take.
2. **Complete the action steps.** Throughout this book I've included sections called "Take Action!" Watch for these and when you get to them, complete each action step. Do them immediately.
3. **Bookmark CEOWARRIOR.com.** You'll find a wealth of resources to help you, including a blog, my upcoming events, and videos.
4. **Sign up for the newsletter at CEOWARRIOR.com.** This is a must-read weekly email newsletter with powerful money-making strategies and tips.
5. **Get the free bonuses.** I reference several free resources throughout this book. You can download all of them at the resources page: **CEOWARRIOR.com/masteryresources**

6. **Connect with me on social media.** Visit **CEOWARRIOR.com** to find all the social media channels we can connect on, including Facebook, LinkedIn, Twitter, and more.

7. **Watch for my next Warrior Fast Track Academy**. Warrior Fast Track Academy is a popular 4-day event to help business owners achieve real change and real success in their business. I share all my best strategies and help you build a road map to implement them. Make it a priority it attend! Learn more at **WarriorFastTrackAcademy.com**

An important note about terminology used in this book: I started out as an electrician and built my business into multiple trade-lines. Then I helped other businesses in the home services industry (such as electrical, plumbing, and HVAC). Then I've gone on to help businesses in many other industries—from dog training to finance to consultants. The truth is, *every business is in the service business*—you may not offer home services like my company but you still serve your customers. So, as you read this book, don't become distracted by a specific reference to my electrical company or to a home service business and assume that those ideas don't apply to you. *All the strategies in this book apply to all businesses.*

INTRODUCTION

I Started In Business Like Many Others Have

Business mastery was not a target of mine when I first became an electrician. I wanted to be a good electrician and the owner of a successful business, but business mastery was not on my mind.

I started Gold Medal Electric with my business partner Rob and we steadily grew the business, experiencing successes and struggles that were similar to what many other service industry professionals face when they start and run their own businesses.

We learned "in the trenches." We worked 18 hours a day, seven days a week. Every morning before the sun came up we'd jump into our van and start working. We'd go non-stop for hours upon hours, taking a quick break for a meal (maybe!) before returning to work.

We were busy but it wasn't good. It was hard work. I often say that it was like a hamster wheel because we were running and running but not really getting anywhere. There was a limit to what we could accomplish because there simply weren't any more hours in the day.

One day my business partner came to me and said that he was leaving the business. He had simply burned out (and to be honest, I was feeling very similar). I thought about how much busier I'd be without him and that forced us to seriously consider whether we should just shut the business down entirely.

As we thought about the business, we talked about the problem: we were too busy and although that seemed like a good thing, running on the hamster wheel was no longer what we wanted to do. It seemed like we had two options: continue to burn out by running around without ever getting ahead, or, shut the business down.

But then I realized there was a third option. So I said to Rob, "Let's make a change... let's do it right." And since Rob knew I was not going to do this business alone, he had a change of heart on leaving. Who would know that my personal destiny and our business destiny would change forever?

It was a turning point for us. Instead of shutting the business down we rolled up our sleeves and tackled the problem. We gutted our business right down to the framework, much like someone would gut a house when renovating. Then we rebuilt the business from the ground up in a way that made sense; **we rebuilt our business to allow us to grow stronger and smarter** without pushing Rob and I to work 18 hour days to do it.

It's been said that successful business owners need to work "*on* their business instead of *in* their business." And this is exactly what we did.

We Changed Our Mindset... And That Changed Everything

Instead of running a two man business and trying to do everything ourselves, we hired employees, we developed processes, and we put ourselves into a management role instead of being the ones driving around in a van serving customers.

We worked *on* our business by developing a stronger, smarter business—one in which we would direct other people to work for us. We no longer worked *in* our business by driving around in that van from sun-up to sun-down!

This wasn't an overnight turnaround. We worked hard (sometimes 18 hour days!) but we had a new target in mind: we would no longer work 18 hour days as technicians but rather **we would structure a business using best practices of other successful organizations**. We looked beyond the service industry to see what other successful businesses in other industries were doing. We looked at Nordstrom and Disney and Zappos and other companies that were at the top of their game in their industry. We took the best practices they were using in their businesses and modeled them in our business in the service industry.

In short, we built a different kind of service business—one that wouldn't burn out its owners; one that WOWed customers so they'd call us back to do more work (and tell their friends about us); one that bucked all the preconceived notions that people have about service businesses.

It wasn't easy; it wasn't instant. But when the transformation took place it was profound; a huge improvement over what it was like before. (And, we continue to transform ourselves—it's a never-ending quest.)

Today (as of this writing) we employ over 190 people, we have over 140 trucks on the road, and we offer many different services to homeowners— electrical, plumbing, heating and cooling, waterproofing, drain cleaning, bathroom remodels, and more. We're also experts in generators, indoor air quality, water filtration, and more. We're the number one home service provider in Central New Jersey with over $30 million dollars a year in revenue.

What a turnaround from that moment when my partner and I felt burnt out and considered shutting the business down! I'm glad we found a third option.

I've Met Many People Who Are Just Like I Was

My experience as an overworked, stressed-out, exhausted electrician is not unique. The service industry is overflowing with tradespeople who are grinding it out every single day, getting up before the sun rises, tiptoeing out of the house before everyone else wakes up, putting in long, long days, and then tiptoeing back home because everyone has already gone to bed.

These same tradespeople are performing an essential service to homeowners in desperate need, but these professionals are doing so at a massive personal cost to themselves and their families. And I suspect that many people (perhaps even you) are getting sick of that hamster wheel—putting in those long days but never getting anywhere.

Maybe you have employees, maybe you're a one-man show; maybe you are brand new to the service industry, maybe you've been at it for decades; maybe you dream of running a small shop that serves a small local area, maybe you dream of owning a national chain serving everyone in America. Whatever your targets and dreams are, this book will help you step off of the hamster wheel and start making meaningful changes to help you achieve those targets.

At the end of the day, if you're able to improve your income, streamline some of the time-consuming aspects of your business, have happier customers, AND spend more time with your loved ones… what would that be worth to you? If you're able to dominate your market and achieve wealth and freedom, how much of a difference would that make in your life? Regardless of your targets, this book can deliver a business improvement that will translate into a significant business (and life!) improvement.

That's a bold promise but I can make it confidently because I first made this change in my own business—from the tiny two-man Gold Medal Electric operation to today's Gold Medal Service operation with 190+ employees. And once I understood what changes needed to be made and how to make them, I started helping others. Through a second business, which you can read about on my website **CEOWARRIOR.com**, I help other businesses—primarily in the service industry but also in other industries—take charge of their businesses and transform them. Through guidance, consultation, and real life examples from what I have done, I help business owners like you break free from the frustrating, limiting problems that hold you back; I help business owners like you start working on your business instead of in it; I help business owners develop mastery over their business so that they control their business instead of their business controlling them. I share my $30+ million dollar blueprint that I used to build my business and I can help you apply it in your business.

This book is all about business mastery—taking ownership of the business you already own!

Like a stagecoach from America's early history, your business is being pulled by several different horses, such as customers, finances, marketing, employees (if you have them), and more. Each horse wants to go in its own direction. And in most service businesses, they do go in their own direction, leaving you, the business owner, struggling to achieve your targets. The business mastery I teach will help you harness those horses together and get them moving in the same direction.

Business success does not have to be elusive. You won't get there by working harder. (When I was working 18 hours a day, I wouldn't have achieved what I've achieved by working a 19th hour each day!) Rather, it is achieved by the principles I teach in this book—business mastery in a few different areas of your business.

Each chapter is a collection of best practices focused on one particular area of your business. Part I of the book is focused on Inner Mastery—a few components that you need to transform within yourself first before you start making changes to the rest of your business. Inner Mastery is absolutely essential if you want to make positive changes that stick. (Skip this part of the book at your own peril because without Inner Mastery any other change is about as effective as slapping a coat of paint on a rotten wall).

Then in Part 2 of this book we focus on Outer Mastery by looking at the changes you need to make in your business. I'll address various components like marketing, sales, customer service, finance, and more.

Mastery Starts With Knowing Your Core 5

As you read, I want you to consider not just how the information will help you in your business but also how it can help your entire life. I believe business change won't be as transformational, effective, or long-lasting if you don't also make changes in yourself. I believe that the very best change—the change that you'll look at years from now and see it as a turning point in your business —starts when you look inward first.

Throughout this book and at my Warrior Fast Track Academy events you'll hear me talk about something I call the **Core 5**, or the **5 Dimensions of Life and Business Mastery**. These are five aspects of your life and business that will guide and inspire you toward success and these Core 5 (or 5 Dimensions) will be rewarded and enriched as you succeed.

The Core 5 are: **Belief, Relationships, Health, Wealth, and Freedom**. These are five equally important aspects of your life that give it meaning, fullness, and a sense of richness. Often, when people achieve success, it's because they understand these 5 Dimensions in their own lives and they've built a life and business that are aligned with each of the Core 5 (or 5 Dimensions). I'll briefly explain each one:

- **Belief** is your core of faith. It's your internal doctrines and principles. Not everyone has faith in a god or a higher power but everyone has belief in something. These are your central ideologies about your existence in this life.
- **Relationships** are just that—the connections you have with others. From your closest relationships (perhaps your spouse, children, and close friends) to your distant relationships (distant relatives, long-lost acquaintances), and everyone in between (employees, customers, vendors, friends). Growing the quantity and quality of your relationships helps you lead a richer life.
- **Health** is your personal well-being. It includes physical health, mental health, and emotional health. These are often ignored or deprioritized in favor of other aspects of life but if you want to have the energy to make positive change in your life and to enjoy the success that comes with it, you need your health.
- **Wealth** is, in financial terms, how much money you own or can create, which gives you a sense of safety and accomplishment, and which allows you to buy whatever you want whenever you want. You'll see me revisit this definition throughout the book.
- **Freedom** is having the time and money to do whatever you want without letting other parts of your life or business deteriorate. For example, freedom is the ability to step away from your business and take your spouse on a month-long cruise while having the confidence that your business will run with excellence while you are away.

Whether or not you realize it, these 5 Dimensions already exist in your life. How you define them right now will be the sum of what you've been taught and decided for yourself even since childhood. These 5 Dimensions make up the internal core of who you are, and all other changes in your life will be influenced by these 5 Dimensions and will influence them.

As you work through this book, I cover 12 areas of mastery in your life and business, one in each chapter. Each of the 12 areas of mastery covered in the following 12 chapters will draw from the Core 5 Dimensions of Life and Business Mastery and they'll contribute to each of these 5 Dimensions as well.

For example, your business contributes to all 5 Dimensions—often by giving you time and money to support those 5 Dimensions. (And, as a business owner, you have employees and vendors who rely on you to help them achieve fullness in the 5 Dimensions of their own lives.)

The more you understand what your 5 Dimensions are now, and the more you align your life and business to what these 5 Dimensions are for you, the more successful you'll be.

Don't worry if this is new to you. I'll explore this more deeply throughout the book and show you how all the pieces fit together. Just keep this concept of the Core 5 (or 5 Dimensions of Life and Business Mastery) in your mind as you read through the book.

I'll Show You How To Transform Your Business… And Your Life

I urge you to read through the entire book—don't just skip to one area of your business that you want to improve. Each chapter in this book provides one part of the picture and meaningful change doesn't happen by only working on one part of your business (just like you don't get in great shape by only working out one muscle-group). Go through this book chapter by chapter and make changes in your business. In the future, you can always go back and review one chapter from time to time to make adjustments but the first and biggest change should occur in all areas of your business.

As you go through this book, you're going to be exposed to new ideas—perhaps ideas that go against what you've thought, heard, or believed. You might learn about techniques that seem difficult or impossible for you to do, perhaps because you don't think your business is big enough yet or that you don't have the finances to make it happen.

These are limiting beliefs and if you go into this book with the walls of your limiting beliefs already set up then nothing I say in this book will have an impact on your business. However, **if you go into this book thinking, "I'll accept that what Mike is saying is possible and I need to keep an open mind and figure out a way to do it," then you'll increase the likelihood of success... even if you're not yet 100 percent sure how you'll achieve it.**

Limiting beliefs hold us back by destroying our ability to believe that we can do something. When we were children we had no limiting beliefs, but as we got older we adopted more and more of them. For example, we learn limiting beliefs like "money does not grow on trees" or "it takes money to make money." Neither of these are true. We learn so many limiting beliefs as we grow up, yet they do nothing but hold us back from achieving our full potential.

Do whatever you can to eliminate your limiting beliefs—they do not benefit you! I actively eliminate my limiting beliefs through exercises like the firewalking and breaking arrows. I've walked across blazing hot coals and not burned my feet because I believed I could do it (while others, who had limiting beliefs, either couldn't walk across the coals or, when they did, they burned their feet). And I've pressed sharp arrows up against my neck— normally these arrows would pierce the skin and cause serious injury but I believed that they wouldn't harm me, and the arrows broke instead of piercing my skin. Your belief systems will determine how much you take from this book and apply to your business and how well you succeed because of them. As Henry Ford said, "Whether you think you can or you think you can't, you're right." Go into this book thinking you can.

At every Warrior Fast Track Academy event I hold, business owners tell me that they like what I have to say but something holds them back from achieving success (they often blame their finances or their market or their business partners or how hard it is to find the right employees). It's not until I open their minds and reveal to them that it's really their own limiting beliefs holding them back that they see massive change start to happen. Commit to yourself that you will no longer be limited by these beliefs, and as you read through this book I'll show you how to destroy these limiting beliefs and replace them with bold, business-growing action.

This Book Is An Action Guide (Emphasis On "Action")

One more thing: I am a martial artist and instructor, and I teach martial arts to others. If I only told my students how to perform a particular punch or kick or blocking move, their effectiveness at performing that move when it mattered would be minimal. Hearing how to do something is only part of the education. I tell them and I show them and then they practice it over and over until it becomes second nature. Only then does the move become an effective martial arts tool for them to use when they need it.

Likewise, many readers will be tempted to read this book and then put the book on the shelf; and then a year or two will slip by with no significant improvement in the business. Reading about how to make the change will not create transformation. **Action creates transformation**—doing the right actions at the right time. As you read through this book, I've included many places where you can immediately take action, so be sure to work through each action step.

In each chapter I have included Take Action sections where I encourage you to pause in your reading and actually turn your reading into action. Each Take Action section contains some of my recommended action steps that you should implement, as well as space for you to add your own actions. Specifically, there are areas to write **actions you will stop doing** (actions you currently do but need to cease), **actions you will keep doing** (actions you currently do now and should continue), and **actions you will start doing** (actions you don't do now but should begin). I've also included space for you to make a note about **when you'll make these changes** and **who might help you do them** (for example, you might delegate to an employee or you might ask someone to hold you accountable to complete the step).

I also recommend that you do your own due diligence and talk to licensed professionals who understand you and your business before making any significant changes. Make sure that the actions are right for your business. Check with your lawyer to ensure that you are following all laws before using any of the ideas in this book. Check with your accountant to make sure that any new idea you implement works with your financial and tax situation.

This book is an investment: perhaps you paid a bit of money to own it and you'll invest a bit more time to read it, and I hope you'll invest a bit more time to make the changes. **The return on your investment can be staggering and it has the potential to improve your business, your income, the lives of any employees you have, and the lives of your family.**

There's a saying that goes, "When the student is ready, the teacher will appear." If you're ready, turn to Part 1 and I'll show you how to master your business and change your life.

INNER MASTERY

Accelerating your business to a higher level starts with you.

In Part 1 of this book you'll learn how to accelerate yourself to a higher level by mastering yourself. Once you've built a strong foundation in yourself, you'll make far more effective, longer-lasting changes in your business.

You opened this book expecting to read about how to transform your business. But then you saw the title of Part 1—"Inner Mastery"—and you're wondering when I'm going to address the business stuff.

I'll get to it, I promise.

But first we need to work on you. I don't say that to be disrespectful to you. Rather, I say it because I know from first-hand experience what you're going through (I was once in your shoes, and today I help other business owners who are currently facing the same challenges you're facing). And I know that there are changes to be made in your business... but I also know that those changes won't take hold if we don't first do some work on you.

After growing my own business yet watching so many other people struggle with growing their businesses, I realized that many people were focusing first on their businesses instead of themselves. However, the better approach is to look inward first and master your own personal growth. When you do that, you'll find business growth will be so much easier.

I promise this isn't fluffy stuff. Real change starts inside and flows out from you. When you start by mastering yourself, mastery of the world around you becomes faster, easier, more effective, and longer-lasting.

Plus, people tell me all the time that the changes they made in their business were good and profitable and highly beneficial, but the changes they made to themselves were profound and far-reaching. I love hearing feedback like that because it confirms my own experience: businesses come and go but true enjoyment of life happens when you are in control of yourself—when you answer only to yourself.

That's what Part 1 is all about: wrestling control of your life back to you again. It's about saying "stop!" to all the different ideas and dreams and demands and responsibilities that are competing for your attention, and then figuring out what really matters.

This isn't just painting over a rotten wall; we're going to tear down and rebuild, transforming your inner self, which will make your business transformation in Part 2 so much better.

Remember the Core 5 (or 5 Dimensions of Life and Business Mastery) that I mentioned earlier? Each of the chapters in Part 1 will help you to understand what your 5 Dimensions are and will help you to align your life with your 5 Dimensions.

CHAPTER 1

MASTER YOURSELF

Want to achieve more in your life than you ever dreamed possible? In this chapter you'll find out step by step how the world's most successful people reach the top of their game.

Introduction

If you look at the most successful people in business, you'll find that they all have one thing in common: no, they aren't born with an extra measure of skill or luck. Only a few inherited the wealth or genetics that put them in the position they enjoy today. Instead, the most successful people in business are masters of themselves.

Before they went out and achieved business mastery, before they created successful businesses, they looked inward and achieved personal mastery. They envisioned greater things for themselves; they were highly motivated to get what they desired; they were highly disciplined to do the work that needed to be done; they chose to succeed and pushed through all obstacles to get there; and they had accountability to see it through to their targets.

The starting point for these people's achievements was not just a desire to be successful but a crystal-clear understanding of who they are and what they want, a willingness to do what it takes to get it, and then they took action. Only after they did the hard work of mastering themselves did they go out and achieve the success they wanted by mastering their business.

For that reason, this chapter is going to be the most important chapter you'll read on your pursuit of success. Some people will skim this chapter or even skip over it, racing to the chapters about how to succeed in their business—those skimmers will focus in on one specific area of their business while thinking to themselves, "I'll deal with the personal stuff later." But I can tell you from personal experience and from observing many other successful people and from helping many business owners get to a new level in their business, that skipping this chapter will reduce the effectiveness of the lessons in the other chapters.

I use the analogy of putting together a puzzle. If you skip this chapter, it's like trying to put together a puzzle with all of the pieces turned upside down so you can't see them. But if you read through this chapter carefully and follow each of the exercises I've described, you'll put together the puzzle of business success with all of the pieces turned so you can see them.

Give this chapter the attention it deserves. Although you should read all the way through the book, I advise most people to spend 90 days working on chapter 1—giving it your deepest focus. This will create the strongest foundation. Master yourself first and then turn your attention to your business and you will transform your ability to succeed beyond your wildest dreams.

We're going to start your journey toward personal mastery by talking about your dreams in life, and then we'll translate those concepts and ideas and aspirations into a solid foundation on which you'll build the rest of the skills explained in this book.

Start With A Dream Of What You Want Life To Be Like

You can only get somewhere if you know where you want to go. When you go on a trip, the very first thing you do is determine the destination! The destination is the target—it's where you want to go.

Then, and only then, do you pull out a map and figure out how to get there. But when it comes to our lives, most people ignore the destination, or they don't even bother thinking about it, or they have a vague idea of what would be nice but they never go deeper. Only those with a clear, detailed dream and a highly-committed decision will ever achieve "success" (no matter how they're defining that term). Everyone else will wander around without any idea of where they really want to go. It comes down to two things: Desire and Choice.

Desire is the drive you have to want something. **Choice** is your decision to go get it. Many people vaguely want something more in life but their desire is not strong enough, nor is their choice to get it strong enough. **Only those who deeply want something bad enough, and then choose to act every day, regardless of the obstacles they face, will achieve their targets. Business owners who have achieved wealth and freedom have done so because they treated their targets like oxygen (so important that they'd die if they didn't reach their targets).**

For example, being a millionaire is a choice. Some people might say that genetics/background or education are determining factors of success, and I agree that those elements can play a part. But in my experience, genetics and education each only contribute about 20% to determine whether or not you will become a millionaire. The other 80% is entirely your choice. If you are not a millionaire, you have chosen not to be (whether you realize you made the decision or not). And let's move beyond the idea of being a millionaire to other aspects of your life as well: your happiness, health, relationships, and lifestyle—from the car you drive to where you go on vacation to who your spouse is—it all comes down to your desire to have a certain quality of life and then your choice to go out and get it.

I want you to start by thinking about what you want in life; specifically, what you aspire to be and what you want to do. I don't just mean in business (we'll get to that later) but in life in general.

I firmly believe that we need to start with the bigger whole-life picture because people who try to achieve success in business, but who don't first totally figure out what they want in life, will struggle to get what they want in business and, if they achieve it, they won't feel fulfilled, happy, or have a sense of congruence with their Core 5—Belief, Relationships, Health, Wealth, and Freedom.

To put it into different terms: when you build a house you start with the foundation. **Build a strong foundation and the rest of the house will sit sturdily on that foundation.** Fail to build that strong foundation and you'll struggle with building the house (and once built, the house won't be very safe). Additionally, building a foundation that is too small will limit the size of the house you can build on top of it. Similarly, personal mastery through understanding what you truly want in life is that foundation.

So, what do you want to be and what do you want to do in life? Let your imagination run free as you think about that question. Consider everything you've ever dreamed of. Reach back into your memory to your childhood. What did you dream about doing when you thought excitedly about being an adult? Think back to your teen years when you wished you had the time and money to do all that fun stuff you wanted to do. Recall your early adulthood, and perhaps your early married life, when you (and your spouse) dreamed big.

Over time our dreams tend to be dampened; they grow faint because of our daily responsibilities and commitments that keep us from achieving them. Here's just one example: we put aside our dreams of an amazing vacation to make sure the kids have new shoes for school. There's nothing wrong with doing this; that's the responsibility that parents accept. But I want you to understand that you can do, have, and be whatever you aspire to… without giving up your responsibilities and commitments.

So, take a moment now and think about your dreams—the big dreams and aspirations you've always had, even the ones that seemed unachievable.

What we're doing is really tapping into what you already believe about your Core 5—your 5 Dimensions of Life and Business. You're reaching into your inner self (sometimes the part that gets locked away because of the busyness and day-to-day responsibilities you have) and you're re-accessing that part of you.

If you need some help thinking about your dreams, think about the Core 5: What beliefs and ideals should define your life? What do your perfect relationships look like? What would perfect health look like for you? What does wealth look like for you? What does freedom look like for you? Write this down in detail.

And, to get more specific, here are some other questions to answer: What does your perfect day look like? When would you wake up? What would you do throughout the day? Who would you do these activities with? Where would you go? Write it all down in detail as if it were in a planner.

And, think about your perfect week, your perfect weekend, your perfect month, and your perfect year. Consider what you would do if money and time were no obstacle. (I mention these two things specifically because money and time are often the two big obstacles that people feel hold them back from achieving their dreams). Write all of those "no-holds-barred" dreams down.

Specifically, I want you to think about wealth and freedom. Wealth is the money you own or have the ability to create, which provides you with a sense of safety and achievement, and which gives you the ability to buy what you want when you want it. Freedom is having the time and money to do what you want while having the confidence that the rest of your life won't diminish or go off-track even though you're not focusing on it.

Now here's a critical point to make: **You need to define what wealth and freedom mean for you. When you define what they mean for you (no one else can define what wealth and freedom mean for you), and when you build them into your vision for the life you want to live, you can structure the rest of your life around creating wealth and freedom for yourself.** This is a powerful concept that I'll revisit throughout this book.

To help you go deeper in this exploration of your ideal life, I want you to build a mind-map. A mind-map is a free-form way to gather your ideas together quickly and comprehensively into one place, and associate those ideas with related ideas. While a list is linear and can sometimes be limiting, a mind-map frees you to brainstorm and make connections.

A mind-map looks a lot like a web, with many ideas branching out from a central point. Write the main idea in the middle of the page and then, as you think of new ideas, draw a line from the main idea and add the new idea at the end of that line. You'll end up with several ideas radiating out from the central idea.

Here's how to build your mind-map: on a blank piece of paper, write the word "Me" in the middle. Then branching out from that, write the words "relationships," "business," "money," "spiritual," "hobbies" and whatever other categories are relevant to your life.

Push yourself to think of all the categories you want to include. Your mind-map might look like this (I've just used four ideas radiating out from the central point; you will probably have many more):

Money
|
Business – [Me] – Spiritual
|
Relationships

Once you have several categories radiating out as a first level from the central "Me," then it's time to build from these categories by writing down specific dreams for each one. For example, under "Money" you might write "I want to be a millionaire" and under "Relationships" you might write "I want to take my spouse on an annual luxury Caribbean cruise."

Draw a line from the appropriate category and write the new dream in. Here's my example mind-map with the two dreams added.

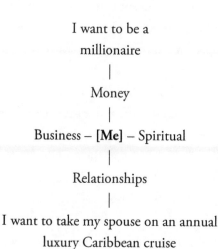

I want to be a
millionaire
|
Money
|
Business – [Me] – Spiritual
|
Relationships
|
I want to take my spouse on an annual
luxury Caribbean cruise

From each of those radiating ideas, write specifically what you want to achieve in each category. You'll probably have several items for each category, so you might end up with a 5-10 categories (I've listed relationships, business, money, and spiritual) and 1-5 dreams branching out from each category.

If you need some help thinking of specific dreams, I'll give you some ideas that are frequently quoted by people, just to prime your pump. Use these to inspire you and place them in the categories in your mind-map:

- "I want to take my spouse on a long Caribbean vacation"
- "I want to pay off my mortgage"
- "I want to restore the same kind of car I owned when I was a teenager"
- "I want to donate more money to a worthy charitable cause"
- "I want to spend less time at work"
- "I want to reconnect with my siblings"
- "I want to spend more time at the golf course"
- "I want to own a vacation home"
- "I want to take care of my parents in their retirement without making too many financial sacrifices"
- "I want to take more time off and spend it with my kids before they go off to college"
- "I want to make enough money to be able to send my kids to any college they choose and not have to rely on student loans to get them there"
- "I want to be a millionaire"

The list could go on and on. I've primed the pump to get you thinking about what you want to do and what you want to be. Take some time to do this exercise. Take as long as you need and don't worry how long it takes. Set aside time in a quiet place to work on this. The more you spend on this, the better. By the end, you'll have anywhere from half a dozen to a couple dozen specific dreams that you want in your life.

But it won't necessarily be easy: as you go through this exercise, I suspect you'll encounter something that most people encounter when they do this exercise—your inner critic. Your inner critic is that devil on your shoulder that says, "You can't do that." Or "It's not possible."

You need to resist this inner critic and I hinted at the reason earlier in the chapter: the reason is that you need to first desire something (such as the list of dreams you've started dreaming of) and then you need to make the choice to do them. **The only way you'll achieve the life of your dreams is by going out and getting that life yourself. No one is going to hand it to you; you need to go take it for yourself.**

How will you achieve these dreams? It doesn't matter yet. (We'll get to that later in this book. In fact, the rest of this book is really about how to help you fulfill these dreams). But first you have to make a choice.

Whatever excuses or reasons or obstacles or challenges you face— you need to desire your dreams more strongly than the strength of the problems you face, and then you need to choose to work through those problems to achieve what you want to achieve.

I'm going to repeat that and I want you to take a moment to think about it: you need to desire your dreams more strongly than the strength of the problems you face, and then you need to choose to work through those problems to achieve what you want to achieve.

It doesn't matter whatever is "handicapping" you—whether it's something physical or mental or a bad choice you made in your past. Your life's dreams are within closer reach than you realize and you can achieve them (even if you don't think you can right now).

It's entirely your choice. If you dream something and don't achieve it, you've unconsciously chosen not to achieve it. **Dream big for a life that you truly want to live, and then make the choice to go get it.**

Take Action!
Recommended actions (add a checkmark beside each one when complete):

__ If you haven't finished the exercise in this section, finish it now. Take as long as you need and make as big of a mind-map as you can, listing everything you want in life. Remember to be detailed and to articulate your dreams as clearly as possible. Keep pushing away that inner critic and focus on what you want to do and what you want to be, not on what that inner critic thinks you can or can't do.

__ Schedule time to revisit this exercise regularly (perhaps quarterly or even monthly) and update this mind-map whenever you think of something else.

__ Create a "stop doing" list of all the ways that you subvert your dreams. Perhaps you tell yourself that you'll never achieve them, or maybe you have a family member who takes pleasure in telling you that you don't deserve the fortune you aspire to have. Add all those things to the stop doing list and remove them from your life.

Add your own actions (add a checkmark beside each one when complete):

__ Stop doing actions (Actions you currently do now but should stop doing)

_____

_____

__ Keep doing actions (Actions you currently do now and should keep doing)

_____

_____

__ Start doing actions (Actions you don't do now but should start doing)

_____

_____

__ Who will do new actions? (Assign the action to yourself or someone else)

_____

_____

__ By when? (When will these actions be complete?)

Build Your Personal Vision, Purpose, And Core Values

You've always had dreams and aspirations for your life, but there's a good chance that you've never before taken the time to sit down and articulate them as clearly and deeply as you just did. These dreams will inspire and motivate you as you work toward achieving them—and you'll enjoy so much more satisfaction in life as you achieve each one.

Dreams aren't the only things that you probably haven't articulated. You also have a vision, purpose, and core values, too, even if you've never articulated those either.

You've probably heard of vision, purpose, and core values before. The concepts aren't unique to me. They are the very essence of a person; the inner drive that gets each one of us up in the morning and helps each one of us to make decisions throughout the day. They keep each one of us focused and moving forward.

A vision is what you see occurring in your life. Your purpose is the reason why you want it. And your core values are the "lane markers" that help you stay focused on achieving your goals. I'll talk more about these in this section of the chapter.

Everyone has a vision, purpose, and core values already, regardless of whether they've thought about them—everyone has them but they let whims and trends and other people decide for them. But, just like my approach with all other aspects of life and business, I believe you need to take control of these and master them. Own them in your life and be intentional about them. When you take this approach you take control of your life. Master them or something else will master you. The fact is there will always be a destination, just maybe not the one you wanted.

Everyone has a vision, purpose, and core values, and when they realize the importance of determining these components, people roll up their sleeves and start defining these for themselves. However, all too often, people develop their vision, purpose and core values in a frenzy of self-improvement and they fail to connect them to real life and to actionable ideas. That's where my approach is a little different. In this section, you'll build off the exercise you did earlier to create your own personal vision, purpose, and core values; however, you'll do so in a way that is fun and memorable, that is truly tied to you (no external purpose is forced on you, for example) and my method below naturally leads to action.

You can identify a dream (as I showed you earlier in this chapter) but we all know that life isn't always simple and the path to success is never a straight line. What happens when we're faced with difficult choices? What happens when the details of everyday life threaten to cloud your aspirations? What happens when the journey becomes difficult? A clearly defined vision and purpose and core values keep us motivated and inspired, they help us make decisions, and they help us stay strong when challenges and obstacles threaten to prevent us from moving forward.

Your vision, purpose, and core values need to be clearly defined because that's the only way you can stay on target to achieve the dreams you listed earlier. Too many people who say they have a dream or vision really don't. What they have is a vague notion of success—"I want to make a lot of money" or "I want to have a successful business"—and they fail to define it clearly enough. There are problems with this approach: it's not very inspiring (not nearly as inspiring as, for example, "I want to have $10 million in the bank") and it's too hard to achieve because without a specific end-result you can't lay out a proper plan.

Earlier in this chapter you've put together a list of all the things you've dreamed about doing and being in life. I hope it's a big list that you find inspiring (even if you're still skeptical about how you'll achieve it all). Some of those dreams might occur sooner, others later.

Now I want you to work with that list and get even more specific. Using that list as a starting point (plus adding anything else you might think of along the way), I want you to answer this question: "If I had a magic wand and could cast the perfect life for myself, what would it look like in three years?"

Craft a description of what your perfect life would be like in three years. Chances are, a good portion of that list of dreams you created will be accomplished or will at least be underway. Write out this three-year "magic wand" description of your life in whatever way is most comfortable for you—either in paragraph form or as a list. But here's what is important: you need to be absolutely clear and ultra-specific. By the time you're done crafting this description—this "personal vision" of your perfect life three years from now—I want you to be able to see, taste, touch, and smell every detail.

So if you want to take your spouse on a month-long luxury Caribbean cruise every year, I want you to be able to see the gorgeous blue water as it flows past the cruise ship; I want you to be able to smell the salt water; I want you to be able to feel the ship gently rocking; I want you to be able to hear the water and the shouts of delight of other vacationers, and the cabana music in the background. Get detailed. Get specific. And "live it" in your imagination.

Warning: this might feel weird for you. As children, we had active, fertile imaginations and used them all the time. But then the reality of adulthood hit and we put our imaginations away. But your imagination is not just a childhood plaything—it's a tool to help you achieve your dreams. Let it out and let it run wild.

Do this rich imagining exercise for every single one of those dreams from your mind-map. Literally "live" each one in your mind.

As you start to think deeply about each one, pull out that mind-map you created earlier and add pictures to it. Cut out pictures from magazines and paste them on your mind-map. For example, if you want to spend more time with your spouse, find a picture of a couple walking hand-in-hand on the beach and cut it out of the magazine and paste it onto your mind-map. If you want to take a Caribbean cruise, find a picture of a cruise ship and cut it out of the magazine and paste it onto your mind-map.

By doing this, you are combining two powerful tools—a mind-map and a vision board. A mind-map is where you gather your ideas together and a vision board is where you envision these ideas for your life. This becomes something I'll call a "vision mind board." This at-a-glance tool connects your initially vague ideas to specific images—both the images you're living in your imagination plus trigger images on this mind-map.

This is your personal vision. It's a clear, vivid, memorable, and inspiring word-picture of what your perfect life is going to look like three years from now.

And while you're doing this exercise, let me also point out: it needs to stretch you a bit. Some people are quite happy with where they are in life and they can't see themselves doing much more in three years than what they're doing now. If you're in that situation, I want you to think even harder about what could be. I have never met anyone who didn't have at least a few areas of their life that they realized they could improve.

The next step is to craft your purpose; what some people call your "life's purpose". The vision you've just created is the "what" you want in your life. It's what you aspire to achieve in life. But behind it is a reason that you're doing it. What is that reason?

To continue with the Caribbean cruise example, it's likely that you're doing that because you want to make your spouse happy and give them something they've been dreaming of, and you want to give it to them as a thank you for supporting and loving you all these years.

Behind every single one of your perfect life dreams lies a purpose; a motivation. As you look at each of your dreams, pull back the curtain and try to spy out the motivation behind it. (Hint: it's probably related to your 5 Dimensions of Life and Business Mastery).

I'll help you understand how your vision and purpose fit together by talking about when humankind started trying to land on the moon. **The moon itself was the vision—the perfect future we wanted to achieve by safely landing there and returning back. The purpose behind it was any number of things—from achieving political dominance in the race to land there, to push science beyond the confines of earth's gravity, to learn something about ourselves, and perhaps even to see if there was other life out there!**

See how the two work together? The vision describes what you want and the purpose is the underlying reason. Now think about your purpose by reviewing your perfect life. You'll likely come up with a list, perhaps a dozen ultimate reasons that you want these dreams. Some common examples include:

- Be a better spouse
- Be a better parent
- Be generous
- Leave the world in a better place for the next generation
- Enjoy life a little after several years of hard work and sacrifice

Then gather those motivations together and synthesize them—this will become your purpose. Combine common ones together. You'll probably end up with three to six of them that drive all of your dreams. Revise this list into a statement—a brief paragraph that summarizes your purpose.

Here are my personal purpose statement and my business purpose statement to give you a couple of examples: my personal purpose is to change the next ten generations of my family, making every generation more of a leader and entrepreneur and able to understand balance and how to create wealth and freedom. My business purpose is to create a movement and change the life of every service business owner so they can have more wealth, freedom, time with their family, and be appreciated in an industry that makes a difference in our comfort and safety and in how we live.

The final step in this exercise: your personal core values. Core values are the parameters that you want to live within. They're like the lines on the side of the road that guide you to live in a way that you feel good about. Your core values are the things you want people to say about you after you die; they're the things that should mark your life.

Many people think of their core values as their ethics, and ethics will certainly play a role in determining your values. However, ethics are only part of the picture. Your core values also bring in your emotions and attitudes, and they list out the things that you think are more important than anything else. These are the "non-negotiables" in your life that must be present in absolutely everything you do or you won't feel good about that particular action or decision.

Build a list of three to five core values that you want in your life. These will help to guide you when things are going great and especially when things are not going so great.

Here are a few core values to get you thinking about them:

- Integrity
- Generosity
- Optimism
- Fairness
- Hard work
- Serve first
- Balance
- Courage
- Clarity
- Accountability
- Freedom
- Wealth
- Leadership
- Mastery

This is just a small list but there are many others. Think about what core values must always be present in your life.

(I hope by now you're seeing how this information not only draws from your Core 5 Dimensions of Life and Business Mastery but also feeds it, sometimes articulating what we've always believed or perhaps correcting and realigning it to where you'd like your 5 Dimensions to be.)

Take Action!
Recommended actions:

__ Craft a vivid, inspiring vision for your perfect life three years from now. Be clear and very, very detailed. Go through each of the dreams you listed that you can see becoming a reality within the next three years.

___ Write a paragraph describing your life's purpose. Remember: this is the "why" and it probably combines several motivations that drive your dreams.

___ Create a short list of three to five core values that must always be present in your life. These are the non-negotiables that may be a combination of ethics, emotions, and attitudes.

Add your own actions:

___ Stop doing actions (Actions you currently do now but should stop doing)

_____

_____

___ Keep doing actions (Actions you currently do now and should keep doing)

_____

_____

___ Start doing actions (Actions you don't do now but should start doing)

_____

_____

___ Who will do new actions? (Assign the action to yourself or someone else)

_____

_____

___ By when? (When will these actions be complete?)

_____

_____

Create A Plan To Achieve Your Personal Vision

A dream is great to have... Unless it only ever remains a dream! There are a lot of people who have thought about their dreams or aspirations—at least vaguely—but they're so caught up in just trying to get through the day-to-day grind that their dreams remain dreams. Unfortunately, many people stop there and they join the ranks of the disappointed—people who are dreamers but who never become doers. Their dreams remain wishes, not targets. What kind of life is that? When you're drawing your last breaths, surrounded by loved ones, and thinking about the life you lived, do you want it to be filled with thoughts of "I wish I had..." or do you want it to be filled with thoughts of "I'm glad I did..."?

Your dreams need to be deeply felt; they need to be inspiring. They need to jolt you awake in the morning and compel you to jump out of bed and get to work, motivating you to work tirelessly throughout the day to achieve them. And when you fall back into bed, exhausted at the end of the day, you need to feel that you moved closer to achieving them. (Please note: I'm not advising you work longer hours in your business. That's not very healthy. In fact, I hope you get to the point where you do just the opposite. Rather, I'm advising you to work long, hard hours on achieving your dreams. See the difference? Working smart, not hard, and working on achieving your dreams, not on business survival, is what this book is all about).

In order to make sure your dreams are deeply felt, you need to spend time thinking deeply and emotively about them. Look at your vision mind board and connect each of those individual dreams to a positive emotion. As you "live" each event in your mind before it happens, don't just watch it passively as if it were a movie in your imagination but experience it emotionally as well. For example, imagine the happiness you'll feel spending more time with your family; imagine the pride you'll feel as you see your children graduate debt-free from the college of their choice; imagine the excitement you'll feel as you watch the money in your bank account increase; imagine the happiness your spouse will have when the two of you are walking hand-in-hand around the deck of a luxurious cruise ship at sunset.

I hope you are perceiving how important I think this step is. I believe that you'll struggle achieving your dreams if you don't have that vivid passion for them. But I'm also a practical person and I think you are too. And I don't really think that you can just sit back and wish for something and it will magically appear. I think you'll agree with me when I say that we need to go out and get what we want (although I've asserted throughout this chapter that we have to first know in detail exactly what we want).

So, now that you have your vision mind board clearly laid out, it's time to take those dreams and do something with them.

On a separate sheet of paper, or better yet, a spreadsheet on your computer, put your list of dreams into a sequence. List them in order from the ones you're farthest away from (or the ones that seem least likely to be achievable to you right now), all the way to the ones that you are really close to achieving already. I advise people to start working on the "sickest" or most distant dreams first. That doesn't necessarily mean you'll achieve them first (you will probably achieve some of those closer ones first).

Once you have them listed in this order, then beside each one I want you to write down some type of measurement—some way of knowing whether or not you have achieved it. You'll need to track your progress to determine how you are doing so make sure you are using specific measurements (because only specific measurements are trackable).

For example, if you want to spend more time with your family in the evening after work, doing activities with them instead of watching television, you should track the number of hours each week that you are doing something together. Or if you want to take your spouse on that month-long Caribbean cruise you've always dreamed about, you may want to measure the amount of money you need to have saved up before you can buy the tickets. Or if you want to have a million dollars in your bank account, you need to measure how much money is there at a specific time each month.

To track effectively, you'll need your beginning measurement (where you are right now as you are doing this exercise) and then your ongoing measurement that you update regularly. This is why I suggest you use a spreadsheet so that you can record month by month or week by week (or whatever frequency your updates are) to see how you are doing.

Your vision mind board and your list of targets with measurements is now a crystal-clear roadmap to what you need to do in life to fulfill your dreams.

Don't worry about how far away some of these dreams are. Even if they are years away, that's okay. Just create your map and start working toward it. You know what you want to achieve and you have the measurements to indicate whether or not you're there.

Just by doing these two things, and nothing else in this book, you will completely transform your life. I promise you that if you have a vision mind board and a spreadsheet in which you are tracking your progress on your dreams, you will vastly increase the likelihood that you'll achieve them.

Here are ways to help you embed these ideas into your life:

- Use apps on your smartphone to keep all of these items at your fingertips so you are always reminded of them.
- Share your targets with everyone so your friends and family can encourage you and hold you accountable.
- Write your targets on sticky notes and put them up on every mirror in your house so you'll constantly see them. Your sticky notes should say: "I will get [target] by [date]," such as, "I will have $3,000 saved up to buy Caribbean cruise tickets for my wife and I by November 1st."

I want to make it even more inevitable that you'll achieve your aspirations. I'm going to push you to go even further: take each of those targets in that spreadsheet and list out the steps necessary to achieve them. In my experience, most targets are multi-step activities. You don't just go on a Caribbean cruise, for example: you need to save up the money, find the time to go, choose which cruise line to take, make sure your passports are in order, book the tickets, and so on. You'll need to list out each of those steps in the order you need to take them.

Be detailed and make sure that each item is a real action you can take (rather than a generic or non-specific idea).

Once you have that list, schedule time to do them. Don't miss this part. Put that list into your schedule so that you set aside the time to do it. Don't skip this part because it's the difference between your dreams remaining dreams and those dreams becoming reality.

The people who attend my Warrior Fast Track Academy tell me that this is one of the most profound and powerful exercises we do because it reignites their passion for their business and their life. They share that it's so easy to get pulled into the day-to-day details of running a business but when they look at their dreams and build a vision mind board, they gain a new level of purpose and motivation. You'll discover this too. Suddenly, you'll wake up every morning excited to tackle the day because each day brings you closer to achieving your dreams.

Take Action!
Recommended actions:

___ Add deeply felt emotion to your vision and repeatedly review your vision in your mind.

___ Craft a vision mind board with pictures that represent your dreams.

___ Create a spreadsheet with each of your targets and add a specific, trackable measurement for each one.

___ Break out each target into actions that you can perform in the order they need to be accomplished.

___ Schedule those actions into your planner right now, (even if it means planning a few weeks or months from now).

___ Schedule time regularly (usually weekly or, at the latest, monthly) to revisit this spreadsheet and update the steps and the measurements.

___ Find a mentor to hold you accountable to your action items. This is a proven way to fast-track your results.

Add your own actions:

__ Stop doing actions (Actions you currently do now but should stop doing)

_____

_____

__ Keep doing actions (Actions you currently do now and should keep doing)

_____

_____

__ Start doing actions (Actions you don't do now but should start doing)

_____

_____

__ Who will do new actions? (Assign the action to yourself or someone else)

_____

_____

__ By when? (When will these actions be complete?)

_____

_____

Getting Things Done

You've determined where you want to go in life and how you want to get there. Now there's one more piece of the puzzle to get this plan out of your head and into reality: you need to take action. You need to put legs to that vision and get things done.

Life is already challenging with the commitments and responsibilities that so easily overwhelm us, so if you don't force yourself to take action on your dreams every day then you'll fall into the same trap that so many people face—their dreams just slip away. Imagine how much easier it is to get up in the morning and know exactly what you need to do today to help you achieve that inspiring dream you've envisioned for your life. No guesswork.

No false starts. No detours. Just an exact, step-by-step action plan that you do to move forward.

That's what you've put together in an earlier section of this chapter: a step-by-step action plan. You turned your vision into a sequence, and then assigned a measurement to each one, and then you created steps for each of those dreams, and then you put those dreams into your planner.

But there's still one step between those dreams and your reality: taking action—doing the steps you've planned, when you planned to do them. Getting them done (while also doing all of the other things you need to do in your life).

Getting things done is not a just a time management issue. We'll talk about time mastery in an upcoming chapter. Rather, getting things done is a personal management issue, which is why I'm talking about it now.

You see, many people make the mistake of putting something into their calendar or planner and their brain gives them a feeling of completeness of the task even though the task itself has not been accomplished. If you want to get things done, you need to be disciplined and persistent at taking action every time you need to take action.

Treat every action you need to take as if someone was holding a gun to your head; treat every action you need to take as important as breathing. (In other words, view each of those actions as if you'd suffocate and die if you don't do them). Think of them as being life-or-death actions. That's the best way to ensure you'll get these things done and, although it takes some hard work, it's also the fastest way to achieve your dreams.

Be accountable to yourself and remember that you don't live in a vacuum. Other people are relying on you (your family, your employees, etc.) and your action—or inaction!—affects them. This level of accountability requires a brutal daily honesty with yourself in which you stop blaming others and you start accepting responsibility for everything you are responsible for. One way to help you stay accountable is to join a mastermind or coaching program to help you stay on track and to provide an external source of accountability.

If you've been grinding it out every day, trying to keep your head above water, your dreams have remained in the background. Let me ask you this:

how are you serving your family and yourself by playing small? Doesn't it make more sense to master yourself and achieve your dreams? It does when you realize that by playing bigger than you have been, you can serve others to a greater degree than you've been serving them so far. Dreaming of your success is not selfish! Your success has positive spin-off results to your spouse, your children, their children, your employees, your employees' families, your vendors, your vendors' families, and so much more.

Along the way, you'll encounter roadblocks and obstacles and challenges. That's okay. Expect it and even embrace it. Remember: if achieving our dreams was easy, everyone would have already achieved all of their dreams. But achieving dreams is not easy. Life's road is full of unexpected detours. Your effort to work toward your dreams is best done by staying flexible and positive, by working tirelessly on each of those scheduled steps until they are complete, and to always, always, always come back to your personal vision—that vision should motivate and inspire you. It should fuel your daily effort and reignite your passion when you are faltering.

Remember that you never have to do it alone. This journey toward your success is not a road you have to travel by yourself. The vision you've created of your perfect life impacts other people so include them. Ask your family, friends, employees, and peers to hold you accountable for the actions that impact them.

And remember this: even though these are your dreams and this is your life, you are not blazing a new path. Many before you have worked to achieve their dreams... And succeeded. Learn from them. There's a saying that goes, "Success leaves clues". When other people are successful, their success provides clues that you can follow. You do not have to reinvent the wheel! Many others have walked through the same journey as you are walking now. Take advantage of their struggle for success by learning from them. Tap into resources like mentors, coaches, consultants, and transformers to help you.

I can't think of a better investment of time or money than to get these seasoned experts to guide you. Mentors are those who have experienced what you have experienced and can guide you by showing you what to do. Coaches can help guide you too, but they also provide some third party accountability to keep you on track. Consultants can even help you as you work on some of your actions, or even do some of those actions for you. And there's a group of people I call "business transformers" or "life transformers" and they have the skill sets and knowledge of all three—a mentor, a coach, and a consultant.

Take Action!
Recommended actions:

___ If you haven't done so already, schedule the actions you identified earlier in the chapter into your planner.

___ Schedule periodic reminders to yourself to "check your head" and make sure that you are accepting full responsibility for your success. Use these times to get on track if you've allowed old habits to rear up and distract you.

___ Get the "stakeholders" in your life—your spouse, children, friends, employees, business partners, etc.—to hold you accountable for taking action on the targets that impact them.

___ Get a mentor, coach, consultant, or business/life transformer to help you take clear, specific actions and to hold you accountable.

Add your own actions:

___ Stop doing actions (Actions you currently do now but should stop doing)
_____
_____

___ Keep doing actions (Actions you currently do now and should keep doing)
_____
_____

___ Start doing actions (Actions you don't do now but should start doing)

_____

_____

__ Who will do new actions? (Assign the action to yourself or someone else)

_____

_____

__ By when? (When will these actions be complete?)

_____

_____

Conclusion

People sometimes struggle to succeed because they think there's a secret ingredient or trick that they just haven't discovered yet. But this is a "lottery" mentality—they think they will eventually strike that hidden jackpot and everything will come together. But the truth is: there is no other secret than what I've written here.

Articulate your dreams for your life—dig deep into your memory and your aspirations to list all of the things you desire. You can have them!

Create a vision, purpose, and core values. Your vision will inspire you with specific targets to work toward; your purpose will remind you of the reason(s) why you have these dreams in the first place; and your core values will keep you working toward the right things and keep you from straying. Living a life with these components in place is freeing and dramatically transformative.

Turn your vision into something you can feel and see with a vision mind board, then convert those dreams into actionable, measurable targets that you can track on a spreadsheet.

Take responsibility for yourself and your future and act every day toward the achievement of your dreams. And, remember that you don't do any of this alone. Get the help of friends and professionals.

Follow the steps. Take action over and over. You'll elevate your life to a point that few people ever achieve: you'll see the complete fulfillment of your greatest wishes, dreams, and aspirations.

It all starts with mastering yourself.

Master Action List For Chapter 1

At the end of each section of this chapter you had actions to perform as well as Start Doing/Keep Doing/Stop Doing lists. Gather those actions together into a Master Action List, add any new actions that you think of, and then go through the questions below to think about how these actions can transform your life and your business:

__ **Is it going to make me money?** Are the actions you've listed going to help you generate more income? (If they are, great. Think about how they might be able to help you generate even more income. If they aren't making you more money then are those actions really as important as you thought they were?)

__ **Is it going save me money?** Reducing how much you spend will help you increase your profit. Are the actions you're thinking of doing going to help you cut back on your expenses without sacrificing the quality of your service? (If they save you money, great. If they aren't saving you money then are those actions really as important as you thought they were?)

__ **Is it going to save time?** Your time is precious and scarce. So the actions you take should help you to save time. Keep the big picture in mind because some actions may take a few extra minutes in the short term but will ultimately help you save time in the long term. (For example, training an employee might be an action that will take a few extra minutes now but will save you a lot of time in the future).

__ **Is it going to help me achieve market domination?** Your business needs to own the market it works in. Whenever someone thinks of the service you provide, they should only think of you. Do the actions you've listed in this chapter support that market domination? What can you change about them to help you dominate the market even further?

__ **How do I start fast to get the low-hanging fruit?** It's easy to say you're going to take action but it's much harder to actually do it. One way to take action and push through to its successful completion is to go for the quick wins—the low-hanging fruit. From the actions you've listed, what low-hanging fruit can you immediately pick?

__ **What's the leverage?** Leverage has a few different meanings but, in this context, I'm talking about how you can motivate yourself. For example, if you commit to complete an action within a certain period of time you can leverage that commitment by saying, "If I don't make that commitment, I'll donate $10,000 to a charity." Since you may not have $10,000, and you'll probably feel some pain donating that much money, you are leveraging your commitment and compelling yourself to complete the actions you said you'd complete.

__ **What's the reward?** For each action, list what you expect to get out of it. If you can't think of a reward for the action, seriously consider whether it is as valuable as you thought. Spend more of your time on actions that have rewards. Two of the best rewards for your actions are below (although there are other rewards you may choose to take action for)…

__ **Is it going to help me achieve wealth?** One of the best rewards you can take action for is to achieve wealth. For each action ask whether that particular action will help you make more money to give you the sense of safety and achievement and allow you to buy whatever you want whenever you want it. If possible, develop the action even further if a stronger, clearer, bigger action will help you achieve more wealth.

__ **Is it going to help me get more freedom?** Another one of the best rewards you can take action for is to get more freedom—the time and financial capacity to do whatever you want whenever you want to (without sacrificing your business). For each action ask whether that particular action will help you get more freedom. If possible, develop the action even further if a stronger, clearer, bigger action will help you get more freedom.

CHAPTER 2

MASTER YOUR RELATIONSHIPS

You don't live in a vacuum. You're surrounded by people—family, friends, employees, vendors, customers, and more. Most people just let these relationships happen on their own, but someone who wants to achieve more in life and business will master their relationships to give more to others and get more from others.

Introduction

Humans are built to be in relationship with others. Even if you're not the most outgoing person, even if you've always been shy or a bit of a loner, you still have valuable relationships that feed your life: immediate family, extended family, friends, vendors, employees, customers. These are the key relationships in your life. Treat them well and they will make your life rich and memorable. Ignore them or take them for granted and you will deal with stress and conflict.

Imagine if you could view the earth from space. You wouldn't just be looking at individual people going about their lives in solitude. You would see cities—a bunch of people in proximity, living, doing business, and interacting. If you could build imaginary webs linking people together, you'd see an amazing explosion of global interconnectedness as people connect with friends and family; with employees, customers, and vendors; with those they meet by chance or those who just happen to be at the gas station or restaurant at the same time. It's complex, and each of those people are connected to others with equal complexity.

There is interconnectedness between humans, and actions that one person takes affect other people. For example, I had a guy who worked for me by cleaning my company headquarters office building. He cleaned my building for over 13 years. When he worked for me, he was no less important than anyone else in my life. If the garbage overflowed and the bathrooms were dirty, these would affect all of us who relied on the clean building to allow us to do what we needed to do. And the wage we paid him to clean our building paid for a roof over his family's head and gas in the car and food on the table. And that money from us, through him, went to other people—like the farmer who grew the food in the first place. We're all interconnected.

It's not surprising, therefore, that the 5 Dimensions of Life and Business Mastery includes relationships as one of its key components. In this chapter I want to show you that the interconnectedness between us creates invaluable and exciting opportunities if we treat those relationships well.

Analyze Your Relationships

Show me the five people you spend most of your time with and I can tell you with great accuracy what you'll be like in a couple of years. People have a profound influence on us, not only with the things they do and say but also in the quality of our relationships with them. Unfortunately, too many people just accept their relationships without thinking about them. I urge you to analyze your relationships to determine how they are influencing your life.

What you will read in the next paragraphs is going to feel uncomfortable; even jarring. And some of you will be tempted to skip this chapter because you don't feel that you can change your relationships, and perhaps you don't even want to analyze your relationships for fear of what you'll find.

But if we are going to be honest with ourselves, and if we want even the faintest hope of achieving our targets, the first thing we need to do is to take a cold, hard look at the people we have relationships with.

Take stock of the people in your life. Start by thinking about the people in your life: get a blank piece of paper (you might need a lot of paper!) and list them out by name. Here are some relationship categories to help you think of specific people in each one:

- Immediate family (spouse, children)
- Extended family (parents, siblings, in-laws, etc.)
- Friends
- The people you think are your friends (like your social connections on LinkedIn, Facebook, Twitter, etc.)
- Colleagues/associates (such as those you might know from the gym or from a club membership or a charitable organization—people who you might not define as "friends" but who you value)
- Personal vendors (such as your barber, stockbroker, dry cleaner, etc.)
- Professional vendors (such as your suppliers, janitorial service, accountant, etc.)
- Employees
- Customers

Most of us are connected, on average, to at least couple hundred people within our "immediate circle" (those listed above). Of course, if you pushed the circle out even further and considered those you might not come into contact with as regularly (cousins, old classmates, distant friends, and past employees) the list grows even larger. But let's just start with the list you've created above because these are the people that have the greatest influence on you, and the people you have the greatest influence on.

Once you've listed them, beside each name, write down how they contribute to your life and how you contribute to their life. Move beyond the obvious: customers don't just provide money; they provide you with a means to fulfill your dream as a business owner and they share their positive experience of you with family and friends. You don't just pay vendors, you feed their families. There is a higher purpose and you need to consider what it is for each of the people you've listed.

I'll warn you right now that this could be one of the hardest exercises you may do in this book because we sometimes do not want to be honest about the value (or lack of value) that others give to us and, perhaps more alarmingly, the value (or lack of value) that we give to others.

Here's what you'll find: relationships only contribute to you at the same level or less that you contribute to them. In very few cases will you find someone contributing more than you do (usually a parent or spouse, but that's it). So if you want to improve the relationship with any of the people you've listed, raise your level of contribution in their life and they'll probably raise their contribution to you. I'll talk more about that in the next section of this chapter but here's an example: I've delivered support, help, and guidance to others without asking for anything in return. The way you behave is the way they will behave in return. (If they don't then it stands out.) When you're aligned and you're working to serve others, they want to serve you in return.

And we may have to be brutally honest about the people that we shouldn't be connected with. Your analysis should identify people who are constantly negative, and people who are so-called "yes men" (who agree with you no matter how bad your ideas). Neither of these people provide good value to you, and they likely never will. You may need to remove them from your life permanently.

Take Action!
Recommended actions:

___ If you haven't completed the exercise from this section of the chapter, do so now. Take the time to list all of your relationships and analyze them based on what you contribute to others and what they contribute to you. It will feel uncomfortable but you will be amazed at what you learn about yourself and others. (And remember that the five people you spend the most time with will reflect what you are like in the next few years.)

Add your own actions:

___ Stop doing actions (Actions you currently do now but should stop doing)

_____

_____

__ Keep doing actions (Actions you currently do now and should keep doing)

_____

_____

__ Start doing actions (Actions you don't do now but should start doing)

_____

_____

__ Who will do new actions? (Assign the action to yourself or someone else)

_____

_____

__ By when? (When will these actions be complete?)

_____

_____

Growing Your Relationships—Quality Plus Quantity

You've spent time analyzing your relationships and determining who has the greatest influence and contribution in your life, and what kind of contribution you add to other peoples' lives. If you just stopped here, your relationships would stagnate and your life would stagnate, returning to the same level it has always been.

But by analyzing the relationships you have and honestly assessing their contribution to your life and your contribution to their lives, you have valuable information to help you build better relationships. And that's what you want—better, richer, deeper relationships.

Sometimes that might mean contributing to your existing relationships at a higher level. Sometimes that might mean eliminating certain relationships from your life altogether. And, sometimes that might mean intentionally forming new relationships. As an example, I started attending a business meet-up group because I wanted to meet people who thought like me and were motivated like me, and who I would not feel strange around or who would not stare blankly when I talked about business. (I ended up meeting one of my best friends, Sameer, at this group). If you want to do something similar, my Warrior Fast Track Academy events are a great way to build relationships with business owners who share your desire to grow in business.

And you not only want to build great quality relationships but you also want a greater quantity of relationships. **A higher quality of relationships and a higher quantity of relationships will provide you with a richer, more meaningful life.** (I'm talking here about all relationships: from rekindling old friendships to developing new relationships with people).

Let's talk about what to do with the relationships you want to grow. Start by asking yourself these three questions about the list of relationships you created in the earlier exercise:

1. **What can you do in the near future to add to each person's life?** Consider how you can selflessly improve your contribution to that person (without necessarily expecting anything in return—because those who truly care will reciprocate). Remember to think more deeply than just a transactional level. As a reminder: your employees are serving you so they can get paid to feed their families—so how can you contribute to them in a way that helps them with that deeper purpose of providing for their families?

2. **How do you deepen the relationships you have?** Along with contributing to the people you're in a relationship with, consider how you can deepen your relationship with them. This does include adding value, as I've discussed, but it also includes learning more about them and becoming more interested in their interests. No, you don't have to go to all of your employees' kids' soccer games from now on but you should at least know that your employees are out there cheering their kids in soccer after spending the day working for you. Ask them about it and pay attention to their answers.

3. **How do you increase the number of relationships that need to be increased?** Not all of your relationships can or should increase in quantity. (You don't need another dry cleaner or barber, and your spouse will kill you if you try to increase that relationship in quantity!) But some

relationships can and should increase—specifically, your customers and employees. Each of these requires a plan to increase in quantity. A little later in this book we'll talk more about it but as you read this book multiple times in the future you should arrive at this section and be reminded that you need to increase the number of relationships in some situations.

Once you've asked these three questions about the relationships on your list, create an action plan around this, identifying specific action steps you can take with each person. For example, as you list the most important, most contributing relationships in your life, consider what specific actions you can take to improve the quality of those existing relationships, and also list actions you can take to improve the quantity of the right relationships.

Then, schedule those action steps into your planner so that you do them.

As you can see, these concepts have a direct connection to your Core 5 (5 Dimensions of Life and Business Mastery)—we're learning and articulating these 5 Dimensions but we're also creating actions to strengthen or even realign these aspects of your life.

Take Action!
Recommended actions:

__ Determine specific action steps you can take to increase the quality of your existing relationships and the quantity of relationships in your life. Be specific!

__ Schedule these actions in your planner.

Add your own actions:

__ Stop doing actions (Actions you currently do now but should stop doing)

_____

_____

__ Keep doing actions (Actions you currently do now and should keep doing)

_____

_____

__ Start doing actions (Actions you don't do now but should start doing)

_____

_____

__ Who will do new actions? (Assign the action to yourself or someone else)

_____

_____

__ By when? (When will these actions be complete?)

_____

_____

Improve Your Life By Improving Your Relationships

We cannot get through life without being in relationship with others. Therefore, **if you want to improve your own life, you need to improve your relationships.** Too many people make futile efforts at improving some aspect of their life (their health, their finances, their business, etc.) but fail to realize that positive changes in relationships will have farther-reaching effect.

For many relationships, improving the relationship means contributing more and getting constant feedback that will help you add even more value to the relationship. But for some relationships, it may mean accepting some uncomfortable truths—such as the need to end some relationships and the need to be fully honest with the person you're in a relationship with. You will be tempted to skip this section but if you commit to working through it at as truthfully and as thoroughly as possible, this section alone will have a shockingly positive transformation in your life.

Constant feedback is absolutely essential in other areas of our lives: the gauges in our car give us constant feedback about how our vehicle is operating. Our business' financial statements give us constant feedback about how our business is operating. Regular check-ups from the doctor and dentist give us constant feedback about our health. Even the bathroom scale gives us constant feedback about whether or not we're mastering our appetite.

We rely on constant feedback in other areas of our lives so it only makes sense that we would also rely on constant feedback on our relationships—one of the most vital areas of our lives. But few people go out and actively seek this feedback because few people want to know the real truth about how they're doing in their relationships. But if you solicit feedback, gain valuable information, and then act on it, your relationships will improve and that will have an immediate, positive impact on your life.

Soliciting feedback is easy (and, as long as you are providing value and contributing selflessly to the relationship, it won't be painful). It should be done through formal and informal surveys.

Survey your family—your spouse and your children. Survey your team. Survey your customers. These are the most important groups. You may end up choosing to survey other groups as well, including your friends and extended family, but if you start with your immediate family, your team, and your customers, the feedback you get will make a profound difference.

For your team and customers, a slightly more formal survey is helpful, giving them the chance to think about and write down their answers, although a face-to-face or over-the-phone survey might be appropriate. For your family, something less formal is probably appropriate. Take each person out individually for coffee and ask them questions.

Ask these people to be as honest as possible and commit to hearing their answers and not judging them. Your survey questions for each group are going to be generally the same—just three simple questions. You want to ask them:

- What is going well?
- What is not going well?
- What can I do differently or better?

As you get feedback, be willing to accept their answers. Take responsibility and don't get defensive. If they give you feedback, don't respond defensively by saying, "that's not true!" Remember that their answers are from their perspective and although you might not like what they have to say, they have perceived something about the relationship that they would like to see improved.

Instead of judging or becoming defensive, take responsibility. Don't be afraid to apologize or take ownership. Accept their feedback and commit to addressing it.

In particular, watch for feedback that is consistent. For example, if one person gives you feedback that you are late to meetings then be extra mindful of your promptness when you meet with them. But if many people tell you that you are late for meetings, you might need to make a deeper change in your life to ensure that you are on time consistently.

Take Action!
Recommended actions:

__ Develop gauges in your life to receive constant feedback. Regularly survey family and friends (informally, of course) and regularly survey employees and customers (formally) to receive constant feedback.

__ Avoid the temptation to push back when you hear something you don't like. Instead, take it to heart and remember that it is the other person's perception. Even if you don't think it accurately describes you, it does describe what the other person thinks so it should still cause you to think about what could change in your life.

Add your own actions:

__ Stop doing actions (Actions you currently do now but should stop doing)

_____

_____

___ Keep doing actions (Actions you currently do now and should keep doing)

_____

_____

___ Start doing actions (Actions you don't do now but should start doing)

_____

_____

___ Who will do new actions? (Assign the action to yourself or someone else)

_____

_____

___ By when? (When will these actions be complete?)

_____

_____

Dealing With Conflict

We are all interconnected but everyone is unique. That means conflict is inevitable. Every relationship will face some conflict at some point, and that's okay. Unfortunately, most people view conflict as a negative. They see it as two opposing views that cannot exist at the same time. However, that is not true. Conflict doesn't have to be bad or have long-term negative consequences.

To draw an example from nature, consider a forest fire. Nothing better describes the chaos and difficulty of conflict better than a raging forest fire, ignited when lightning strikes a dry area. But environmental scientists will tell you that a forest fire, when naturally ignited is a positive thing (I'm not talking about when a careless smoker throws their cigarette butt out the window). Forests need forest fires to clear out an in-grown, overly-dense forest and to make room for a strong, well-nourished new forest.

Likewise, positive conflict in relationships helps to clear out misconceptions and wrong-thinking and makes room for stronger growth. And, in some cases, conflict ends relationships that need to end, and that's sometimes a good thing. Therefore, even though conflict seems uncomfortable, conflict doesn't have to be bad. Don't avoid conflict.

This is an excellent point to illustrate how critical it is that we align our lives with the 5 Dimensions of Life and Business Mastery: The quantity of our relationships doesn't give us a life of fullness. If that were the case, we'd simply just go out and meet as many people as we could. Rather, it's healthy, mutually-beneficial relationships that give us a life of fullness. Therefore, when those relationships are in discord and conflict, they're out of alignment. That's why dealing with conflict is so important: it helps to put the relationships in our lives back into alignment with the Relationships Dimension of the Core 5 Dimensions.

I'll show you how to navigate your way through conflict to turn it into something positive that can grow the relationship.

First, address conflict head-on. If you detect some discomfort between yourself and someone else, don't let it fester and grow worse. Call it out. Say something like, "I sense that there is an issue that is causing some discomfort. I'd like to address it so that it doesn't turn into a larger issue."

Second, during conflict, listen. Listen closely. When the other person is speaking, try to look past their emotions to the facts. Remember that perceptions are everything, so even if the facts say one thing, someone's interpretation (perception) of the facts may influence how they feel. Listen carefully without interrupting and let them say everything they need to say. Prompt them to continue if they pause. Many conflicts could be cut off before they become worse if one person was able to fully air their feelings. Sometimes even just the speaking of the issue out loud is enough to solve many conflicts.

Remain carefully in control of your emotions. Even if the other person is becoming increasingly upset, do not allow yourself to be dragged into a yelling match. You are in control of your own emotions but if you descend to the other person's emotional level, you are giving control of your emotions to them. Make the conscious decisions not to. As you listen to them, and as you prepare to speak, always be careful to separate fact from feeling. Stick to the facts because facts are incontrovertible.

Third, when it is your turn to speak, respond politely and firmly. If you need to tell the other person that they are wrong, carefully explain how the facts are wrong—be careful that you don't imply that they or their feelings or perceptions are wrong.

As you speak, avoid logical fallacies to support your position. If you want to become better at conflict, learn about logical and rhetorical fallacies like relying on anecdotal evidence, using "the straw man" in your argument, mistaking correlation for cause, and many others. These fallacies are often used as desperate crutches during conflict but they are ineffective and they weaken your position.

And, don't ever back down from the truth. Too many conflicts are allowed to persist because someone preferred to take the easy way out. It is better to tell a hurtful truth than a comforting lie. All a comforting lie does is put the conflict "on pause" until it becomes worse.

Conflict seems uncomfortable so many people avoid it, ignore it, or let it build up before it explodes. But a person who has mastered themselves and their relationships embraces transparency and doesn't fear conflict. Instead, they tackle it head-on, dealing with it when necessary.

Take Action!
Recommended actions:

__ Retrain your brain to accept conflict as a good, healthy part of a relationship.

__ Learn to navigate through conflict firmly, responsibly, and gracefully, using the process I've listed above.

__ When you are alone, practice responding to typical conflict-starting statements you might hear. For example, if you often hear something from an employee or customer that gets your heart racing and your defenses up, role-play the conflict in your head ahead of time using the approach I've outlined here; practice a calm approach to the conflict in your mind before dealing with it in person.

___ Study logical and rhetorical fallacies so that you can become better at conflict.

Add your own actions:

___ Stop doing actions (Actions you currently do now but should stop doing)

_____

_____

___ Keep doing actions (Actions you currently do now and should keep doing)

_____

_____

___ Start doing actions (Actions you don't do now but should start doing)

_____

_____

___ Who will do new actions? (Assign the action to yourself or someone else)

_____

_____

___ By when? (When will these actions be complete?)

_____

_____

Conclusion

As humans, we are interconnected. We depend on others and they depend on us. Our relationships form a complex web, which means that our choices and actions influence the lives of others—and vice versa. Therefore, someone who has mastered themselves and wants to live a fuller, richer life needs to also master their relationships.

Invest the time to analyze your relationships and seek to add to the quality of your existing relationships and to the quantity of your relationships.

By understanding and adding value to others, you will enjoy more meaningful relationships. By seeking ongoing feedback from the most important relationships in your life, you'll have an easy way to ensure that you are adding the best value you can. And, by dealing with conflict fearlessly whenever you need to, you'll minimize the negative consequences and enjoy even deeper relationships.

After you've mastered yourself, mastering your relationships is essential to mastering all other aspects of your life.

Master Action List For Chapter 2

At the end of each section of this chapter you had actions to perform as well as Start Doing/Keep Doing/Stop Doing lists. Gather those actions together into a Master Action List, add any new actions that you think of, and then go through the questions below to think about how these actions can transform your life and your business:

___ **Is it going to make me money?** Are the actions you've listed going to help you generate more income? (If they are, great. Think about how they might be able to help you generate even more income. If they aren't making you more money then are those actions really as important as you thought they were?)

___ **Is it going save me money?** Reducing how much you spend will help you increase your profit. Are the actions you're thinking of doing going to help you cut back on your expenses without sacrificing the quality of your service? (If they save you money, great. If they aren't saving you money then are those actions really as important as you thought they were?)

___ **Is it going to save time?** Your time is precious and scarce. So the actions you take should help you to save time. Keep the big picture in mind because some actions may take a few extra minutes in the short term but will ultimately help you save time in the long term. (For example, training an employee might be an action that will take a few extra minutes now but will save you a lot of time in the future).

___ **Is it going to help me achieve market domination?** Your business needs to own the market it works in. Whenever someone thinks of the service you provide, they should only think of you. Do the actions you've listed in this chapter support that market domination? What can you change about them to help you dominate the market even further?

___ **How do I start fast to get the low-hanging fruit?** It's easy to say you're going to take action but it's much harder to actually do it. One way to take action and push through to its successful completion is to go for the quick wins—the low-hanging fruit. From the actions you've listed, what low-hanging fruit can you immediately pick?

___ **What's the leverage?** Leverage has a few different meanings but, in this context, I'm talking about how you can motivate yourself. For example, if you commit to complete an action within a certain period of time you can leverage that commitment by saying, "If I don't make that commitment, I'll donate $10,000 to a charity." Since you may not have $10,000, and you'll probably feel some pain donating that much money, you are leveraging your commitment and compelling yourself to complete the actions you said you'd complete.

___ **What's the reward?** For each action, list what you expect to get out of it. If you can't think of a reward for the action, seriously consider whether it is as valuable as you thought. Spend more of your time on actions that have rewards. Two of the best rewards for your actions are below (although there are other rewards you may choose to take action for)…

___ **Is it going to help me achieve wealth?** One of the best rewards you can take action for is to achieve wealth. For each action ask whether that particular action will help you make more money to give you the sense of safety and achievement and allow you to buy whatever you want whenever you want it. If possible, develop the action even further if a stronger, clearer, bigger action will help you achieve more wealth.

___ **Is it going to help me get more freedom?** Another one of the best rewards you can take action for is to get more freedom—the time and financial capacity to do whatever you want whenever you want to (without sacrificing your business). For each action ask whether that particular action will help you get more freedom. If possible, develop the action even further if a stronger, clearer, bigger action will help you get more freedom.

CHAPTER 3

MASTER YOUR HEALTH

As you journey toward success you'll want to give yourself every advantage possible. One of the best advantages you can give yourself is to master your health—to achieve a higher level of health and well-being so you can operate at a higher level. The benefits will impact all areas of your life!

Introduction

Life is already busy enough and it's not going to lighten up any time soon. A lot of people are relying on you to think quickly and act forcefully at any given moment. You'll also find that the more successful you are, the more you are called upon to perform at peak levels—for longer and with the expectation of greater results. If you want to reach those levels of peak performance, you must be healthy.

Health is easily ignored for the sake of the busyness of life. When our schedules are packed full of activities, it can be easy to cut out healthy choices and activities in order to find more time. Instead of eating healthy, you choose less healthy foods. Instead of exercising, you do some other activity that seems like a better use of your time (but is it really a better use of your time?).

Your success hinges on your health, perhaps more than you realize. If you ignore your health, the rest of your efforts at mastery will be thwarted. Maintaining a healthy lifestyle gives you the fuel and clear-headedness to run your business. In this chapter I will show you why health mastery must be a priority, and I'll show you how to master your health.

Again, health is so important that it's one of the Core 5—the 5 Dimensions of Life and Business Mastery.

Reasons To Be Healthy

Have you ever made a health-related New Year's resolution? Many people do—perhaps they want to exercise more, eat better, or quit smoking. Those are some of the most common resolutions. Most people would say that they'd like to be a little healthier. But few resolutions last longer than the end of January, and by February many people are looking for the fried chicken buffet to load up on greasy, salty foods.

We know we need to be healthy and we sometimes think we should make positive changes to our lifestyle but we don't really take our resolutions seriously for very long, nor do we enable ourselves to actually make good, long-lasting changes.

I think health is more important than most people realize. **Everything else in your life hinges on your health.** Someone who is unhealthy will struggle and fail… if not now, eventually. Someone who is healthy will have a greater chance of succeeding: not only because good health helps you to navigate life a little more easily but also because the disciplines you acquire in your effort to be healthy will translate into positive disciplines for other areas of your life.

I believe that health is an indicator of success. Show me a healthy person and I'll show you a successful person… Or one who will inevitably be successful very soon. Conversely, show me an unhealthy person and I'll show you someone who will struggle to be successful.

That's because the qualities required to be healthy—discipline, planning, pushing boundaries, temporary self-sacrifice for a bigger purpose—are the exact same qualities that a successful person uses to reach their targets.

Let's look at some of the reasons to be healthy:

One reason to be healthy is that you'll think more clearly. You'll enjoy clearer thinking and better decision-making. A business master is bombarded with decisions to make throughout the day. A clear head allows you to think through each decision analytically and quickly, exploring all possibilities and selecting the best choice. (Compare this to someone who is unhealthy—their thinking is dampened and slow and foggy.) Your good health helps you be more focused. Working hard requires prolonged focus. When you are healthy, you have more focus because focus is a skill you develop while you are getting healthy.

A second reason to be healthy is that you'll be more productive. As a result of these qualities of clear thinking, better decision-making and improved focus, you'll get more done. Getting more done will allow you to achieve your targets faster and have more time at the end of each day to enjoy some downtime. If your scheduling is filling up because of the exercises you did in the previous chapters, you don't have to wonder where the time will come from. When you master your health, you'll have no problem finding the time because you'll actually get more done with the time you have.

A third reason to be healthy is that you'll be more resilient and you'll have less stress. Stress creates a negative life and it can even be a killer. Unhealthy lifestyles cloud your ability to think clearly, which increases stress. But when you are healthy, you'll think more clearly and you'll be more resilient and, as a result, you'll reduce your stress. It's a fact that healthy people can cope with far greater stresses than unhealthy people.

A fourth reason to be healthy is that you'll reduce pain and injuries and you'll be safer. This is a multifaceted reason: part of it has to do with your clearer thinking and even faster reflexes, which will reduce workplace injuries or mishaps with tools. Part of it has to with a stronger body that can stand up to hard use without experiencing pain, and can heal faster when injuries do occur.

A fifth reason to be healthy is that you'll lower your costs. There's a saying that goes, "you pay for your health, either now or later." It means that you pay for good health right now by spending time to maintain good health, or you pay for your bad health later with expensive medical costs and even, perhaps, a shorter life. You're going to pay one way or the other so why not make the less costly investment of time and effort right now to make healthy choices instead of the far more expensive choice later?

A sixth reason to be healthy is that your relationships will improve. You'll be friendlier and more positive, which will make people want to spend more time with you. Your positivity will add more value to your relationships, which will enrich those essential relationships, as I talked about in the previous chapter. (Added bonus: your sex drive will increase, and so will your sexual performance).

A seventh reason to be healthy is that your good health will improve the quality of your work-time and your down-time. If you end the day exhausted and sore, and all you want to do is snooze in front of the television until bed-time, what kind of quality of life do you have? Imagine how much better it will be to work even harder through the day but end up feeling good enough by the day's end to do quality activities with your loved ones instead.

I've just listed seven great reasons to be healthy; you can probably think of more. If you don't have good health as one of the important dreams on your vision mind board, add it in!

Take Action!
Recommended actions:

___ I've listed some general reasons why you should be healthy. Now I want you to personalize them. What are the exact benefits of health for you? And, what are the exact costs of being unhealthy?

Add your own actions:

___ Stop doing actions (Actions you currently do now but should stop doing)

_____

_____

___ Keep doing actions (Actions you currently do now and should keep doing)

_____

_____

___ Start doing actions (Actions you don't do now but should start doing)

_____

_____

___ Who will do new actions? (Assign the action to yourself or someone else)

_____

_____

___ By when? (When will these actions be complete?)

_____

_____

What Do I Mean When I Say "Healthy"?

So when I say "healthy," what do I mean? What does it involve? I can tell you that some readers will read this most of book but hope they can skip this chapter. If that's you, maybe you're afraid that you have to give up that big bowl of chips you eat in front of the television to unwind every night. Don't skip this chapter.

Good health is essential. Good health will not only change your body, it will change your mind and that will have a transformative effect on many other aspects of your life. Yes, it will take sacrifice but if you have a vision of your life that you truly desire to achieve, you will have no trouble making the choice to give up a few things now to get what you want later.

If you want to enjoy a fulfilling relationship with your spouse well into retirement, and if you feel that dream with enough motivation, then giving up the bowl of chips in front of the television is not really a sacrifice at all. Your dream will inspire you to switch to fresh vegetables and to perhaps take a walk with your spouse instead of watching TV. (See how the Core 5 Dimensions all work together? Your health will contribute to the other Dimensions—such as your relationships, wealth, and freedom.)

So let's talk about what good health really is. There are a number of factors. I'll list them here. Take some time to personally assess your health against this list.

- **Fitness level and weight**: I'm not going to tell you that you need to be a specific weight or that you need to have a specific Body Mass Index (BMI). Both of those are imperfect measurements, partly because muscle weighs more than fat. But when I'm talking about your fitness level, I'm talking about what kind of shape you're in. Are you flabby? Lose that flab. Your weight should be lean-to-average. Resist the temptation to find excuses about your weight ("but it's glandular" or "but I'm big-boned"). You know what a healthy weight is for you and if you're not at it right now, you need to make some changes. And here's the news that no one likes to hear: you consume calories with food and you lose weight by burning calories. So burn more than you consume and your weight will drop off. It's a simple solution but few people are willing to accept the discipline required.

- **Exercise**: related to the above. You need to exercise. I don't care if you are active at work; that's not a replacement for exercise. Exercise is meant to push your physical limits and, in the repair of muscles, you'll get stronger. And stronger muscles burn more calories. Remember that there are two types of exercises: strength-building exercises that push your body's main muscle groups and cardio exercises that pushes your body's heart and lungs. You need to do both types of exercises.

- **Intake**: when I say "intake" I mean diet but I also mean much more. You need to manage what you put in your body. Your food should be healthy. A lot of vegetables, a reasonable amount of meat. Less fat, salt, and sugar. Watch your carbs (carbs are good but it's easy to overload on them). And intake also includes hydration. Your brain needs to be wet and most people go through the day starving their bodies and brains of liquid. Drink plenty of liquids (preferably water) and you'll be surprised at how much clearer you can think. Intake also includes other things we put into our bodies: tobacco and drugs and even prescription medicine. Unless it's required by a doctor for you to live (such as an insulin injection for a diabetic), don't put it into your body. Period. You already know this (how many years have you been making the same New Year's resolution?). Now it's time to stop. (If you have a medical issue, hire the best health coach to help you get results.)

- **Posture**: your posture is an under-appreciated aspect of your health. Good posture ensures that you breathe deeply and it encourages circulation and the proper use of muscles. It decreases issues like back pain and headaches. And there are social benefits to posture, too: you command a room when you walk in with good posture.

- **Rest**: rest is a critical part of health. Most people need somewhere between six to eight hours of sleep a night. If you oversleep or if you undersleep, you pay the penalty the next day. Your fatigue will hamper your decision-making abilities and your attitude and your relationships. Get good rest.

- **Clean**: keep yourself clean. Shower daily. Maintain a well-groomed appearance. Your skin is an organ, which means that it needs to be clean and free of foreign matter in order to do its job, just like any other organ. Not only is this healthier (fewer infections, for example), it will also have benefits to your relationships. Your employees and customers will respect you more because you maintain a neat, tidy appearance.

- **Whole body**: a lot of health experts stop with the things I've written so far but you should also not neglect other parts of your body that require good health habits, like your eyes and teeth. Get both checked regularly.

- **Mental health**: if you take corrective measures on all of the above tips, your mental health will skyrocket. But you can still gain even more health benefits (especially with clear thinking and stress-reducing resiliency) by taking care of your mind. For this I would advise adopting a practice of meditation. Don't get scared off by this as some kind of weird, mystical activity that is parodied on television. Meditation is nothing more than the intent to accomplish something by the guidance of a quiet mind. Periodically stop what you are doing and close out all distractions, and then center your thoughts. You should also consider scheduling days in which you turn off all electronics—you'll be surprised at the benefits to your mind and your relationships when your mobile device and laptop are locked away and ignored for one full day.

When most people think "health" they think of their body but your health is so much more—it's your mind and your general well-being—and it affects so much more than your body too.

Take Action!
Recommended actions:

___ As you read the list in this section you probably thought of a few areas in your life that could use some improvement. Go through the list again and outline exactly what "healthy" means for you—perhaps include a specific weight or level of fitness, how much sleep you should be getting, how many calories you should consume each day, etc.

Add your own actions:

___ Stop doing actions (Actions you currently do now but should stop doing)

_____

_____

___ Keep doing actions (Actions you currently do now and should keep doing)

_____

_____

___ Start doing actions (Actions you don't do now but should start doing)

_____

_____

___ Who will do new actions? (Assign the action to yourself or someone else)

_____

_____

___ By when? (When will these actions be complete?)

_____

_____

How To Be Healthy

By now I hope you've seen the reason why I'm so adamant that good health is essential. And, most importantly, I hope you see that good health has a closer tie to the success of your business than perhaps you first realized. Now I want to lay out a solid, common-sense plan for you to attain good health. Most of this plan will apply to most people but I recommend that you talk to your doctor about your health and discuss any health-related lifestyle changes you intend to make.

I can recommend good advice that I know works. But if you read this chapter and don't make positive changes in your life then you need to go back and read chapter one of this book again and go through the visioning process more deeply to get a more inspiring vision for your life—and you need to especially consider how better health can help you enjoy all the other great things you're thinking about enjoying. On the other hand, if you did go through chapter one and came away with a deeply felt dream of what you want your life to be then you'll read this section of the chapter and nothing will seem too difficult to adopt.

I'm going to lay it out really simply for you. If you want to be healthy, stop looking for a magic pill or a quick fix. Just do these things and you will get healthy. It's that easy.

- Eat less than you are right now and workout more than you are right now.
- Eat your larger meals earlier in the day—your biggest meal for breakfast, a lighter meal for lunch, your lightest meal for supper. Better yet, if your schedule allows it, stop eating three meals a day and instead eat five to six smaller meals spaced out through the day.
- Choose balanced food with more vegetables than you have been eating.
- Eat less fat, grease, fried foods, salt, and sugar.
- Drink more water… way more water.
- Workout during your day, especially in the morning or afternoon if possible.
- Do a combination of strength training and cardio training.
- Stretch before and after each workout.

- Warm up before each workout and cool down after each workout.
- Go for a walk in the evening with your spouse. (That shouldn't replace your exercise but you'll get a bit of extra exercise, some fresh air, and some quality time in your relationship.)
- Get a good sleep each night—six to eight hours.
- Stop smoking.
- Drink in moderation.
- Shower daily.
- Floss more often.
- Schedule appointments with your eye doctor and your dentist.
- Meditate daily.
- When things get stressful, meditate again.

People spend a lot of money on workout routines and gym memberships and diets… but don't follow through with them. All you need to do is make the changes I've described above. As you read that list, you should immediately see what you aren't doing that you need to do (and what you are doing that you have to stop doing). It really is as simple as making a change and choosing to start and/or stop the right things.

One of the healthy activities that I love and strongly recommend to others is martial arts. Martial arts is great physical activity but martial arts is so much more: It is a discipline, and it helps you to be more disciplined in other areas of your life as well. If martial arts like karate or taekwondo is not your thing, you'll find similar exercise-plus-discipline benefits from yoga or tai chi. Ultimately, you want to find something that supports your health and growth; something you can integrate into your lifestyle easily, and something that is enjoyable yet challenging to do.

With today's technology, integrating exercise into your life has never been easier. For example, you can hike and listen to a podcast, or you can ride a bike and have a conference call, or you can invest in a desk with built-in exercise machine. The key here is to find how you can integrate activities into your lifestyle that contribute to health and growth.

The best way to get started in your health is to identify your baseline. What is your health like right now? Use real numbers, such as weight, blood pressure, or even how many stairs you can do before you get winded. With this baseline, start working on your health and then measure regularly to test your results. **You may not see immediate results but if you stick with positive changes, you'll start to notice results and they will build over time.**

In the next section, I'll give you some additional tools to help you get healthy.

Take Action!
Recommended actions:

__ Now we're getting more specific. Drawing from the list above, what exact steps do you need to take right now to get healthier? Schedule time in your planner for those things right now.

__ Identify your baseline health. This is the measurement of where you are right now. Perhaps you'll want to use your weight and blood pressure as a starting point but there might be other numbers you can measure as well (such as the number of cigarettes you smoke in a day or how many stairs you can climb before you get winded). Post these numbers where you can see them frequently and work at improving them.

Add your own actions:

__ Stop doing actions (Actions you currently do now but should stop doing)

_____

_____

__ Keep doing actions (Actions you currently do now and should keep doing)

_____

_____

__ Start doing actions (Actions you don't do now but should start doing)

__ Who will do new actions? (Assign the action to yourself or someone else)

__ By when? (When will these actions be complete?)

The Most Important Thing About Being Healthy

I've talked about health so far in this chapter but here's the real reason I'm talking about health: good health starts with good habits and discipline… and the habits you develop while getting healthy will not only help your health, they'll also help the rest of your life and business. I want to talk about developing good habits and I'll apply them here to your health but believe me when I tell you that the same principles apply to other areas of your life. If you want to develop a habit in anything, do the same thing I describe here.

If you read any philosophers—modern or ancient—and if you've observed the most successful people in history, you know that self-mastery is the most profound, transformative quality to have. When you master yourself, everything else will seem easy.

So the best place to start to master yourself is with your health habits. Master your health habits and you'll not only live a healthier life, you'll also regain control of your life.

You probably already know what habits you need to change in your life to achieve better health. Even if you don't know absolutely everything there is to know about good health, that doesn't matter. You already know enough to start making positive changes right now. Start planning those positive changes. Pick a few areas of your health where you want to improve and make a plan to improve them. If you can't make a massive change, then just start eating better. Do it daily for 30 days until it becomes a habit then adopt something else (without letting the first thing drop).

Don't put them into your planner to start next week or next month or next year. Start them today or, at the very latest, tomorrow. Make positive changes by creating small habits that you can act on daily. Remember that this has nothing to do with a specific weight number. Rather, this is a holistic approach to healthier living to provide you with personal and business benefits, outlined earlier in this chapter.

Challenge yourself. Push yourself to get better. Set reminders to yourself to be reminded why you're doing this and review those reminders regularly (because there will be times when you are tempted to break your habits). Be accountable to others: get the help of family and friends to remind and encourage you. And ask the person in your family who does the grocery shopping to help you out by buying fewer of the foods you shouldn't eat and more of the foods you should eat.

And don't forget that good health can be fun, too. Adopt martial arts, yoga, sports, or even just a simple change like walking the dog with your spouse in the evening.

One of the best ways to motivate yourself is to think about how your health contributes to the other Core 5, and to remind yourself of that whenever you're faced with a choice between healthy and unhealthy options.

Take Action!
Recommended actions:

__ List several positive, healthy actions you could do (such as exercise, studying martial arts, eating well). Then write down reasons from the 5 Dimensions that will help to motivate you. For example: "Eating well will help me live a longer life and therefore enjoy better relationships by giving me more time with my family."

Add your own actions:

__ Stop doing actions (Actions you currently do now but should stop doing)

_____

_____

__ Keep doing actions (Actions you currently do now and should keep doing)

_____

_____

__ Start doing actions (Actions you don't do now but should start doing)

_____

_____

__ Who will do new actions? (Assign the action to yourself or someone else)

_____

_____

__ By when? (When will these actions be complete?)

_____

_____

Conclusion

Show me a healthy person and I'll show you a successful one. If you want to be successful, start with your health because the healthy habits you adopt will have a huge impact on the rest of your life.

And remember that it takes time and persistence. Good health doesn't change overnight. Someone who is out of shape didn't get to be that way from just eating one cheeseburger; it took months or years of poor eating choices. To create positive change, it takes persistent, positive actions that you stick to even when it's tough. You'll start to notice some changes within a day or two, within a week, and then within a month or two. Keep at it. Keep pushing. Healthy living is a great reward itself but the spin-off benefits to your relationships and your business will also motivate you.

Master Action List For Chapter 3

At the end of each section of this chapter you had actions to perform as well as Start Doing/Keep Doing/Stop Doing lists. Gather those actions together into a Master Action List, add any new actions that you think of, and then go through the questions below to think about how these actions can transform your life and your business:

___ **Is it going to make me money?** Are the actions you've listed going to help you generate more income? (If they are, great. Think about how they might be able to help you generate even more income. If they aren't making you more money then are those actions really as important as you thought they were?)

___ **Is it going save me money?** Reducing how much you spend will help you increase your profit. Are the actions you're thinking of doing going to help you cut back on your expenses without sacrificing the quality of your service? (If they save you money, great. If they aren't saving you money then are those actions really as important as you thought they were?)

___ **Is it going to save time?** Your time is precious and scarce. So the actions you take should help you to save time. Keep the big picture in mind because some actions may take a few extra minutes in the short term but will ultimately help you save time in the long term. (For example, training an employee might be an action that will take a few extra minutes now but will save you a lot of time in the future).

___ **Is it going to help me achieve market domination?** Your business needs to own the market it works in. Whenever someone thinks of the service you provide, they should only think of you. Do the actions you've listed in this chapter support that market domination? What can you change about them to help you dominate the market even further?

___ **How do I start fast to get the low-hanging fruit?** It's easy to say you're going to take action but it's much harder to actually do it. One way to take

action and push through to its successful completion is to go for the quick wins—the low-hanging fruit. From the actions you've listed, what low-hanging fruit can you immediately pick?

___ **What's the leverage?** Leverage has a few different meanings but, in this context, I'm talking about how you can motivate yourself. For example, if you commit to complete an action within a certain period of time you can leverage that commitment by saying, "If I don't make that commitment, I'll donate $10,000 to a charity." Since you may not have $10,000, and you'll probably feel some pain donating that much money, you are leveraging your commitment and compelling yourself to complete the actions you said you'd complete.

___ **What's the reward?** For each action, list what you expect to get out of it. If you can't think of a reward for the action, seriously consider whether it is as valuable as you thought. Spend more of your time on actions that have rewards. Two of the best rewards for your actions are below (although there are other rewards you may choose to take action for)…

___ **Is it going to help me achieve wealth?** One of the best rewards you can take action for is to achieve wealth. For each action ask whether that particular action will help you make more money to give you the sense of safety and achievement and allow you to buy whatever you want whenever you want it. If possible, develop the action even further if a stronger, clearer, bigger action will help you achieve more wealth.

___ **Is it going to help me get more freedom?** Another one of the best rewards you can take action for is to get more freedom—the time and financial capacity to do whatever you want whenever you want to (without sacrificing your business). For each action ask whether that particular action will help you get more freedom. If possible, develop the action even further if a stronger, clearer, bigger action will help you get more freedom.

CHAPTER 4

MASTER YOUR TIME

We all get the same amount of time each day and yet some people seem to achieve so much while others barely have enough time to do anything. In this chapter you'll discover the secrets to master your time so that you can be most efficient in your working time and also maximize the amount of time you spend with loved ones.

Introduction

Have you ever wished you had more time? Sure you have; everyone does at some point in their lives. They pack things into their schedule so tightly and they feel ridiculously busy… and yet, many people don't accomplish as much as they want. (And, as you've read the first three chapters of this book, I've been asking you to put even more into your schedule!)

The next time you feel way too busy, I want you to look around and consider some of the most successful people in life and some of the least successful people in life. Do you know what they have in common? They both have the exact same amount of time each day. No one gets more; no one gets less. The Steve Jobs and Elon Musks and Tony Robbins of the world (often considered successful) have the same amount of time in their day as the homeless guy sitting on the street begging for change. **It's how you use the time that makes all the difference.**

Every day we wake up with an asset in our "time bank" and we spend that asset throughout the day. Perhaps you spend a few minutes here on one activity and a few minutes there on another activity; perhaps you spend an hour for lunch; perhaps you spend a couple of hours in front of the television in the evening. Some of the time you spend on business activities; some of the time you spend on personal activities. Everyone gets the same amount of time each day. How do you spend your time?

As usual, I'm going to say something that some people will find bold and many will even find offensive: since everyone has the same amount of time—from the most successful to the least successful—you need to decide what kind of person you want to be and then you need to use your time in the same way as the people you aspire to be like. I promise you that Elon Musk doesn't watch four hours of television every night.

If your personal vision is as aspirational and stretching as I suggested it should be in an earlier chapter then you need to figure out how to use your time more effectively to achieve it. In this chapter I'll show you how to master your time so you have enough to do it all.

Not Just Time Management... Time Mastery

"Time management" is a misnomer. People focus on managing their time and they look to time management gurus to help them. Time management books are constant bestsellers. People think that if only they could manage their time better they would achieve everything they want in life. There are several things wrong with that mindset and in this section I want to tell you what you need to do to shift your mindset.

The first thing wrong with the time management mindset is this: it places your schedule as the item of highest importance in your day. When that happens, your schedule starts to dictate what you should be doing. Time masters, however, dictate what their schedule should contain.

The second thing wrong with the time management mindset is this: attempting to manage your time will inevitably fail. That's because we all have the same amount of time in the day and you can't manage your time. What you should really should be doing is managing yourself and your situation. That's how you'll achieve time mastery.

The third thing wrong with the time management mindset is this: time management is often about trying to squeeze more and more stuff into the small amount of time you have. But **time mastery is about freeing up your**

schedule so that, eventually, your time can be filled entirely with things that you want to do. In other words, time management focuses on trying to get more done in the same amount of time, while time mastery focuses on trying to do the right things so that you have more time.

I'm very passionate about time mastery because I see so many people at risk of burning themselves out because they feel that they are short of time. I want to show you how to make the most of the time you have so that you not only feel that you have enough time to do whatever you *need* to do, but you also have enough time to do whatever you *want* to do.

Take Action!
Recommended actions:

___ Make a big list of everything you do in your day. You might need to take a notepad with you and actually record your daily actions in 15 minute chunks throughout the day to get a true picture of what you do. And, you might want to do this exercise for a few days or even a week to get a clearer picture of what a typical day looks like.

___ Using the list you created above, identify which specific daily tasks contribute to your 5 Dimensions of Life and Business Mastery, and how they contribute. Chances are, you'll find that several tasks do not contribute very much at all.

___ Using the list you created above, think honestly about your time and determine who (or what) is in control of your time? Are you mastered by your schedule? Do you delegate to others? Do your customers, vendors, employees (or someone else) tell you what you should be doing? Analyze what you could weed out, what you love to do, and what you hate to do.

___ Make a list of things you wish you could do in life (probably drawn from the vision for your life that you created in chapter 1) but don't have the time to do.

Add your own actions:

__ Stop doing actions (Actions you currently do now but should stop doing)

_____

_____

__ Keep doing actions (Actions you currently do now and should keep doing)

_____

_____

__ Start doing actions (Actions you don't do now but should start doing)

_____

_____

__ Who will do new actions? (Assign the action to yourself or someone else)

_____

_____

__ By when? (When will these actions be complete?)

_____

_____

A Simple Plan To Time Mastery

Forget trying to manage your time. Instead, work toward time mastery—this isn't just scheduling things properly, it's about understanding yourself and how you work, and learning to use the right tools to get more done. Don't think of this chapter as an alternative to other time management methodologies. Instead, think of this chapter as a total transformation of how you understand your ability to accomplish the things you need to do.

It starts with your personal vision, which you created at the beginning of this book. What do you want in life? You need to know that answer first because that will influence what you spend your time on. The same with your business vision (which I'll show you how to create later in this book).

Use your personal blueprint (which you created with your vision mind board and the spreadsheet of targets) to help you determine what you spend your time on. After all, it's a clearly laid-out step-by-step plan of how you will achieve your vision. And the same goes for your business, too. You'll create a business blueprint (similar to a personal blueprint) later in this book and it will also help you determine what you spend your time on.

And that's it. Those are the only things that should be influencing your schedule. You'll have specific tasks that fill each of your days but every single one of those tasks should contribute in some way to your plan to achieve your vision. You should see the faces of people who attend my Warrior Fast Track Academy events when we talk about this topic. There's a huge level of amazement at the new-found freedom they discover when they build their schedules in this way.

Here's how to schedule your day: first, it's important to plan early. I'm always building my schedule at least the day before. You don't need a fancy app or an expensive, branded calendar. I used to fall into the trap of using those things but when I started to master my time I switched to a simple blank pad of paper. Nothing fancy. This forces me to write a new schedule every day and, as I'm writing it I'm forced to think about it. (Compare this to a calendar app on your phone or computer where you just input appointments as they come up—there's very little control or awareness over that kind of schedule.)

On your pad of paper (or whatever you decide to use for your schedule), block out your day into a few different chunks. These chunks should include:

- Any appointments you have scheduled for the day
- The top three things you absolutely must accomplish that day (more about this in a moment)
- A couple of open spots for unknowns

So, you might end up with four to eight chunks in your day, each filled with something (or, at least a placeholder for the unknowns). These chunks of time can be as long as you need them to be—anywhere from 30 to 60 minutes. Don't schedule these chunks to butt up immediately against the other. Leave a bit of space in between, just in case one of the activities takes longer than you expected.

You should also keep a list of things you can do that aren't scheduled because if you find yourself with some spare time between those scheduled chunks you can probably knock out a couple of additional tasks.

In your daily list of chunked appointment times, I mentioned that you need to set aside time for the top three things you absolutely must accomplish that day. For me (and I recommend this for you, too) these top three priority items are the things I do to move the needle: these are business-building times. This is where you are thinking about your business, focusing on building stuff, developing strategies, developing processes, and evaluating how your previous initiatives have done.

A lot of business owners feel that this is too difficult to do. They look at the list of things they think they need to do in a day and they don't see how they can cut it down to *only* three of the most important things to do... it feels like they've got three *dozen* most important things to do each day! If that describes how you feel, here is my advice: take a cold, hard look at yourself and your business and decide whether or not you actually do all the things you want to do in the day. In my experience, business owners list all of the things they think are important, only do a few of them, and then just move the rest to the next day. It's a vicious cycle. (By the time you're done reading this book, I think you'll find that you have far fewer tasks you consider to be most important. So even if you have a hard time figuring out how to narrow your actions down to only three right now, just keep reading through this chapter and by the end of the book you might find that it's a lot easier.)

If you're not sure which of your many, many tasks you should schedule for today, I advise that you **choose the tasks that will have the highest pay—the biggest return on investment (ROI)**. Business owners do all the right things at the wrong time. They need to make money but they're focused on something else, like systemization. Here's the ROI ranking I use: I list out everything I'd like to do and rank it on a scale of 1 to 10 based on what's it going to do for saving me money or making me money. That's it. When you think in those terms, your most important tasks become clear and they should go into your schedule into one of the top three priority "chunks" that you absolutely must finish that day.

As you create these chunks and fill them with activities, make sure everything you do meets at least one of these four criteria:

- This activity will be fast to implement.
- This activity is easy to do (if it's not easy to do, you might procrastinate. Break it up into easy tasks).
- This activity is balanced between cost and quality. (You don't necessarily need to choose the cheapest option, nor the most expensive.)
- What is it going to grow into? (Are you planting a seed for an oak tree or are you planting a weed?)

As you look at your schedule, everything else that does not fit must be ruthlessly eliminated!

Now I want to talk about a related concept—multitasking. I'd like to break the myth of multitasking. It's virtually impossible for humans to multitask. When you multitask, your brain toggles back and forth from one activity to the other. The more you force your brain to switch, the less focused your brain is on the task at hand. Even if you are one of the rare people who is great at multitasking, imagine this: if you went from being a great multitasker to a great single-tasker, you would be even more effective.

When I talk about the "cost" of multitasking, I'm not just talking about switching from one important work-related task to another important work-related task. You definitely shouldn't multitask that way. But I'm also talking about multitasking between anything—for example, don't switch between a work-related task and a social media site like Facebook. Treat every task with singular focus—whether it's a critical work task or a light and inconsequential task. When you give each task its full focus, you'll do a better job and it will take less time.

Here's the bottom line when it comes to creating a schedule, choosing what goes on it, and being productive and present throughout your day: **you need to focus on one thing at a time and you'll get a lot more quality work done when you spend time on a single task and work at it until it's completed.**

Doing quality work isn't just a nice concept. It's measurable. When you measure your productivity, you can master it and become more productive.

As with your health, your time mastery requires a baseline to provide you with a starting point so you can measure how productive you are. Find measureable numbers around your productivity (and procrastination!) that reveal your existing level of time mastery. For example, how often do you check Facebook? Are you taking phone calls from friends during the day? What are the patterns of your day (for example, do you get your morning tasks done easily but your afternoon ones are a struggle)? You'll need to find numbers that measure your existing level of time mastery so you have a baseline—a starting point—from which to improve.

As you improve them, you'll find a direct improvement to your 5 Dimensions of Life and Business as well. For example, more time helps to contribute to more freedom. It also helps you to work at a higher level in your business and make more money (which contributes to your wealth). And, more time with your family enhances your relationships.

By now you should have an understanding of what time mastery is and how this mindset shift should set you free from the misguided concept of time management and actually make you more productive. With those ideas in mind, I want to show you how to create a winning day. These are the same techniques I use—I've used them as I built my business from the ground up into the number one rated service company in New Jersey, serving over 125,000 customers!

Take Action!
Recommended actions:

__ Get a pad of paper and put together a schedule as I've described in this section of the chapter. Try it for a week and I promise that you'll notice a difference—you'll feel more in control because you're forced to think through your schedule for each day. You'll also love the sense of accomplishment because you end up crossing off all of your tasks by the end of the day (instead a sense of failure as you move your uncompleted tasks from one day to the next).

___ Make a list of everything you'd like to do and need to do... and then rank those things on a scale of 1 to 10 based on how likely (or unlikely) they are to save or make you money. The more likely they are to save you money or make you money, the higher priority they should be and the greater focus they should they should get on your schedule.

___ Starting with the next couple of days, chunk them out into four to eight sections (remember to leave some flex space between each chunk).

___ Create a list of things you can do in between those chunks—things that need to be done but don't need to be scheduled.

Add your own actions:

___ Stop doing actions (Actions you currently do now but should stop doing)
_____
_____

___ Keep doing actions (Actions you currently do now and should keep doing)
_____
_____

___ Start doing actions (Actions you don't do now but should start doing)
_____
_____

___ Who will do new actions? (Assign the action to yourself or someone else)
_____
_____

___ By when? (When will these actions be complete?)

_____

_____

Action—The Missing Link

Another huge issue people face when dealing with the flawed concept of time management is procrastination. Many people know what they need to accomplish—the important stuff is jam-packed into their daily schedule. But they find themselves wasting away the afternoon on a task that suddenly seems important (even though it's not on their list) or they burn through the evening hours watching television instead of wrapping up some tasks they know they should be doing.

So let's address this concept right away: you absolutely have to take action on your schedule. **Once you have created your schedule, you MUST take action on it and do each item when it's scheduled, and attempt to complete it within the time allotted, and you must do that daily. Period.**

If you create your schedule in the way I showed you and then take action to work on each of those items in your schedule, there will be absolutely no stopping you or the trajectory of your business.

But now let's talk about reality: sticking to your schedule doesn't always happen, does it? Chances are, something else happens: you need to do something on your schedule but you choose to do something else instead. Sometimes that "choose to do something else" is your own choice (and we often call that "procrastination") and sometimes that "choose to do something else" is when other seemingly critical tasks suddenly demand your time (and we often call that "putting out fires"). Regardless of the reason, the result is the same: you don't do your work and you choose to do some other task.

As soon as you break from the schedule you've created, you are choosing to break from a successful path and you risk hurting your business.

Now, I realize that there will be times when some emergency crisis rears its head and you have to deal with it right away. But many business owners often accept any *seemingly* urgent interruption as a crisis that demands their full attention at the cost of everything else they had scheduled. In my experience, only a tiny portion of real crises should actually tear you away from your pre-established schedule. Wife having a baby? House burning down? Sure. Deal with those important events. Everything else can wait for the hour or so that you are working on the task you planned to do.

If you have the common tendency to do something else instead of your scheduled work, here is my best advice to solve that problem: you need to realize the consequence of putting off your scheduled work to do something else. Doing your work now is going to help your business grow bigger and become more profitable; doing your work now will help you move closer to your personal vision and your business vision; doing your work now will contribute to your Core 5 Dimensions of Life and Business Mastery. However, any kind of delay (whether you label it procrastination or something else) will make the problems in your business grow. When you make that comparison, the desire to do your work tends to reappear!

While you're thinking about the consequences, don't just admit that there are vague consequences but go deep and get specific: I like to put leverage on everything that I'm doing; my leverage is my family. If I'm not efficient at getting things done, if I decide to slack for a little while, I'm affecting many people, including my family. (I'm also affecting my customers, employees, vendors, and all of their families as well.)

As you take action on your scheduled "chunks" of work, focus on each one and work through to completion. If you find that you just can't complete it in the time you chunked out for it then consider whether you can complete it in the "free space" between the chunks in your schedule. If you can, do so. If you can't, immediately reschedule the work.

Take Action!
Recommended actions:

___ Set up some kind of reminder to yourself throughout the day (maybe have a trusted friend ask you periodically) if you are sticking to your schedule or if you have moved off of it. If you've moved off of it, get back onto it as soon as possible.

__ Find or hire an accountability partner to help you keep on track until you've developed a habit.

__ Make a list of the things that have pulled you off of your schedule and determine how you can avoid having those things pull you off of your schedule in the future. (For example, perhaps locking your office door or not looking at email will help you to focus on another task.)

Add your own actions:

__ Stop doing actions (Actions you currently do now but should stop doing)

_____

_____

__ Keep doing actions (Actions you currently do now and should keep doing)

_____

_____

__ Start doing actions (Actions you don't do now but should start doing)

_____

_____

__ Who will do new actions? (Assign the action to yourself or someone else)

_____

_____

__ By when? (When will these actions be complete?)

_____

_____

Leverage

At the end of the previous section I hinted at one of the best ways to achieve time mastery: create leverage. Leverage is using a small amount of power, intelligently applied, to achieve a comparably larger result. And there are several very powerful ways that you can leverage your time to achieve even more than you thought possible. Here are the ways I use leverage in my business to get comparably larger results:

Automation and technology: leverage your time by using technology and by automating parts of your business. I use Skype in my business in a number of different ways—to communicate with my team and to educate them. This cuts down on the time-consuming and money-consuming face-to-face meetings and a well-planned Skype call keeps us on task.

Email is another way you can use technology to communicate but I should warn you that email can sometimes become a burden if you're not careful. Set up systems and boundaries (more on that in a couple of paragraphs) to help you use email well instead of letting it master you.

YouTube is another great way to leverage your time with technology: if you record something once and then post it on YouTube you can use it over and over without having to deliver the same thing in person. Here are some ideas of what you can post on YouTube:

- Videos your sales staff can use in their sales efforts
- Training videos for new employees (Not all videos are public videos so you can post videos that only specific people will see)
- Updates to existing employees to update them and inspire them

Apps allow you to turn your phone into a recording device so you can record your thoughts while you are on the road. This leverages your travel time and allows you to create communications and training for your team that can later be transcribed.

Delegation and outsourcing: leverage others to help you achieve more in less time. When I say "delegation" most business owners think of getting their team to do the work that the owner once did. And that is true—your team can and should do a lot of the technician work you once did. But there is so much more to the concept of delegation and outsourcing.

I delegate absolutely everything I possibly can. For example, I refuse to be the cleaner around my home or my office so I hire them. Here are just a few of the long list of people I delegate to:

- The staff in my business (of course! This is the obvious one)
- House cleaners
- Landscapers
- Home and business upkeep (such as painters, etc.)
- Dry cleaner

Understanding your personal rate per hour will help you decide what to delegate. If you make $100 an hour, why would you do cleaning that you could hire someone else to do for $25 an hour?

You should delegate whatever is not your expertise. Never spend time on something that someone else can do faster. There is even a service that will receive your mail, open it for you, and scan it so you can review it virtually.

Let me give you three examples of how extreme I am on my delegation:

- I don't drop off my clothes at a Laundromat; I found someone who will pick it up for me at my doorstep and drop it off when they're done.
- I have my vendors participate together on a monthly call *without me.* They don't need me there. They know what I want and they work together to do it.
- My accountant and vendors come to visit me (instead of me visiting them), to save me time.

When it comes to delegation, there are often two concerns that business owners have. I'll address those concerns and resolve them for you right now:

1. "But It costs money to delegate," someone might object. My response: how much is your own time worth? If you are mowing your lawn, you are losing money. Why give up the opportunity to do whatever you want

to do with an hour of your day when you can pay someone to cut your lawn? Or do you pack your lunch because you don't want to spend the money on lunch? "Delegate" your lunch purchase to a restaurant and take meetings at lunch. The extra cost of the meal will be easily replaced by the time you spend on your business.

2. "But they won't do it as well as I could," someone might object. My response: it's good to have high expectations of other people. But a small up-front investment of training, along with clear communication of your expectations, plus some follow-up, will help you achieve the result that is nearly as good—or oftentimes better—than what you could do.

I'm only scratching the surface of delegation because I want to expand your mind to the possibilities. But later in this book I'll go deeper on this topic when I talk about mastering your team.

Add value and motivation: Here's another way I use leverage. Whenever I have an important task to do, or when I'm holding someone else accountable for an important task they need do, I add leverage: I identify something of value that will either provide a higher reward if the work is completed or a higher cost if the work is not completed.

As I mentioned in the previous section in this chapter, I add leverage to my workday by understanding that each action contributes to my wealth and freedom, which allows me to spend more time with my family. If I do the work, I will ultimately get more family time; if I don't do the work, I'm causing my family to suffer and I'm taking away from the time I can spend with them.

Another way to add leverage is to apply a cost to a project if it is not completed on time. So you might say that if you do not complete a project within a limited timeframe, you'll donate $10,000 to a charity of your choice. Since $10,000 might be a difficult amount to give away, it adds extra leverage to the task to help you ensure that you'll complete it on time.

For every task you have in your schedule, add leverage: identify the reward for completing on time and the cost if it takes longer.

Take Action!
Recommended actions:

___ Make a list of activities that you do right now that you can delegate to others. Put a lot of focus into this list. After you've made your list sit down and examine your life closely to determine if there are other areas that you can delegate. Look deep into your life to see where you can delegate (you might be surprised). For example, you might hire a personal driver so you can get work done instead of driving.

___ Start a list of items you want to delegate right now. These should be things that someone else can do better than you, or that simply cost less to hire out than if you do them yourself.

___ Start a list of items you would like to delegate someday (but can't delegate immediately for some reason). Identify what needs to happen in order to delegate these out and use that list as an action list. (For example, perhaps you want to delegate your marketing so you need to hire a marketer to do it. Therefore, an action item should be to hire a marketer.)

Add your own actions:

___ Stop doing actions (Actions you currently do now but should stop doing)

_____

_____

___ Keep doing actions (Actions you currently do now and should keep doing)

_____

_____

___ Start doing actions (Actions you don't do now but should start doing)

_____

_____

__ Who will do new actions? (Assign the action to yourself or someone else)

_____

_____

__ By when? (When will these actions be complete?)

_____

_____

Other Ways To Master Your Time

Every day you wage war: the hours in your day are the front lines. On the one side of the battlefield you are working to accomplish your targets. Fighting against you is not just one enemy but many enemies—each one hoping to take some of your time.

Now that I've showed you how to build a simple but powerful plan to achieve highly productive days every day, now I want to talk about other ways to master your time. These are time mastery best practices that I use daily to achieve more in my business and in my life.

Reduce interruptions: interruptions are a scourge on your schedule. They will flood in relentlessly and if you are not equally as relentless in stopping them, avoiding them, and pushing back on them, then everyone else's priorities will overtake your more important priorities. Not only will interruptions make it harder for you to complete your work, everyone else in your company faces the same challenges, too. To counteract that problem in my company, I've created a list of 10 practices that I've implemented—for myself and for my staff—to reduce interruptions for everyone. Here's the list:

1. Do things on time: you will have things completed and moved on to others before they feel the need to follow up (interrupt) you to find out why information they were expecting has not been given to them.
2. Don't interrupt others: if you have a habit of barging in and interrupting others this sends a message to do the same to you. More often than not, people treat us exactly as our actions show that we want to be treated.

3. Look before you leap: learn to look and see what people are doing, and decide if your interruption is merited. Most conversations can easily be delayed without negative consequences.

4. Set appointment times: people tend to interrupt because they are not sure when they are going to have access to you. Whether it be ten minutes in the morning with your assistant or a follow-up on that big project that requires multiple meetings throughout the week, set appointment times in your calendar so there is clarity for all involved that there will be time to meet and talk.

5. Tell them you are busy then immediately set a time to meet: if appropriate, consider meeting/talking after normal business hours or over a scheduled lunch. You may want to schedule time as a repeat appointment with those who have routine access to you.

6. Take a stand: allowing someone to sit down in your office inevitably will mean a longer interruption. If you stand up and walk to your office door or cubicle entrance, an interruption will take less time.

7. Turn off visual and audio email notifications: your email system allows you to turn off these interrupters. Setting times throughout the day to manage email eliminates the need to use notifications.

8. Batch communication: keep a file for every person you interact with frequently and place notes of non-urgent issues you wish to discuss with them during your scheduled appointment times. These "batch files" will minimize the need for non-scheduled interruptions.

9. Do things right: handle communications completely and correctly the first time to reduce others' need to get clarification.

10. Leave complete phone messages: expect to get voicemail when you call someone and be prepared to leave complete information in your message. Request that others do the same for you.

Another useful system I've put in place to shield myself from interruptions is the 1-3-5 system. Everyone who comes to my door or texts me or emails me knows to always include a ranking of 1, 3, or 5 right off the bat. This is a ranking of the severity of the situation: 1 is "just looking to bullshit,"

3 is "I need to chat by end of day," and 5 is "I have an issue that is money-threatening or business-threatening".

So, someone might knock on my door and say, "Hey Mike, I've got a level 5 situation here" and I know to drop everything and deal with it because it's a money-threatening situation. But someone else might text me: "Got time to talk? 1" and I can see at a glance that they're just looking to bullshit for a bit and I can decide if now is the best time to talk.

Set up boundaries: setting up boundaries in your business establishes a level of predictability in your business, which gives people limits, confidence, security, and an understanding of how things should work. One boundary in my business is the 1-3-5 system that I mentioned above. People know that a 5 is only used for the most dire money-threatening event and it's okay to interrupt me with that. A 1 is inconsequential and although I'm happy to talk to someone else, there are no expectation on me to drop everything immediately.

But there are other boundaries, too. You should understand who you are talking to (no matter if it's a client, employee, vendor or whatever) and determine what are the safe places to go in the conversation.

Another boundary is the split between business and non-business, and what is allowed in each. For example, my wife isn't in my business so she's not going to tell my employees what to do. My wife knows that, my employees know that, and it creates a better work environment.

Focus your day: there are different types of days you should create. You can still use the chunking method I described earlier in the chapter but the overall "theme" of the day might be one of the following types of days:

- Money days—these are days where you are focused on making money. No, I don't mean that you are actually out there selling, I mean that you are thinking about *how* you make money in your business; you're focusing on conversion rates and offers and promotions, and you're strategizing with your coach or mastermind group about how you can make more money in your business.

- Logistical days—these are the days you're doing backstage stuff. You're handling logistical items, you're building processes and systems for your business to make it run better. And, you're also checking in and seeing how the existing system is running or you're shadowing existing employees to see how things are going.

- "My day" Free days—for doing what you want and only what you want. On these days you can do anything you want! You aren't on your computer doing work; you aren't taking work calls. This is all about you and spending time doing the things you love with the people you love. My family is so important to me so I think of these as family days and I spend all my time focusing entirely on my family during these days. This is also my day for when I want to focus on personal growth in all areas of my life.

These are the three primary types of days you should be scheduling, but you'll often find that a fourth type of day needs to take place from time to time:

- Floater days—these are when you have days filled with meetings, or when you go on a trip, etc. These are days for the unforeseen, the crazy accountant meetings, or checking out a new vehicle for fleet.

And here's the whole point of time mastery summed up: your free days should grow and your logistical days should eventually be handed off to your team. Ultimately, you should get to the point where you are working almost exclusively on money days (when you're working) and also enjoying many free days regularly.

Earlier in the chapter I suggested you plan your day the day before. It's helpful to plan these types or theme days a week or two ahead of time so you know in advance what kind of days you'll have—this will allow you to plan more effectively. For example, if you receive a meeting request, you can recommend that it be held on one of your "floater" meeting days. As different tasks come up, you can add them to the appropriate day and then, the day before, you can rank them and decide which activities you'll do.

Rethink how you define your work: I like to use the terms "working *on* your business" and "working *in* your business", and perhaps you've heard those terms before. Understanding the difference can help you redefine your work and think differently about what tasks are important to you. Working *on* your business is thinking of the big picture of your business and leading it; working *on* your business is what you should be doing during your money days. Working *in* your business is actually doing the work that your business does (such as: plumbing if you're a plumber). It could also be pushing papers, or doing the mundane items. Items you can easily hire for. The target of time mastery—and, in fact, all of business mastery—is to do more working *on* your business and to do less working *in* your business.

Take Action!
Recommended actions:

___ Implement a system similar to my 1-3-5 system in your workplace to help you manage interruptions.

___ Plan your next couple of weeks by identifying some money days, logistics days, and yes, even some "my days." Be bold and decide to really jump in with both feet and make this change. (Some of you reading this will be tentative and will prefer to ease into it—but I don't think it will be as effective or rewarding!)

___ Look at the list of tasks you do every day. Review which ones are working *on* your business and which ones are working *in* your business. How can you increase the tasks of working *on* your business and how can you decrease the tasks of working *in* your business?

Add your own actions:

___ Stop doing actions (Actions you currently do now but should stop doing)

_____

_____

__ Keep doing actions (Actions you currently do now and should keep doing)

_____

_____

__ Start doing actions (Actions you don't do now but should start doing)

_____

_____

__ Who will do new actions? (Assign the action to yourself or someone else)

_____

_____

__ By when? (When will these actions be complete?)

_____

_____

Conclusion

Your time is an invaluable asset that is spent once and you never get it back. A key component of mastering yourself is mastering your time. Don't let anyone else take control of this priceless commodity—it's yours and you can make huge transformations in your life and business if you first master your time.

It starts with a change in how you view time (mastery instead of management) and how you schedule it. And it takes your full effort and focus to implement these changes and make them stick.

Master Action List For Chapter 4

At the end of each section of this chapter you had actions to perform as well as Start Doing/Keep Doing/Stop Doing lists. Gather those actions together into a Master Action List, add any new actions that you think of, and then go through the questions below to think about how these actions can transform your life and your business:

__ **Is it going to make me money?** Are the actions you've listed going to help you generate more income? (If they are, great. Think about how they might be able to help you generate even more income. If they aren't making you more money then are those actions really as important as you thought they were?)

__ **Is it going save me money?** Reducing how much you spend will help you increase your profit. Are the actions you're thinking of doing going to help you cut back on your expenses without sacrificing the quality of your service? (If they save you money, great. If they aren't saving you money then are those actions really as important as you thought they were?)

__ **Is it going to save time?** Your time is precious and scarce. So the actions you take should help you to save time. Keep the big picture in mind because some actions may take a few extra minutes in the short term but will ultimately help you save time in the long term. (For example, training an employee might be an action that will take a few extra minutes now but will save you a lot of time in the future).

__ **Is it going to help me achieve market domination?** Your business needs to own the market it works in. Whenever someone thinks of the service you provide, they should only think of you. Do the actions you've listed in this chapter support that market domination? What can you change about them to help you dominate the market even further?

__ **How do I start fast to get the low-hanging fruit?** It's easy to say you're going to take action but it's much harder to actually do it. One way to take

action and push through to its successful completion is to go for the quick wins—the low-hanging fruit. From the actions you've listed, what low-hanging fruit can you immediately pick?

__ **What's the leverage?** Leverage has a few different meanings but, in this context, I'm talking about how you can motivate yourself. For example, if you commit to complete an action within a certain period of time you can leverage that commitment by saying, "If I don't make that commitment, I'll donate $10,000 to a charity." Since you may not have $10,000, and you'll probably feel some pain donating that much money, you are leveraging your commitment and compelling yourself to complete the actions you said you'd complete.

__ **What's the reward?** For each action, list what you expect to get out of it. If you can't think of a reward for the action, seriously consider whether it is as valuable as you thought. Spend more of your time on actions that have rewards. Two of the best rewards for your actions are below (although there are other rewards you may choose to take action for)…

__ **Is it going to help me achieve wealth?** One of the best rewards you can take action for is to achieve wealth. For each action ask whether that particular action will help you make more money to give you the sense of safety and achievement and allow you to buy whatever you want whenever you want it. If possible, develop the action even further if a stronger, clearer, bigger action will help you achieve more wealth.

__ **Is it going to help me get more freedom?** Another one of the best rewards you can take action for is to get more freedom—the time and financial capacity to do whatever you want whenever you want to (without sacrificing your business). For each action ask whether that particular action will help you get more freedom. If possible, develop the action even further if a stronger, clearer, bigger action will help you get more freedom.

OUTER MASTERY

In Part 1 of this book you looked inward to build a strong foundation in yourself. Now in Part 2 it's time to look outward and build on the successes you created earlier to improve your business and take it to a higher level.

Chances are, you picked up this book because you wanted to make some changes to your business. But building a new home on a shaky foundation is a bad practice. That's why I devoted the first four chapters of this book working on your foundation—on mastering yourself—to ensure that you are in total control of who you are, where you want to go, and how you want to get there.

This is the missing piece. After growing my own business yet watching so many other people struggle with growing their businesses, I realized that the missing piece is personal growth. If your personal life is not aligned with your business life, you will struggle. But if you do the personal growth piece (from Part 1: Inner Mastery) first, you'll find it so much easier to grow a sustainable business.

I will assume that you've gone through those first four chapters with your full-attention and followed all of the Take Action activities. If you haven't, I urge you to go back and do that now. Inner mastery is a journey that you'll never complete but it's so important to get started and headed in the right direction before you try to master your business.

Now let's turn our attention to your business. You'll discover that many of the Inner Mastery principles and skills and strategies established in Part 1 of this book will clearly translate into your business.

Together, we're going to roll up our sleeves and get to work on your business, putting you firmly in control. It won't be easy, especially since there are employees or customers who have perhaps grown accustomed to how things have worked and won't like the changes. But the changes you'll make in Part 2 of this book will create a stronger, more resilient, more flexible, more profitable business that will take less time to run and will be immeasurably more enjoyable to own.

And the changes you make in your business will have an impact on your life. You'll find that a positively transformed, growing business will enhance and contribute to the 5 Dimensions of Life and Business Mastery, and will ultimately help you achieve whatever you define as success.

CHAPTER 5

MASTER YOUR BUSINESS

Now that you've looked inward at yourself, it's time to turn your attention outward. Many of the inner mastery strategies you've learned so far will inspire and guide you to business mastery. In this chapter, you'll follow the step-by-step process to create a blueprint that can lead you to a stronger, more successful business.

Introduction

Just like our personal lives, businesses are more successful when they have a clear, well-defined purpose that they are working toward. Roman galleys were rowed by slaves transplanted from all over Europe who didn't speak the same language and, of course, didn't want to be there. In spite of this, Roman galleys were fierce fighting machines on the water in the ancient Mediterranean.

Although the Roman Empire's treatment of its slaves was deplorable, this concept provides an excellent metaphor for business vision: businesses, like Roman galleys, take disparate and seemingly unconnected elements and bring them together to create a business that moves unswervingly forward.

Your business faces the same challenge: there are many moving parts, many different ideas, many great new opportunities, many ways you can grow… and it's tempting for the business owner to pursue one after another. But the result is about the same as buying a lottery ticket: you end up with nothing gained. And something else happens: business owners often end up being mastered by those same ideas and opportunities instead of mastering them.

However, **you can master your business by putting under your control all of the different pieces that contribute to your business. Rather than allowing yourself to be mastered by different parts of your business, you bring them under your mastery.**

Start With A Dream Of What You Want Your Business To Be Like

The first place to start in your business is very similar to the first place you started in yourself: start with a dream of what you want your business to be like. It's a similar first step to what you did earlier in the book when you crafted your personal vision, because your business is kind of like a living thing.

Dream about your business. What will it look like? What will you do? How will you go about your day? Who works there? What will your head office look like? What will your customers be like? What will your employees be like? What kinds of products or services will your company offer?

Dream big! Will you expand into new markets? Will you gain national recognition for your philanthropy? Will your employees be like loyal family who invite you to their family events? Will you leverage your business success into a speaking and consulting career? Will you be so successful that you regularly take your executives, management, and top-producers, along with their families, on cruises?

Start dreaming; dream big for your business. When I say "dream big for your business" I don't mean that you need to dream of a big business because that's not what everyone wants. But even if you want a small business serving a small, local market, **dream big in terms of highly loyal customers, highly loyal employees, record-breaking profitability, and so on. Don't hold back!**

This dream will come out of part of your personal vision. You have envisioned what you want your life to be like, and your business should contribute to that vision by giving you the resources to make the other parts of your personal vision come true. This dream will also come out of your 5

Dimensions of Life and Business. As you understand these 5 Dimensions for yourself, they'll guide you to think about your business.

For example, if you envision spending time with your family on regular extended vacations, your business needs to contribute: your business needs to give you the financial resources to allow you to do that, plus provide you with the time and energy to go and fully participate (rather than sitting on your laptop and cellphone all day while the kids are at the beach), and your business should be able to run without your constant attention while you're away.

Creating a personal vision is one thing but if you don't build a business that contributes to it, your personal vision is meaningless. Make sure that you dream of a successful business that is closely connected to what you envision in your personal life. Avoid the temptation to think of the two separately. As you dream, constantly ask yourself, "Is this dream congruent with my personal vision?" If you're dreaming of building a business that requires you to be there 12 hours a day *and* you're dreaming of spending more time with your family, there is incongruity there and one of those dreams will suffer.

Silence your internal critic who might tell you: "You'll never achieve that," or, "You can't get the capital to make that happen," or, "Your marketplace isn't big enough to sustain what you're dreaming about." Those are not helpful right now. Although there will come a point in this process when you'll need to deal with these challenges, now is not the time. At this point, your only task is to think of what you want your business to be—without any boundaries.

As you dream about your business, include the short-term dreams but don't forget to dream about what you want to do with the business in the future when you're ready to exit it. (For example, will you sell the business? Give it to your kids? Will it be a large corporation that you hand off to another CEO? And so on.)

Create a mind-map with your business in the center and various components of the business around the outside. For example, you might have components like: "Profitability," "Employees," "Customers," "Market area," "Services offered," and so on. (I've listed five but there are many you could use here.) Here's an example mind-map with four items added:

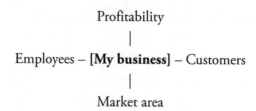

Profitability

|

Employees – **[My business]** – Customers

|

Market area

Then, just like your personal mind-map, add specific dreams to each of those components. For Employees, you might add something like, "I have 100 loyal employees working for me," and under Market area you might add a dream like, "I'm the biggest service business in my state."

To help you add specific dreams to your business vision mind-map, use a similar practice as when you built your personal vision: ask yourself this magic question: "If I was to look out three years from now and could wave a magic wand to have anything I wanted, what would my business look like?" Here are some further ideas to help you:

- How much time do you want to spend in the business? (For most of us, the target is likely going to be less time than we're spending now.)
- How much money do you want the business to make, and, how much money do you want to earn?
- How big will your business be? (How many employees? How many customers? How many calls per day? Etc.)
- What will your head office look like?
- How will your employees like working at your business?
- How will your customers feel when they buy from your business?
- What will your marketing be like?
- How will you give back?

Take a holistic approach and consider all aspects of your business. For example: don't just focus in only on generating huge profits and ignore everything else. You should also consider how your employees will love coming to work because they feel fairly rewarded and appreciated, and your customers will happily pay your fair price because they are stunned by how amazing your service is.

As you build your vision think deeply and visually about your business. Create a vivid mental picture of what your business will look like. This vision should be accurate for now and for the future.

When I say, "accurate for now and for the future," I don't mean that you've necessarily attained the vision in its fullness now, but rather that the vision isn't so far off course that you can't work toward achieving it. For example, if you are an electrician on the east coast of the United States but your vision is to be a plumber in New Zealand then that might be a long-term desire that you keep in the back of your mind but it wouldn't be a business vision that is very accurate for now or for the next three years (nor would you want to share it with your staff or customers!)

The more you can see, feel and taste the vision, the better your mind will work to take it as a GPS target to move towards.

Take Action!
Recommended actions:

__ This action is fun: Start dreaming about your business. Think about what you want to accomplish. See yourself building the business exactly the way you want. Dream big for your business (no matter what size of business you want).

__ Get out your personal vision that you put together in Part 1 of this book and reflect on what you envisioned for your personal life and how your new business vision can contribute. Adjust your business dream to support and contribute to your personal vision.

__ Think about how each of the components you listed in your business mind-map are connected to the 5 Dimensions of Life and Business. For example, money gives you wealth and freedom, the employees and customers are your relationships, etc. This is a great exercise to help you understand the depth of the 5 Dimensions in your life and business!

__ Schedule time to revisit your vision periodically to ensure that it is on track and still congruent with your life. (Over time, perhaps your life changes and your business vision may change—such as might happen if you started your business young and then later got married and had children. So make it a point to review your business vision regularly to ensure congruence with your personal vision.)

Add your own actions:

__ Stop doing actions (Actions you currently do now but should stop doing)

_____

_____

__ Keep doing actions (Actions you currently do now and should keep doing)

_____

_____

__ Start doing actions (Actions you don't do now but should start doing)

_____

_____

__ Who will do new actions? (Assign the action to yourself or someone else)

_____

_____

__ By when? (When will these actions be complete?)

_____

_____

Create A Blueprint To Achieve Your Business Vision

The most successful people in business, politics, sports, and in many other arenas of life, succeed because they have a vision for what they want to accomplish and they take action with a well-defined blueprint. With your business vision created, now it's time to put together a blueprint to turn that vision into reality.

Once you have your business vision written you can reverse engineer your plan. Again, it's just like how you used your personal vision to create a personal blueprint.

Here's how to create that business blueprint:

First, identify the big pieces of your vision. For example, you might have a specific high revenue number and a specific large business size as two areas you envision for your future, and you may also have employees, customers, vendors, and charity as four others. Perhaps there's more on your list.

Second, with each of these big pieces of your vision, figure out what you need to do in order to achieve that particular part of your vision. For example, you might realize that your vision of higher revenue might require you to invest in better systems and higher quality equipment, do more staff training, raise your rates, and do more advertising to acquire more customers. You're just thinking about the general ideas that needs to take place to make your vision a reality.

Third, once you've thought about what needs to happen for each part of your vision, list the steps to complete each one. In the example above, to realize your vision of higher revenue, I suggested you might need to invest in better systems and higher quality equipment, do more staff training, raise your rates, and do more advertising to acquire more customers. Those aren't steps in and of themselves; you need to create steps from them. Step one might be: "Identify systems I need for customer service." And step two might be: "Identify systems I need for financial management." And so on. List out as many steps as you need. Expect to have dozens, perhaps hundreds of steps—that's okay. Don't be overwhelmed by the number of steps because you don't have to do them all at once.

Fourth, put those steps in order. Do the best you can and remember that some flexibility is required because you might start achieving a higher level in your business and realize that there were steps in your blueprint you simply didn't know about earlier.

Fifth, now that you have a big list of steps, put them in your schedule and do them. Work tirelessly on each step until it is done. And by the time you've reached the end of your list of steps, you'll have achieved your vision.

It really is as simple as that. Many people mistakenly believe it's more complicated than that but it's not. As I mentioned in a previous chapter, there is no other secret that you haven't "got" yet. It's as simple as creating a vision, developing a blueprint, and then acting on that blueprint relentlessly.

Sound daunting? I think it should sound a little daunting—this is your life and your business, after all, and you need to take those things seriously because people are relying on you. Fortunately, you don't have to do it all alone. You can get help in various ways: get encouragement from family and friends, delegate different steps to employees or vendors, and get guidance and direction from experts, mentors, consultants and transformers.

Don't forget: as you create a blueprint to fulfill your vision, consider how each step contributes to your Core 5 Dimensions of Life and Business. For example, a more automated business gives you more time in your relationships and more freedom to spend on the things you enjoy.

Take Action!
Recommended actions:

___ Follow these steps to convert your business vision into an actionable blueprint. Put it into a spreadsheet so you can track it. Assign specific measurable numbers to each strategy to help you measure your progress.

__ Schedule time to revisit your blueprint and make sure you are on track. You may need to add new steps or reorder steps as your business changes.

Add your own actions:

__ Stop doing actions (Actions you currently do now but should stop doing)
_____
_____

__ Keep doing actions (Actions you currently do now and should keep doing)
_____
_____

__ Start doing actions (Actions you don't do now but should start doing)
_____
_____

__ Who will do new actions? (Assign the action to yourself or someone else)
_____
_____

__ By when? (When will these actions be complete?)
_____
_____

The Inside Functions Of Branding

In your personal life, you created a vision and then a blueprint. With a business, there's one more step: you need to build your brand.

I'm not just talking about a logo or a slogan. Certainly that's part of the brand but a brand is so much more. **A brand is the "face" of your company. It's what everyone experiences when they look at or think about your company. It's the part of your business that they'll remember when you're**

not in front of them. It's the attitude and appeal of your business. It's what your customers expect when they hire your business. It's the vision of your business, communicated in an easy-to-remember way.

Think of a brand this way: if a new customer needed your service and had never heard of your before, they should see your brand on the side of your truck or in your advertising or even in how one of your employees talks about your business, and that new customer should be able to accurately summarize what your business stands for, believes in, promises to others, and envisions for the future.

Here are the elements that go into a brand. I've divided them up into specific elements but there is a lot of overlap between them.

Core values: everyone has values that they live by—sometimes these values are stated, sometimes they aren't. Every business, as well, has values that they operate by. Some common values include:

- Honesty and integrity
- Fairness
- Profitability (yes, that's a value)
- Customer satisfaction

There are many others. Core values are the most important "non-negotiables" in your business. They're the very cornerstones that drive how you do everything—from pricing your services to firing and hiring to marketing to customer service, and more. Even if you've never thought about them before, your business operates on certain values… likely stemming from your own personal values.

Whether you've ever thought about your business' values or not, now is the time to state those values. List them out and choose a few that are very important and memorable and use those as part of your brand. Let people know what they are, hire from them and fire from them, make business decisions from them.

Brand identity: your brand identity is how your business should look and feel—how it is positioned strategically in your market. I'm not just talking about your business name; I'm talking about who your business is and what it's all about: are you a low-cost provider? Do you offer the very best customer service? Do you offer more services? Do you focus on one specific thing as THE go-to expert? Do you perform a service in a way that no one else does? All of these make up your brand identity. It's what people think of when they think of you. It's what people say about you to their friends.

Your brand identity needs to be unique. If you're a plumber, and you advertise yourself as a plumber, this will cause confusion amongst your prospective buyers because there are already many plumbers in the marketplace. Find a way to position yourself uniquely in the market: for example, be the plumber who specializes in homes over 100 years old. See the difference? Be unique. And don't just say you are something—be it! (Many businesses say they give great customer service but very few actually set a standard and live up to it. I'll talk more about this specific problem later in the book.)

Once you have established this part of your brand identity, name your brand. Even if you are an existing business, you might consider renaming your business to reflect your brand identity.

Brand promise: this is the promise to the market. It's the promise you're making that you're going to deliver to everyone you serve. It's your commitment to your customers.

A brand promise makes a great slogan for your business so you may consider making it that, but it should be much more than a slogan. It should be your mindset and the mindset of each and every employee on your team. It should encapsulate your values and it should guide all of the decisions made in your business every day.

I'll illustrate with an example: in my company: our brand promise is "we do more." When we're in a customer's home to look at their leaky faucet, if we notice that one of their door knobs is loose then we'll quickly fix it for free. See how we live up to that "we do more" promise?

Here are some ideas about what you might make your brand promise:

- Reliability
- Great customer service
- Friendly attitude
- Speed of service
- Expertise
- Accurate estimates

Your brand promise will stem not only from your brand values but also from your brand identity.

Some business owners think a brand promise is just bullshit because they already deliver what they feel to be great service. But I believe that a brand promise isn't bullshit, it IS the shit! It is the foundation of the business and business growth. It is also sometimes the "X factor" that drives a business to grow past their competitors and take over market share.

Brand image: brand image is what a lot of people think about when they think of brand. This is the visual aspect of your brand. It's your logo but it's more than that. It's the condition of your vehicles; it's how your employees are dressed and how they act and do their work; it's how your website works; it's all of your printed materials—from your flyers and ads to your estimate sheets and invoices.

All of these should look the same. A customer should be able to look from your flyer to your service vehicle to your Yellow Pages ad to your business card to your invoice—and everything should look like it came from the same business. The frequency of your brand image builds trust, so the more people are exposed to your brand, the more they trust you.

Here's how to create a great brand image:

- Have a logo designed that describes your business. Ignore the generic swoosh or lines or dots—these elements don't say a thing about your business. Instead, have a logo created that explains what you do. If you offer fast service, your logo might include a clock. If you're the plumber who specializes in homes that are 100 years old, perhaps you want a stately-looking old house in your logo. My company, Gold Medal Service, has a gold medal as its logo.

- Incorporate your business name into everything. Ideally, you would incorporate it into your logo but if this is not possible (because the size of your business name, for example), it should always be placed near your logo.

- Own a color. Choose a color that closely reflects what you do and own it. Make sure everything in your business has that color on it. Again, in my business, our color is yellow and we make sure it's present in all aspects of our brand image—from our vehicles to our printed material to the name badges on our employee's uniforms. The color and look needs to be planned very strategically to make sure it does not just blend with other companies. It should stand out from other companies in your area.

Brand penetration: here's the last part of building a brand—brand penetration. Brand penetration is the amount of depth into the market that your brand achieves—just like market-share. Instead of trying to get more people to know you, go deep with brand penetration and instead get more customers who you would like to work for.

My advice is: put your brand on everything because that creates a consistent experience for your customers and your employees. Incorporate those elements in the following places:

- Your service vehicles
- Your business signage
- Your employee uniforms
- Your marketing
- Your follow-up paperwork (estimate sheets, invoices, etc.)
- Emails, social media, forms

But that's just the beginning. All of the brand elements I've talked about so far will also inform the following:

- How you market and sell
- How you deliver your service
- How you provide customer service and ensure customer satisfaction
- How your employees act when dealing with a customer
- What your employees say when they answer the phone

I want to wrap up this brand-building section by saying this about creating a brand: your brand creates an emotion—it attracts or repels. If I start a plumbing company that is primarily pink, it may attract women but may push away men. What you say and what you do during every interaction—that creates part of your brand and it, too, can attract or repel. Pay attention to your brand and build one that attracts the right customers. And don't underestimate the power of a brand: if you pay attention to brand in the beginning, you can make a one truck company look like a 50 truck company, and the reverse is true, too.

Take Action!
Recommended actions:

__ Start thinking about your brand. If you have an existing brand, consider what changes need to be made to elevate it to the next level. If you haven't put in much time and effort into your brand so far, you're starting with a blank slate and can create something powerful.

__ Ask your employees, customers, and vendors for their thoughts about your brand. Ask them for input such as: "When you need our services, what is it about us that you like?"

__ Develop your core values, brand identity, brand promise, brand image, and brand penetration. As you do this, you might end up with several possible elements (such as multiple logo ideas, multiple color ideas, etc.) Narrow these down and choose one that most expresses your business vision—what your business will be like in the future.

Add your own actions:

__ Stop doing actions (Actions you currently do now but should stop doing)

_____

_____

__ Keep doing actions (Actions you currently do now and should keep doing)

_____

_____

__ Start doing actions (Actions you don't do now but should start doing)

_____

_____

__ Who will do new actions? (Assign the action to yourself or someone else)

_____

_____

__ By when? (When will these actions be complete?)

_____

_____

Setting Up Your Business

A business vision, blueprint, and brand is essential. But a business is more than that. A business is built on taking smart actions in a way that grows the business without ever letting it get beyond your control. In this section, I'm going to talk about setting up your business, and I mean turning the idea of your business into an actual business. Don't skip this section if you already own a business—you'll still learn some really useful advice about how to grow your existing business.

I'm not here to talk about the legal or financial aspects of your business—whether you should incorporate or where, or things like that. There are financial and legal experts who should be giving you that advice. Besides, it doesn't matter for what I'm talking about here. (It's important but the exact details aren't important to what I'm talking about here.)

Instead, I want to talk about how to actually set up the business so that it starts making money. Think of these not as a step-by-step list but rather a list of best practices around starting a business. Even if you are running a business already, you can still apply many of these best practices to grow your business.

Test the market first: put your little toe in first. Then go big. Try something out and see how people respond. If it's possible, make that effort bigger and permanent. For example, if you're going to send direct mail, test it with a little piece and, if you get results, you can magnify it. If you go into a trade line, test a little piece. Consider what McDonald's restaurants do: they don't just look at a piece of land and think that it should be a good place to put a restaurant. By the time you see a store going up, they've already tested the market and surveyed the market and determined that people would want it.

Set up systems and processes: do this early and put these into all aspects of your business.

- A system is usually one thing that has to be done all the time. For example: at the end of the day when you're closing up, you need to lock the doors and turn on the alarm.
- A process is a sequence of operations and an order to do things. For example, you should create a process around customer interactions so that every customer experience feels the same for every customer. Create checklists for everything.

I can't stress the importance of systems and processes. Every successful business has many of these in place while every struggling business lacks them. If you do the same thing more than once, or if there's an aspect of your business that is causing pain or challenge, or if you want a desired result for a particular aspect of your business, you need a system or process.

I needed to mention systems and processes here as part of mastering your business but I've devoted an entire chapter to it later in the book. I'll give you some specific examples there of systems and processes you should set up in your business.

Do more than you think you need to do: although you might dream of living on a beach and going to work only a couple of days a week, you're not there yet. You need to work relentlessly in your business to get to a point where you can do that and, in every business I've ever seen or coached, it always took more than the owner initially thought. Don't be discouraged by that—be inspired!

Don't stop generating leads and prospects: think of your business as a conveyor belt. At the beginning are leads and they move along the conveyor belt to eventually become customers. If you only intermittently put leads at the beginning of the conveyor belt, or worse yet, if you stop altogether, you won't have enough customers regularly rolling off the conveyor belt at the end.

Look at customers along every area of the belt and ask what can be done to help them convert more and be lifetime customers.

Take Action!
Recommended actions:

__ Think about new markets or trade lines you want to enter. Test the market and determine if it is right for you. Schedule new tests (of different markets or different trade lines) to occur regularly in your business.

__ Make a list of systems and processes you need in your business. Start the list now; we'll come back to it in a later chapter.

__ Find a mentor, coach, consultant, or transformer who can help you stay inspired and energized to do more than you think is required to reach your goals.

__ Lead generation and prospecting are one of the most important activities in your business. These activities ensure that your business thrives. Let everyone in your company know that they contribute to this through their behaviors and actions. And make sure you schedule time daily to do more lead generation and prospecting (if you own a small business this might be an activity that you do personally; if you own a larger business and have staff to do this for you, you should still be involved in lead-generation and prospecting but at a higher level).

Add your own actions:

__ Stop doing actions (Actions you currently do now but should stop doing)

_____

_____

__ Keep doing actions (Actions you currently do now and should keep doing)

_____

_____

__ Start doing actions (Actions you don't do now but should start doing)

_____

_____

__ Who will do new actions? (Assign the action to yourself or someone else)

_____

_____

__ By when? (When will these actions be complete?)

Decision-Making Criteria

There's a knock on your office door and someone says: "You need to decide on a new angle for our marketing." Later in the day another person says: "You need to decide on the healthcare plan for our employees." Still later in the day someone else says: "You need to decide on that new hire we were talking about." The business owner's day is filled with decisions.

Unfortunately, many business owners discover that decisions are one of the hardest parts of running a business. You are called upon through the chaos of your day to make instant decisions in a fairly rapid turnaround that often have far-reaching consequences.

It's not easy to make decisions: it can be time-consuming to make decisions and some decisions end up being based on emotion rather than logic. It's tempting to delay a decision because you think that there are aspects of the decision you don't have yet, or that deciding locks you into one path that you cannot extricate yourself from. Fortunately, business mastery allows you to make smarter decisions, faster (and to quickly correct decisions that turned out to be not quite right the first time).

Not all decisions need to be made by you. The larger you get, the fewer decisions you should make personally and the more decisions your staff should make. Empower all staff to make decisions that are appropriate for their position and help them to make those decisions in alignment with the company's core values and targets. For example, your cleaning staff shouldn't have to come to you to ask which cleaning scent they should use. Your field experts shouldn't have to come to you to ask whether more materials need to be ordered. Some of these "low level" decisions should be done by staff. However, to help maintain mastery over your business (and control over your costs), you should set up some decision-making criteria to help your staff know what to do so that they make informed decisions that are aligned with the business.

An example is a customer service situation. In many businesses, if a customer has an issue, the front-line staff member is not empowered to address the customer service issue. Therefore, the issue goes unresolved or the staff member needs to knock on the boss' door and ask for a decision to be made about how to resolve the issue. In my business, my employees have a basic criteria to help them make instant decisions about customer service issues and they are empowered to make things right immediately if there ever is an issue. Of course, for larger issues, the manager may be involved but smaller scale issues can and should be solved on the spot.

Building a decision-making process for your business will have a profound impact on your ability to make decisions, your confidence in those decisions, and how much time you spend making decisions.

To help you build a decision-making process, here is what I use: **most business decisions can be made by collecting the available evidence and then running through a decision-making criteria.** The criteria I use is a list of questions that I ask myself whenever I face a decision:

- What does it do for customer needs?
- What does it do for employees?
- What does it do for the company?
- Does it overcome a weakness?
- Does it provide a return on investment?
- How much time will it take?
- What does it do for the business owners?

Learning to make decisions on the fly, in the rapid-fire environment of a business, requires that you trust your decision-making ability and then you move forward confidently that you made the best decision based on the available data. Not using a process could cause blind spots or keep emotion as part of the hidden process. When you use a process, emotion is removed and then you can make smart decisions. For example, a pilot never takes off without going through a checklist first. This keeps the pilot's focus on the task and ensures that every item is reviewed; it removes emotion and human error from the equation.

Take Action!
Recommended actions:

___ Think about the decisions people ask you to make throughout the day. Build a system that will allow them to first determine whether it's a decision you need to make at all. Empower your staff to start making decisions that are appropriate for their level. (And if they make a mistake, that's okay. It happens. Adjust the criteria or help them to understand how to apply the criteria correctly.)

Add your own actions:

___ Stop doing actions (Actions you currently do now but should stop doing)

_____

_____

___ Keep doing actions (Actions you currently do now and should keep doing)

_____

_____

___ Start doing actions (Actions you don't do now but should start doing)

_____

_____

___ Who will do new actions? (Assign the action to yourself or someone else)

_____

_____

___ By when? (When will these actions be complete?)

_____

_____

Improving Your Business

There's a well-known saying that I love: "If you're not moving forward, you're moving backwards." This is true in so many areas of life, including your business. If you are not moving your business forward, you are allowing your business to be battered backwards by the whims of the market. If you're not aggressively pushing to improve your business then other factors—such as your competitors, the economy, the industry, or your employees—will push you back. Even if you think you're standing still, eventually you will move backwards. **You need to constantly and actively improve your business. I would even go so far as to say that, once you've set up your business, improving your business is the most important task you have.**

When a business wants to improve quality control, they often stick a manager in the truck to ride around with an employee and see how that employee performs. But we all know that this doesn't really work. The employee will be on their best behavior, often doing things the way they're supposed to do them because they know someone is watching. This method of quality control is flawed.

One of my favorite ways to improve a business is to mystery shop. This is the best form of quality control because you get to see your entire business in action. You can hire a company to mystery shop for you or you can get your friends (those who your employees don't know are your friends) to mystery shop. Give them a list of criteria that you want them to watch for and have them go through the entire process of calling up your company, scheduling service, interacting with your employees, hiring them, and having them complete the work. This is the best way to get accurate feedback on how your staff are doing.

You can also improve your business by mystery shopping your competition. In this case, you might do this yourself. (Let me clarify that when you mystery shop the competition, you are not doing it to steal their ideas.

Rather, you are evaluating what their processes and service is like and examining whether they have a competitive advantage that you are missing.)

Look at how they compare against your business and how can you improve your business to be the business of choice in your market. This is not a new concept; it's just new to some industries. Large retail stores, though, have been doing this since the beginning of time.

Take Action!
Recommended actions:

___ When was the last time you assessed your business? Immediately perform a mystery shop on your staff this week. Schedule regular mystery shops of your business and compare them against the benchmark set by the first mystery shop. Use the information from each mystery shop to improve your business.

___ List your competitors and make a plan to mystery shop them. Again, you're not doing this to steal their ideas but to assess their advantages over your business.

Add your own actions:

___ Stop doing actions (Actions you currently do now but should stop doing)

_____

_____

___ Keep doing actions (Actions you currently do now and should keep doing)

_____

_____

___ Start doing actions (Actions you don't do now but should start doing)

_____

_____

__ Who will do new actions? (Assign the action to yourself or someone else)

_____

_____

__ By when? (When will these actions be complete?)

_____

_____

Conclusion

We've covered a lot of material in this chapter! You started by dreaming big about what your business could be and we progressed to the point where you are assessing your business with mystery shopping.

This chapter has a lot of "big picture" elements in it—visioning, planning, branding, decision-making—but they are all part of mastering your business as a whole.

Invest weeks or months on this because everything else in the following chapters is driven by the choices you make here.

Your journey toward achieving your personal vision is fueled in part by how your business operates. Working on the elements in this chapter will help build a better, stronger, smarter, more profitable business that will then contribute to your personal vision.

Master Action List For Chapter 5

At the end of each section of this chapter you had actions to perform as well as Start Doing/Keep Doing/Stop Doing lists. Gather those actions together into a Master Action List, add any new actions that you think of, and then go through the questions below to think about how these actions can transform your life and your business:

__ **Is it going to make me money?** Are the actions you've listed going to help you generate more income? (If they are, great. Think about how they might be able to help you generate even more income. If they aren't making you more money then are those actions really as important as you thought they were?)

__ **Is it going save me money?** Reducing how much you spend will help you increase your profit. Are the actions you're thinking of doing going to help you cut back on your expenses without sacrificing the quality of your service? (If they save you money, great. If they aren't saving you money then are those actions really as important as you thought they were?)

__ **Is it going to save time?** Your time is precious and scarce. So the actions you take should help you to save time. Keep the big picture in mind because some actions may take a few extra minutes in the short term but will ultimately help you save time in the long term. (For example, training an employee might be an action that will take a few extra minutes now but will save you a lot of time in the future).

__ **Is it going to help me achieve market domination?** Your business needs to own the market it works in. Whenever someone thinks of the service you provide, they should only think of you. Do the actions you've listed in this chapter support that market domination? What can you change about them to help you dominate the market even further?

__ **How do I start fast to get the low-hanging fruit?** It's easy to say you're going to take action but it's much harder to actually do it. One way to take

action and push through to its successful completion is to go for the quick wins—the low-hanging fruit. From the actions you've listed, what low-hanging fruit can you immediately pick?

___ What's the leverage? Leverage has a few different meanings but, in this context, I'm talking about how you can motivate yourself. For example, if you commit to complete an action within a certain period of time you can leverage that commitment by saying, "If I don't make that commitment, I'll donate $10,000 to a charity." Since you may not have $10,000, and you'll probably feel some pain donating that much money, you are leveraging your commitment and compelling yourself to complete the actions you said you'd complete.

___ What's the reward? For each action, list what you expect to get out of it. If you can't think of a reward for the action, seriously consider whether it is as valuable as you thought. Spend more of your time on actions that have rewards. Two of the best rewards for your actions are below (although there are other rewards you may choose to take action for)...

___ Is it going to help me achieve wealth? One of the best rewards you can take action for is to achieve wealth. For each action ask whether that particular action will help you make more money to give you the sense of safety and achievement and allow you to buy whatever you want whenever you want it. If possible, develop the action even further if a stronger, clearer, bigger action will help you achieve more wealth.

___ Is it going to help me get more freedom? Another one of the best rewards you can take action for is to get more freedom—the time and financial capacity to do whatever you want whenever you want to (without sacrificing your business). For each action ask whether that particular action will help you get more freedom. If possible, develop the action even further if a stronger, clearer, bigger action will help you get more freedom.

CHAPTER 6

MASTER YOUR NUMBERS LIKE AN ENGINEER

Everything you do in business can be quantified with real numbers. And the more you measure these numbers and use them to influence your decisions, the more you will master your business. In this chapter, learn which numbers are most important and how they can help you.

Introduction

Most professionals start their businesses because they have been working at their profession or specific trade-line for a while and want to work for themselves instead of for someone else. They are experts at whatever specific service they know well but what they might not realize is that running the rest of the business is a numbers game. When you make the switch from technician to business owner, you are not a carpet cleaner or an electrician or a plumber anymore. (Yes, you still do those things and that's why you get paid) but rather, you are a numbers person.

We live for numbers in our personal lives: our income and our expenses are two numbers we're familiar with. The temperature outside is another number we're familiar with, especially if we have to work outdoors. Our body temperature is a number we tend to ignore until we get sick. Even our leisure time—such as watching our favorite sports team or participating in a fantasy football league—is all numbers.

Numbers drive a business, too. Numbers quickly and clearly tell you just how well your business is performing with zero guesswork or

interpretation. **You can look at a number and, when you understand it against other numbers or number trends, you instantly know how things are going and you can act accordingly. Numbers are the pulse of a company in a positive way or negative painful way.**

Before you started your business you may not have been very focused on the numbers. But now that you are a business owner your job is not only to perform the trade you have been hired to perform, you also need to understand the numbers that drive your business. And you need to start now to master your numbers even if you have a small business, because the bigger your business gets, the more you'll need to know, understand, and master your numbers.

Numbers Are Your Business

In the introduction of this chapter I said that numbers drive your business. Another way to put this is: numbers ARE your business. Without key numbers, your business will be completely lost. You will be blind to how your business is working.

So, what numbers am I talking about here? You can probably guess at some of them. Chances are, you're thinking about some of them even if you haven't attained mastery yet. But you probably aren't thinking about all of these and perhaps you're also considering ones that aren't as important.

These are the numbers you need to master in your business:

- **Leads**: This is the group of people in the area you are marketing to. You have their names and contact information and you use marketing to convince them to enquire further.
- **Prospects**: When you market to your leads, some of them will reply to you and indicate that want more information. These are prospects—people who have indicated that they are interested in possibly doing business with you.
- **Customers**: Customers are prospects who have hired you. Even if they haven't paid you yet, as soon as they book an appointment to have your experts come to their home, they are customers.

- **Conversion rate**: This is the number of prospects who become customers. Not all prospects who enquire for more information will become customers. You need to track this ratio and improve it.
- **Sales**: A sale is made as soon as a customer agrees to a service. You'll provide the service and they'll pay you, and the sale is complete. (Note: My definition of sales is associated with the exchange of service for money. Later in the book you'll see how I redefine the act of selling quite differently. But sales, as a number, has to do with the sale of a service.)
- **Average transaction**: This number measures the average amount of money that occurs in each sale, and it is determined by adding up all the dollar amounts from sales over a period of time and dividing by the number of sales. If you earned $5,000 in a week from 5 sales, the average transaction was $1,000 per sale.
- **Revenue**: Revenues are any incoming money you earn in your business.
- **Expenses**: Expenses are any outgoing cost you have to pay in order to run your business.
- **Profit**: When you subtract expenses from revenue, your profit is what's left over.
- **Assets**: Assets are the things you own. As a measurable number, it's the dollar value of these assets. In accounting terms, some assets depreciate (reduce in value) over time.
- **Receivables**: Receivables are the amounts that customers pay you. Whenever a sale is made, a receivable is created. If the customer pays immediately, the receivable is paid. At the end of each week or month, you'll have a list of unpaid receivables that will need collection. Keep your receivables under control!
- **Payables**: Payables are the amounts that you owe your vendors. Your payables are your vendors' receivables. Keep your payables paid on time to ensure a positive, mutually beneficial relationship between you and your vendors.
- **ROI**: This stands for Return On Investment and it measures how much you receive in from a particular investment. For example, it might measure the amount of revenue you generate from a specific marketing effort.

- **KPI**: Key Performance Indicators (KPIs) are the numbers you track on a daily, weekly, or monthly basis that give you an at-a-glance view into the health of your company. I'll talk more about KPIs later in this book.

- **Breakeven**: Your breakeven is the amount of money you would need to earn just to pay your bills. The number is derived by adding up all of your expenses. If you make enough money to pay your expenses, and not a penny more, you'll be at breakeven. Anything you earn above this is profit.

- **Employee retention**: This measures how long, on average, your employees stay with you, from the day they were hired to the day they stop working for you. Your goal is to increase your retention number.

- **Employee satisfaction**: As the name indicates, this number measures how satisfied your employees are to be working for you. Don't just rely on anecdotal evidence. Measure this number using surveys to get an actual, trackable number.

- **Customer satisfaction**: As the name indicates, this number measures how satisfied your customers are with the service they receive from your company. Again, don't just rely on anecdotal evidence but use surveys to get an actual, trackable number.

- **Website traffic**: Website traffic measures the number of people who visit your website. (There are other website numbers you may want to track as well, including the number of users versus new users, whether those users are on desktop or mobile browsers, how long they're on your site, or what their bounce rate is).

- **Mailing list size**: This is the number of people you're mailing to. As you'll learn elsewhere in the book, size doesn't matter as long as you are deeply penetrating a specific market. Of course, over time, you'll want to grow your mailing list size but don't make a big list your top priority because it may hint that you are not penetrating your market deeply.

- **Market demographics**: These are the numbers around what your market is like. How many households are in the specific geographic area you've chosen? What is the average number of people per household? What is the average value of their home? What is their average income? I cover other demographic information in the chapter on mastering your marketing and sales.

- **Labor:** This is the average rate per hour that you pay your employees for their labor on a job. Since this number can rise quickly, you'll need to strike a balance between paying your employees well and keeping a lid on these costs.

Each of these numbers represents a key component of your business. Combined, this entire list gives you a snapshot of your business; remove any number from this list and you don't get a complete picture. (This is a starting point for your numbers. I go in-depth into these at the Warrior Fast Track Academy—my 4-day hands-on intensive training event.)

I can't put it any more simply than this: **master these numbers and you will master your business**. And although you might not see the connection at first, if you master these numbers you'll contribute to your 5 Dimensions of Life and Business Mastery: each of these numbers gives you information about the quality and quantity of some of your employee and customer relationships, how much wealth you're generating, and how close you are to true freedom.

Here's an exercise to see how well you know your business: write the above list of numbers on a piece of paper and then try (without looking at any other paperwork) to accurately write down what your numbers are right now in your business. Then, compare your answers against your paperwork for accuracy.

You'll reveal a couple of things in this exercise: first, there's a good chance that you won't be aware of many of these numbers. And second, you'll also discover that the information stored in your paperwork is likely scattered and hard to find. (Maybe you had to find a list of assets and add them up, for example.) I want your business to get to the point where, if I were to walk in and ask you to assess the health of your business, you could write this list from memory and then I could easily check in only a couple of places to discover the answers—and you'd be pretty damn close to correct on every single one. That is the goal of number mastery. Work toward it and by the time you get there, I promise that your business will be running VERY differently!

Take Action!

Recommended actions:

___ Do the exercise listed above. List those categories of numbers, guess each number, then try to find whether you're accurate or not.

___ Create a spreadsheet with the categories (above) along the top and the months of the year down the side. Use your current numbers (from the exercise above) as this month's numbers. Then schedule time each month to update the spreadsheet. You can download a Microsoft Excel Spreadsheet template for your business from the free resources page: **CEOWARRIOR. com/masteryresources**

Add your own actions:

___ Stop doing actions (Actions you currently do now but should stop doing)

_____

_____

___ Keep doing actions (Actions you currently do now and should keep doing)

_____

_____

___ Start doing actions (Actions you don't do now but should start doing)

_____

_____

___ Who will do new actions? (Assign the action to yourself or someone else)

_____

_____

___ By when? (When will these actions be complete?)

_____

_____

Master Your Numbers By Glimpsing The Future

By now I hope I've convinced you about just how important numbers are to your business. Now I want to show you how to make sure that you are getting the best numbers in your business.

When someone asks me how they can master their numbers, here's what I tell them: **you need to see the future—the outcome of your business (your business vision and blueprint) —and then live it in reverse. And you need to put some numbers around it.**

After you see the future, you rewind what needs to be done to get there. You will also spot past trends that point to potential roadblocks you need to be aware of. For example, if your goal is to build wealth but you notice a trend where your expenses rise faster than your revenue, then this diminishing profit will be a roadblock to building wealth. But this is only something you'd notice if you have put some numbers around your vision and blueprint.

See how everything is tied together? Your vision doesn't exist apart from your numbers; they're connected. Your vision inspires you to move forward, your numbers help you stay on track and give you measurable feedback about your progress. And they all work together to contribute to your Core 5 Dimensions of Life and Business Mastery.

Mastering your numbers is not an academic exercise, it's how you will ensure your business survives and grows. And that leads me to the last point I want to discuss in this section: your numbers don't just guide you on their own, they help you understand your business when you look at them altogether.

Here's what I mean: you need to earn a certain amount of money in revenue to pay your employees and your expenses and yourself, and retain a bit of profit. You also need to retain enough to add to future growth. In order to earn that revenue, you need to make a certain number of sales at an average transaction per sale. In order to make that many sales, you need to convert a certain number of people from prospects to customers. In order to get those prospects, you have to get a certain number of leads. In order to get those leads, you have to do a certain amount of marketing.

Although there are many steps between the marketing you do and the dollars you ultimately earn in revenue, there IS a link—a series of links, like a chain, and each link has a number attached to it. At first, these numbers might not make sense to you but over time these numbers become predictable. You'll know exactly how much marketing you need to do in order to get the right number of leads to get the right number of prospects to get the right number of sales to get the right amount of revenue to pay everyone and to have some profit predictably left over. Your mastery of numbers drives this. Otherwise, it's unprofitable guesswork.

Take Action!
Recommended actions:

__ Think about your business vision and blueprint, and the numbers you have wrapped around it. Now, reverse-engineer those numbers—"rewind" your business from the ideal future to the current state—and determine what the numbers look like as they change in between now and the future.

__ Next, determine what actions you need to take—perhaps daily, weekly, monthly, or annually—to influence those numbers in the direction you want them to go.

__ See if you can make an educated guess in your business about how much specific marketing activities you need to do in order to get one sale. Determine what the marketing cost was to derive just one sale from your efforts. Now calculate what happens when you invest ten times or one hundred times that amount of money to get ten sales or one hundred sales.

Add your own actions:

__ Stop doing actions (Actions you currently do now but should stop doing)

_____

_____

__ Keep doing actions (Actions you currently do now and should keep doing)

_____

_____

__ Start doing actions (Actions you don't do now but should start doing)

_____

_____

__ Who will do new actions? (Assign the action to yourself or someone else)

_____

_____

__ By when? (When will these actions be complete?)

_____

_____

Growing Your Business With Numbers

I've given you an overview about how you want to understand some of the key numbers you have in your business, and why; and I've showed you how to discover your targets based on your vision for the business. Now I want to give you some powerful ways to use numbers in your business to improve it.

Create Key Performance Indicators (KPIs): KPIs are the measuring stick of what you want to achieve at various levels in your company. It boils down performance to just a couple of numbers so that anyone can tell at a glance how that particular part of the company is doing. KPIs should be tied to the most important numbers I've shown you earlier.

You should create KPIs for every part of your business—each role should have KPIs that they are evaluated against, each department should have KPIs that they are evaluated against, and the business itself should have some overall KPIs that help you see how the business as a whole is doing.

Get the KPIs down to a level where each person can see what they are supposed to do in their job and how their job contributes to the bottom line. This is not just for experts who are out there performing calls at customers' homes, it's also for the drivers, the customer service experts, the financial department, etc. Everyone should have a measurement and a result they need to deliver and be ranked against.

Here are some examples:

- A business might have revenue and profit as one of their KPIs
- The sales department might have customer conversions as one of their KPIs
- An individual employee might have customer feedback on a scale of 1-5 as one of their KPIs

KPIs on their own are helpful but here's how you can make them even more helpful: set minimum standards and winning standards. Minimum standards are the lowest acceptable level. As long as you're achieving this, you're doing a good job... but not a great job. If you fall below these levels, it is time for an intervention—so a business KPI that falls below the minimum standard might require a company-wide recalibration, or an employee KPI that falls below the minimum standard might require some additional training or that employee may ultimately need to be let go. Winning standards are targets that are superior. When you're achieving this level of KPI, things are great and expectations are being exceeded.

Create scorecards: exactly as the name suggests, scorecards give an at-a-glance view of how your business is doing. They should contain the key numbers and KPIs that you are paying attention to. Keep them all on a single page. This is the pulse of the company and it should tell you at a glance how many customers you have compared to how many you need, what your revenue, profit, conversion rate, and average invoice numbers are. You can download a copy of a KPI scorecard template that I use in my company from the free resources page: **CEOWARRIOR.com/masteryresources**

Communicate this information to your staff regularly: staff should receive their scorecards with their own employee-level KPIs regularly but they should also receive department and company scorecards as well so they can see how their efforts are contributing to the larger picture.

As much as possible, keep your team informed in real time. Leverage technology like email or text to help you get the word out about your company's KPIs as they change. In my company, for example, we send out a daily text to let our staff know about our company's most important KPIs.

So far I've talked about KPIs as a way to grow your business with numbers but there are other ways. Here's one more powerful way to grow your business with number:

Rank your customers: another way to grow your business with numbers is to rank your customers. Although you should value all of your customers and treat them all professionally, not all of them are the same and you shouldn't treat them all the same. Rank your customers by levels and then over deliver for that level.

For example, I recommend that you rank your customer by potential lifetime revenue and then create levels of service for that particular group. Here are some numbers as an example:

- A+ customers—these customer will send you $20,000 of business or more.
- A customers—these customer will send you $10,000 to $19,999 of business.

- B customers—these customers will send you $5,000 to $9,999 of business.
- C customers—these customers will send you $2,000 to $4,999 of business.
- D customers—these customers will send you $0 to $1,999 of business.
- F customers—these are Fired customers who no longer fit your business practices and plan.

Of course you should treat every customer professionally but each of these levels of customers might receive different things from you. For example, your sales department might have a different sales funnel for the bigger customers; or you might give your A+ customers a special number to call to get directly to a special contact person, like a concierge, while the D customers would call through to your regular line.

There are many different ways you can add value to each level but the important thing is to create an appropriate promise that you make to each level and then over deliver on that promise.

Ranking customers helps us manage relationships and quickly deliver a certain level of pre-defined service to the right customer.

Please understand this is a brief overview of numbers, since numbers are different for each business, and this section alone could become an entire book. I recommend that you determine which numbers are important to your business and then seek the very best business-transforming experts in the world to help define things deeper. Business is full of numbers so if you lack a strong foundation of how the numbers work, you could be in for a painful (or instant!) destruction of your business.

Take Action!
Recommended actions:

__ Create KPIs for your business, including KPIs for your overall business and for each role. Schedule time regularly to update these KPIs and share them on scorecards with employees.

__ Create a spreadsheet to rank your customers, as I've listed above. (You may need to adjust the dollar figures for your business.) Then determine what you'll do for each level of customer. Then, file all of your customers into the appropriate ranking and instruct your team to begin delivering the level-appropriate service for each customer.

Add your own actions:

__ Stop doing actions (Actions you currently do now but should stop doing)

_____

_____

__ Keep doing actions (Actions you currently do now and should keep doing)

_____

_____

__ Start doing actions (Actions you don't do now but should start doing)

_____

_____

__ Who will do new actions? (Assign the action to yourself or someone else)

_____

_____

__ By when? (When will these actions be complete?)

_____

_____

Conclusion

Your business might be made up of products and services and employees and customers… But it's really the numbers that are your business.

Numbers are ruthless because they won't give you a second chance or turn the other cheek. They bare everything—your triumphs and your failures. Some people might not like how cold-heartedly honest numbers are but that's exactly why I like them. Numbers won't lie to you. Numbers tell you exactly where you are and they help you to assess how close or far you are from achieving your target numbers. Numbers are an honest guide that will never lie to you or tell you what you want to hear.

And when you master your numbers, you master your business and will push your business higher, faster.

Master Action List For Chapter 6

At the end of each section of this chapter you had actions to perform as well as Start Doing/Keep Doing/Stop Doing lists. Gather those actions together into a Master Action List, add any new actions that you think of, and then go through the questions below to think about how these actions can transform your life and your business:

___ **Is it going to make me money?** Are the actions you've listed going to help you generate more income? (If they are, great. Think about how they might be able to help you generate even more income. If they aren't making you more money then are those actions really as important as you thought they were?)

___ **Is it going save me money?** Reducing how much you spend will help you increase your profit. Are the actions you're thinking of doing going to help you cut back on your expenses without sacrificing the quality of your service? (If they save you money, great. If they aren't saving you money then are those actions really as important as you thought they were?)

___ **Is it going to save time?** Your time is precious and scarce. So the actions you take should help you to save time. Keep the big picture in mind because some actions may take a few extra minutes in the short term but will ultimately help you save time in the long term. (For example, training an employee might be an action that will take a few extra minutes now but will save you a lot of time in the future).

___ **Is it going to help me achieve market domination?** Your business needs to own the market it works in. Whenever someone thinks of the service you provide, they should only think of you. Do the actions you've listed in this chapter support that market domination? What can you change about them to help you dominate the market even further?

___ **How do I start fast to get the low-hanging fruit?** It's easy to say you're going to take action but it's much harder to actually do it. One way to take

action and push through to its successful completion is to go for the quick wins—the low-hanging fruit. From the actions you've listed, what low-hanging fruit can you immediately pick?

__ **What's the leverage?** Leverage has a few different meanings but, in this context, I'm talking about how you can motivate yourself. For example, if you commit to complete an action within a certain period of time you can leverage that commitment by saying, "If I don't make that commitment, I'll donate $10,000 to a charity." Since you may not have $10,000, and you'll probably feel some pain donating that much money, you are leveraging your commitment and compelling yourself to complete the actions you said you'd complete.

__ **What's the reward?** For each action, list what you expect to get out of it. If you can't think of a reward for the action, seriously consider whether it is as valuable as you thought. Spend more of your time on actions that have rewards. Two of the best rewards for your actions are below (although there are other rewards you may choose to take action for)...

__ **Is it going to help me achieve wealth?** One of the best rewards you can take action for is to achieve wealth. For each action ask whether that particular action will help you make more money to give you the sense of safety and achievement and allow you to buy whatever you want whenever you want it. If possible, develop the action even further if a stronger, clearer, bigger action will help you achieve more wealth.

__ **Is it going to help me get more freedom?** Another one of the best rewards you can take action for is to get more freedom—the time and financial capacity to do whatever you want whenever you want to (without sacrificing your business). For each action ask whether that particular action will help you get more freedom. If possible, develop the action even further if a stronger, clearer, bigger action will help you get more freedom.

CHAPTER 7

MASTER YOUR MARKETING AND SALES

Service businesses struggle at marketing and sales; they simply don't do enough of each and they don't do it very well. Mastering your marketing and your sales will have a profound, long-lasting impact on your business. Read this chapter to discover how you can become more effective at marketing, and I'll also redefine your concept of sales.

Introduction

Open the Yellow Pages and you won't be surprised to discover not one, not ten, but usually dozens of service businesses. It doesn't matter the size of town or city you live in, it doesn't matter whether you're a plumber or HVAC specialist or pest control expert or you offer services in all the service business lines, there will be competition.

Now put yourself in your prospective customer's shoes. One day, they find themselves in need of a particular service. They turn to the Yellow Pages, or they search online, or they ask a friend, or they spot a billboard—they turn to whichever marketing channel they trust and find convenient, and they search for someone to help them.

Will they find your business? Will they find your competitor? How will they tell the difference between the two? What will compel them to call you instead of any of your competitors?

Customers have a lot of choice out there so all business owners know they need to market. I've never met a business owner who didn't know the importance of marketing. However, where most business owners fall short is that they don't market enough, nor do they market as effectively as they should.

Many businesses that don't spend the time thinking strategically about marketing and sales mastery commit the following business-killing error: they throw away thousands of dollars every year on wasted marketing efforts and that, in turn, throws away tens of thousands or even hundreds of thousands of dollars in potential income from customers. You might as well just write your competitors a check and gift wrap it and deliver it to them in person because that is essentially what you are doing if you do not have marketing and sales mastery.

And we can't talk about marketing if we don't also talk about sales. They are tied together. You can't have one without the other. There's some overlap. Marketing is about building awareness, promoting yourself, getting people to listen to you. Sales is about getting people to commit to hiring you; "closing the deal", etc.

Before we continue, though, I want to make a point of distinction about sales: Sales tends to feel aggressive and inauthentic, and the focus of the sale is on the transaction; on getting the customer to hand over their money. Instead of selling, I like to talk about serving, and will use that term throughout the rest of this chapter. Serving takes the focus away from the financial transaction and puts it where it should be—on you helping your customer. Of course you still get paid for this help but my focus is on helping. So I always talk about serving instead of selling.

I make this distinction for a few reasons: first, the service business industry has a bad reputation when it comes to serving customers; second, people simply don't trust a slick salesperson as much as they trust someone who is obviously helping them; third, and the most important reason, serving builds your relationship with your customer over the long-term, creating lifetime value customers who will keep calling you whenever they need help.

In this chapter, I'm going to talk about marketing first and then I'll talk about serving (instead of selling). Pay attention to both of these components because some business owners are really good at marketing but fall short on serving while other business owners are really good at serving but fall short on marketing. In both cases, those businesses are on the fast track to failure. You need marketing and serving mastery to successfully attract prospects so you can help them.

As you market and serve, you grow your business but you actually do more than that: you build the quantity and quality of your customers, which builds wealth, and that creates freedom in your life. That's right: effective marketing and serving contributes to the Core 5 Dimensions of Life and Business Mastery. So let's look at marketing and serving...

Marketing: Why And How

The activity of marketing is terribly misunderstood and business owners end up thinking that they are marketing but then they're left scratching their heads and wondering why the phone isn't ringing. Before I get into specifics, I want to be crystal clear about why you should be marketing and I want to give you a high level overview of how to do it.

If you're already marketing in your business but you're not getting the results you want, I hate to break it to you but you might not actually be marketing at all. You might be *thinking* that you're promoting, advertising, communicating to your marketplace but in reality you're not.

Marketing should do three things (and if your marketing doesn't do these three things, you're just wasting your money):

1. **Marketing should promote your brand as the go-to brand for whatever you're offering.** Your marketing should explain why your business is the only business to call to solve the problem that the customer is having.
2. **Marketing should promote your brand to the right audience.** There are many audiences out there but not all of them are the ones who will take action to buy from you. You need to find the right audience and connect with them.
3. **Marketing should get people to take action**—to compel them to reach for the phone and call, expecting to receive service and expecting to pay for it. Your marketing should motivate people to call immediately.

Unfortunately, many businesses fail to create marketing that does these things. Here are some examples of how service industry businesses frequently get it wrong:

- A plumber might think he is marketing but he isn't promoting his brand as the go-to brand. To his prospective customers, they can't tell the difference between his plumbing service and every other plumbing service out there.
- An electrician might think he is marketing but he isn't promoting his business to the right audience. His audience doesn't need the services of an electrician.
- An HVAC professional might think he is marketing but he is putting out information that doesn't prompt his audience to take action. They see his ad and then forget it and move on.

Good marketing, then, should promote your brand as the go-to brand for the right audience, and also prompt them to take action.

What makes it particularly challenging to market (in the service business especially) is that people don't always see your marketing when they have a need. You need to do enough marketing that they'll remember you when they do have a need.

Don' be afraid of doing too much marketing. Many service businesses do just enough marketing to stay in business (but not more than that). But, the more marketing you do (assuming that it follows the three parameters I described above), the more your marketing frequency builds trust.

When it comes to marketing, I recommend budgeting a substantial portion of your projected income each month towards marketing—and be sure to use every drop of that budget. Don't do just enough marketing to get by; spend every cent (wisely, of course) to grow your business. And the bigger your business grows, the more money you should put toward marketing.

Take Action!
Recommended actions:

___ Go through your records to review your marketing efforts, your marketing expenses, and your marketing results. Find out what worked and what didn't. Your goal should be to create marketing that is increasingly predictable and effective. Schedule time to revisit this exercise periodically as you deploy new marketing tactics.

___ If you haven't allocated a line in your budget for marketing, do so now. If you do have a line in your budget for marketing, sit down with a calculator and rework your numbers to increase that marketing line as much as possible. Schedule time to revisit this budget item regularly to ensure that your marketing expense grows as your business grows.

Add your own actions:

___ Stop doing actions (Actions you currently do now but should stop doing)

_____

_____

___ Keep doing actions (Actions you currently do now and should keep doing)

_____

_____

___ Start doing actions (Actions you don't do now but should start doing)

_____

_____

___ Who will do new actions? (Assign the action to yourself or someone else)

_____

_____

__ By when? (When will these actions be complete?)

_____

_____

Good Marketing Starts With An Avatar

Next, I want to talk about how to put together a marketing system that actually achieves the three parameters I mentioned above.

I want you to start by building something called a "customer avatar." An avatar is a representation or an icon or an ideal—a single thing that reminds you of all others like it. Therefore, a customer avatar is an ideal customer—a very detailed word-picture of exactly the kind of customer you want to get business from—your iconic perfect customer. In other words, I want you to describe your exact perfect customer as if they were one person.

You cannot get too detailed in this exercise. The more detailed you can get, the closer you'll be to defining the people who will pay you the most money, they'll pay you the quickest. I want you to describe the following characteristics about your perfect customer:

- What do they look like?
- How old are they?
- Where do they live?
- What kind of home do they live in?
- How old is their home?
- Do they have kids?
- How old are their kids?
- Do they like to pay with credit? Cash?
- Where do they shop?
- What's their favorite color?
- What kind of car do they drive?
- What kind of job do they have?
- How much money do they make?
- Where do they hang out?

The list can go on and on. The more detailed you make it, the easier it will be to find your perfect customer and then to create marketing that connects directly with them.

To connect with your audience, you'll create marketing that speaks in the way they understand; that demonstrates your awareness of the things that are important to them; that shows how you are the exact expert to serve them and solve their problems. **Create marketing as if you are talking to just one person and show them how you can help them.**

Creating marketing is simple, actually, after you have built your perfect customer avatar. Here's how to do it: tell people what benefit they gain from hiring you. That's it.

Now, I should clarify something: many people who are new to marketing mix up features and benefits. A plumber might say that their plumbing service is what people gain when they hire the plumber but that is not true. People gain a clean, dry house, peace of mind that their water is available when they need it (and drains the way they want it to), and the freedom to spend their time doing what they want (instead of thinking about plumbing issues). That's the real benefit people get when they hire plumbers.

Here's a classic marketing example that perfectly illustrates the difference between features and benefits: when someone is buying a drill, they're not buying it because it's a drill. They're buying holes—the holes that the drill can create. Your marketing needs to be built around the same concept. When someone hires you for the service you provide, they're hiring you because you're a licensed, experienced plumber, electrician, HVAC pro, pest control specialist, appliance repair expert, etc. They are hiring an expert that fits their needs and one they can trust and connect with.

That's why you need to figure out who your perfect customer avatar is; because when you know that, you can more easily determine why they would hire you and then you can create marketing specifically for them.

Some of you might be reading this and wondering: "If I create marketing that only one type of customer would find compelling, won't I be pushing away other prospective customers?" To which I answer: "Yes! That's exactly what you want!" If you spent enough time building a detailed avatar of your perfect customer, you won't want to attract any other kind of customer. Your avatar is your low-hanging fruit and all other customers will be more time consuming, less profitable, and slower to pay.

Once you have created marketing messages that connect with this avatar, deploy those messages frequently and in many different ways. I call this "stackable marketing" and I'll talk about it in greater detail in the next section in the chapter.

The goal of this effort is to move customers emotionally so that they remember you and also choose you when they need a job done—and you do that first by creating a customer avatar and creating marketing for that avatar.

Take Action!
Recommended actions:

___ Think about your ideal customer. Perhaps consider the customers you have served in the past who were among the best customers you've ever served—the ones that made you say, "I wish all my customers were like that one!" Write down the qualities and characteristics of this ideal customer. Be as detailed as possible. By the end you should have a very clear description of who this customer is and what they are like.

___ Start creating marketing messages for this ideal customer by focusing in on the benefits that they will gain by hiring you. Note: this will probably not come easy because you have to break bad habits and ways of thinking that are so common among service industry business owners.

___ Review other marketing to your ideal customer. It doesn't matter if the marketing you review is for products and services that you don't offer, the marketing will help you to get into the head of your ideal customer and understand what else they are buying and why they are buying it.

Add your own actions:

__ Stop doing actions (Actions you currently do now but should stop doing)

_____

_____

__ Keep doing actions (Actions you currently do now and should keep doing)

_____

_____

__ Start doing actions (Actions you don't do now but should start doing)

_____

_____

__ Who will do new actions? (Assign the action to yourself or someone else)

_____

_____

__ By when? (When will these actions be complete?)

_____

_____

"Stackable Marketing"

If I tell you something once, you might remember or you might forget. If I tell you something more than once, it's possible that you'll probably remember. But if everywhere you turn I'm telling you the same thing over and over and over again, you won't ever forget.

Market to prospective customers so that they *never* forget! We don't always have the ability to market to a customer when they are in dire circumstances and desperately need the service of a plumber, electrician, HVAC professional, pest control professional, etc. We need to lodge ourselves in the minds of our prospective customers now, and continuously, so that they never forget us; so when the need arises, they won't think of anyone else.

Unfortunately, most service professionals do just enough marketing and no more, thereby achieving very little in terms of making themselves memorable. Those service professionals wonder why other service businesses—like my own—get so many calls.

The reason is something I call "stackable marketing". **Stackable marketing is a strategy I developed because I didn't want to do just enough marketing. I wanted to dominate my market so that whenever someone thought they needed the services that my business offered, they were compelled to pick up the phone and call my business because that was the only one they could think of.**

The best way to explain my stackable marketing strategy is to give you an example—this is a typical example of what I do in my business and what I advise other businesses to do. The exact sequence or media might vary but the illustration will show you what I mean: let's say I have a list of people, along with their email, home address, and phone number. First I send out an email that says, "Keep an eye on your mailbox for a special message worth $1000." People often ignore emails but I promise you that most people will be going to their mailbox every day to see what comes.

I mail out the offer, which might be a coupon offering $1000 off of work above a certain amount of money. Some people respond and some people don't. Among the people who don't respond, I send them another email that says, "Did the postman steal the postcard?" And later, I might call them and ask, "Is everything okay?"

Along with that direct campaign, I'll also pick a five mile circumference around the geographic area I'm targeting and along with my direct mail (and email and phone calls), I'll also do billboards, social media, Pay Per Click (PPC) marketing and so on.

Some skeptical service business owners will look at all of that and say, "Isn't that too much?" but I promise you that the results will speak for themselves. You can target a specific area and flood that area with stackable marketing; and because your stackable marketing is bombarding your prospective customers with the same message, you'll likely see a higher response and a higher marketing ROI, compared to spending the same amount of money to spread out your message to a larger geographic area.

And other business owners will look at this and say: "I don't have the money to do this." Well here's the good news: you don't have to start in a large area as I described above. (If you did, you'd probably have more work than you'll be able to handle anyway.) Start small—do you have enough money to do this on just one street? Send out postcards and direct mail and other stackable marketing techniques over and over to all the house on just one street. Your costs will be low and you'll be amazed at how much work will come in from that street.

(Bonus benefit to you: imagine the additional marketing impact you'll have when everyone on the street sees your company truck stopping at one house one day, and then another house a second day, and then another house the third day, and so on!)

Start small with what you can afford and grow from there. Focus on one area—whatever you can afford—and stack your marketing in that area. **It's better to do stackable marketing to a smaller area than to spend the same amount of money and spread your marketing over a larger area.** Going deep in an area before going wide is always better than going wide first. Going wide results in more travel, thinner penetration, and less brand impact. Go deep first!

Stackable marketing allows you to mix and match any number of marketing methods and media in any way that works, allowing you to get your message out over and over to your marketplace. Use a combination of the following:

- Direct mail—including letters, postcards, etc.
- Voice broadcasts
- Email blasts
- Outbound calls
- Websites
- Business cards
- Video

- Pre-recorded messages
- Affiliates
- Social networking—including Facebook, Twitter, etc.
- Blogging
- Web TV
- Loyalty programs
- Referral programs
- Stickers
- Yard signs
- Folders
- Magnets
- Pens

And some service business owners will say: "Whoa, that's a lot. I can't afford all of that, even if I sent it out to a small geographic area." So my advice is to start small with one of the simplest stackable marketing systems: send out one postcard to your targeted group. Then send out a second postcard five weeks later to the same targeted group. Then send out a third postcard five weeks after the second one, and so on. Just send simple postcards every five weeks to the same group of people. You can easily automate this; just put the list into a program to send postcards to each person regularly.

And if you want to really bump up response on your postcards, increase the sense of urgency among readers by saying: "You're losing money. The price went up by 20%." They'll realize that they need to act fast before the price goes up again.

The secret to creating successful stackable marketing is to create great marketing (with a message that resonates with your ideal market, which I discussed earlier in this chapter) and then owning your marketplace by making your message appear in many locations so your prospective audience can't help but see and hear it over and over and over again. If you send generic messages and/or if you send it to the wrong market or don't bother trying to own a marketplace, your marketing will get lost.

This model of marketing frequency and deep penetration should be built into your marketing budget and you should aim to make your marketing more frequent and penetrate more deeply every single year.

Stackable marketing is something we build out in my Warrior Fast Track Academy events, so if you've ever been to one of my events then you've probably participated in some stackable marketing development. It's a popular part of my events and really hands-on.

Think of your marketing like the beginning of a romance: a meaningful relationship takes time—you meet and then you start to date and then you get engaged and then you get married. It doesn't happen all at once; it happens over a period of time and with several points of contact. In your business, your marketing gets you the introduction to meet your customer and over time you build a relationship with them. Unfortunately, most service business owners do it wrong by trying to create "one night stand" marketing that throws away money, rarely works, and never creates a long-lasting relationship.

Take Action!
Recommended actions:

__ Find out where your ideal customer tends to live in the geographic area you serve. (Chances are, many of them are located in a few communities—they never live "everywhere" in a city).

__ Outline a stackable marketing plan to use in your marketplace. Use postcards, as well as many of the ideas I listed in this section of the chapter, to create repeated marketing exposure.

__ Now look at your budget and see how big of a geographic area you can afford to deploy this stackable marketing strategy into. It might be a radius of a few miles, it might be a single neighborhood, or it might only be one or two streets. That's okay. Don't spread your marketing too thin. Do as much stackable marketing to a specific geographic area as you can afford.

Add your own actions:

___ Stop doing actions (Actions you currently do now but should stop doing)

_____

_____

___ Keep doing actions (Actions you currently do now and should keep doing)

_____

_____

___ Start doing actions (Actions you don't do now but should start doing)

_____

_____

___ Who will do new actions? (Assign the action to yourself or someone else)

_____

_____

___ By when? (When will these actions be complete?)

_____

_____

"Marketing On Steroids"

I've told you about who you need to market to, and I've showed you how to construct marketing messages from that, and then I've introduced the concept of stackable marketing. If you do just those things, you should see a dramatic increase in the effectiveness of your marketing.

But now I want to show you how to take your marketing to another level by implementing something I call "marketing on steroids." This is where you make your marketing even more effective. It's a series of concepts, tips, tactics, tricks, and strategies that I've found to really rocket marketing results.

Use voice blasts. This is when you get the phone numbers for the geographic area you are targeting and you send out a pre-recorded call. When you add this into your stackable marketing, it's very powerful because it's not just printed material (like so much other marketing is) but it brings in another sense. (Note: check with your lawyer to make sure that voice blasts are legal in your area.)

When using voice blasts, keep it simple and personal. Say "hi" and then tell them your name. This builds trust. Then offer them something or use an awareness message. For example:

- "Hi, I'm Mike Agugliaro of Gold Medal Service. I'm calling to let you know that we're offering you and your neighbors 25% off of all plumbing work for the next week. If you have leaky pipes or low water pressure, now is the perfect time to get it fixed."
- "Hi, I'm Mike Agugliaro of Gold Medal Service. In just a month or two, the summer heat will be blazing and you'll need your air conditioner more than ever. Air conditioners should be serviced at least once a year. This is a friendly call to remind you to service your air conditioner."

You can also use this for existing customers, as well, by sending out a voice blast to anyone who you have served in the past. Here are a couple of scripts for that:

- "Hi, I'm Mike Agugliaro of Gold Medal Service. Winter will be here soon so make sure you test your heating system before the cold snap. Don't wait until the cold snap to find out if your furnace works."
- "Hi, I'm Mike Agugliaro of Gold Medal Service. The local weather station is issuing a major storm warning for the area and I want to share that information with you. Make sure all your windows and doors are closed, and stay safe and dry."

These messages are still marketing messages even though they aren't necessarily promoting a specific offer. They're providing a valuable service to our existing customers and reinforcing the value we provide. And, they result in calls. For example, the "Winter will be here soon" voice blast can lead to calls for furnace service before the cold snap (which can turn into a busy time as people discover their furnace needs work), and the storm warning voice blast is a nice service-oriented one that positions you as someone who truly cares for your customers.

Here's a bonus way to use voice blasts, even though this isn't necessarily used for marketing: You can send out voice blasts to your employees to make them aware of great things that are happening in your company. The bigger your company becomes, the more important these additional communications are to help your employees feel connected.

Own a color or color combination and use it in your marketing: in a previous chapter I talked about owning a color as part of your brand. Since your marketing is an extension of your brand, that color should be prominent throughout your marketing. Not only should your brand display that color in everything (business cards, vehicles, uniforms, etc.) but so should your marketing—whether that marketing is a billboard or a flyer.

This color or color combination tightens up your brand and helps create a bigger impact when your prospective customers see your marketing. It also makes it easier to remember, especially when a customer sees a future marketing piece or one of your vehicles drive by.

Use video: video is a powerful medium and, thanks to the web and portable devices, it's never been easier to record video and share it with others. Here are some ways to use video:

- When you've finished with a customer, invite them to share a video testimonial and record it for them.
- Record yourself talking about new products or services.
- Record your staff introducing themselves.
- Use video to explain the company story or core values.

Record these videos, create a channel on YouTube and post them there, then embed them on your company website and social media.

And here's a bonus idea: You can also use videos to help educate your employees, especially with activities they need to repeat. For example, you might want to create a video for your employees about how to fill out an invoice. It's a great way to train them without being physically in front of them.

PR like a ninja: marketing is the promotional efforts you create (such as advertising, direct mail, etc.), while public relations (PR) is often exposure from information about your company that is newsworthy or has public value. The web is blurring these definitions but it's a good rule of thumb if you're just starting to think about marketing and PR.

PR has excellent value to your business, not only to generate immediate attention to the services you provide but also to help position you as an expert in the future.

Good PR comes in different ways: some kind of charitable act or donation, public service announcements, and opinion interviews. One great way to do PR like a ninja is to get interviewed by the local media on different topics. You don't have to speak only on a topic directly related to your area of business. Rather, you can be interviewed on any number of topics that could be tied back to what you do. For example, if your area is prone to flooding in the spring, and you're a plumber, this might be a good topic to be interviewed by the local news about. You can share some useful tips about how to prepare for a flood, from a plumber's perspective, and that will position you as an expert. Or, here's another example: I was interviewed on MSNBC. Although the interview was about my business' growth, it was a great opportunity to generate some PR about the business and the services we offer.

PR can also make a one truck company look like a 100 truck company simply by shaping people's perceptions of your company. If you are a well-groomed, professional, uniform-wearing expert, people will see that depiction of you in the media and think very differently about your company than if you show up in a beat-up old truck wearing jeans and a stained shirt.

PR gets your face into the media and noticed in the communities. It's a very effective way to promote and grow your business. I use it extensively now but I wish I had pursued it as vigorously in my business right from day one.

Marketing checklist: this is a checklist that I use before every marketing piece is sent out from my office, no matter what type of media I'm using. Whoever is sending out the marketing will use this checklist to make sure that these parts are all dealt with and nothing is missed.

1. **Envelope format/Layout**
   a. Teaser: are you using the entire envelope? Or,
   b. Blind: can you tell that it is direct mail?
2. **The headline- The top**
   a. Does your headline catch the reader's attention and demand that he reads the rest of the ad?
   b. Are you using a subhead that supports the headline?
3. **The salutation- Greeting**
   a. Did you properly personalize your mailing? Or,
   b. If using a generic salutation, did you clearly define the group the mailing is going to?
4. **Getting your copy read- demand attention**
   a. Did you give your offer a name?
   b. Did you make a "why wouldn't they buy" list and answer them?
   c. Did you create an interesting and arousing opening sentence?
   d. What does the reader gain if he responds or lose if he doesn't?
   e. Did you end all pages in incomplete sentences?
   f. Use short sentences and short paragraphs?
   g. Use graphic enhancement to make your mailer easier to read?
   h. Have a middle-school aged child read your copy to make sure they understand all words?
   i. Tell the reader their advantages to respond?
   j. Include all pertinent info? (including: method of payment, sizes, location, hours, etc.)

5. **The deadline- when and why**
   a. Is your deadline by time or amount?
   b. Did you ask the reader to respond several times in the mailing?

6. **Testimonials- social proof**
   a. Did you put in as many as you can?
   b. Did you properly identify them?

7. **The illustration-visuals create emotion**
   a. Do you have room for an illustration?
   b. Does the illustration tell a story?
   c. Is the illustration properly captioned?

8. **Free gift- teaser to take action**
   a. Are you offering a free gift or gift with purchase?
   b. Have you properly described the gift to maximize its perceived value?
   c. Do you have room to show a picture of your giveaway?

9. **The guarantee. Is it strong? Ask why.**

10. **The P.S.**
    a. Does your P.S. re-state your offer, your guarantee, your giveaway, your deadline?
    b. Do you have room for more than one P.S.?

11. **The list. Are you mailing to the people most likely to respond?**

This list is a high level starting point for you and you can start using it right away. If you want to go deeper into each of these, my Warrior Fast Track Academy events push you even deeper into marketing effectively with this checklist.

These points won't always apply in every marketing situation but it's good to go through the checklist each time to make sure that your marketing does address everything it can.

You can download a copy of this marketing checklist from the free resources page: **CEOWARRIOR.com/masteryresources**

Go deep then wide: as I mentioned earlier in this chapter, you really reduce the effectiveness of your marketing (or, put another way, you really increase the cost of your marketing!) by spreading out your message to a wide audience. Yet, that's what many service businesses do: they cast a wide net. I take a different approach: I prefer to go deep first and then wide.

Going deep first means to target a specific geographic area. I recommend about five miles in circumference, although the exact size will depend on the density of the population where you live as well as your ability to serve the people who contact you—this is something you'll figure out by testing. Ultimately, you need to penetrate the market street-by-street, and don't move out further until you have market-share in that area. Once you've targeted one geographic area then build a stackable marketing campaign that targets this geographic area.

Consumer awareness guide: a consumer awareness guide is a short document, perhaps in the form of a checklist, that makes the customer aware of the things they should think about when buying the kind of service you offer. I learned this method from Joe Polish, who used it in the carpet cleaning industry. This is a powerful document you can hand your customers when you give your quote. It's a subtle marketing piece that positions you as an expert because it demonstrates how helpful you are, especially when the customer sees that your service meets all of the qualities described in the guide.

Customer packet: a customer packet is a packet of information that every field expert gives the customer when they first start working with the customer. I'll explain what's in my customer packet but if you ever want to see one, this is something I share in detail at the Warrior Fast Track Academy events. The customer packet contains the following:

- An attractive, full-color 4-page brochure about our heating and air conditioning consultation, which outlines what the customer can expect, what we look for, a bold promise, and an "instant rebate" offer.
- An attractive, full-color double-sided page with home maintenance checklists for every season.

- An attractive, full-color multi-page brochure that outlines our TotalCare Club, as well as a page of coupons for club members.
- A number of forms that the homeowner can fill out if they need chimney work, Freon repair, and other environmentally sensitive or highly regulated service work done.
- An attractive, full-color multipage brochure with additional products and services we offer (such as home generators, basement waterproofing, tankless water heaters, etc.)
- A detailed page explaining our warranty.
- A blank sales receipt, which our service staff can use when on a service call.
- A checklist of helpful emergency safety information—including what to do in the case of a fire, as well as a place for them to write emergency contact information.
- A brochure for a helpful pipe-clearing product we recommend and use.
- Stickers (with our phone number) that say "emergency shut-off" and can be placed on furnaces, main water lines, gas mains, etc.
- Stickers (with our phone number) to be placed on various units—such as a furnace or air conditioner or water heater, etc.
- A magnet, which includes helpful household information (ours gives cooking conversion tips but you can use any information that people find helpful) as well as a coupon right on the magnet.
- A water-analysis kit (so customers can take a sample of their drinking water and send it in to be analyzed) along with a form they fill out and a postage-paid envelope to send it to us.
- A pen with our logo on it.

There's a lot of great stuff in there and it's a combination of immediate and long-term information, and a combination of marketing content with high-value free information. It is a value builder and everything in the customer packet has a reason for being here—to serve the customer.

This customer packet is kept altogether in a nice, branded folder with the company's contact information on it. It looks really sharp and immediately positions the field expert—and the company—as a professional operation that provides superior value. (Even if you are a one-person company, a nicely produced customer packet hand-delivered by you in a clean uniform can make you look like a large, national organization).

Note: You don't have to create a customer packet with all of these things in them. If you're a small business on a budget you can build it slowly. Just having a folder (even if it's a plain, one-color folder) with some high quality information can separate you from the rest of your competitors.

Automated gifting: do you give gifts to your customers after you've completed a job for them? You should. For our customers, our gifting program looks like this: for every job that costs less than $500, the customer gets a thank you card. For every job that costs between $500 and $5000, the customer gets a thank you card, cookies from Cookies For A Cure, and $50 off their next service.

Just giving these thank you gifts will transform how customers view you but if you really want to put this part of your marketing on steroids, here's how to automate it (this is what I do): every week, pull together the names of the customers you've finished during that past week, put their names and addresses into a spreadsheet, and then pass that spreadsheet off to someone else—an employee or a vendor—who takes care of it for you.

And when you use a service like I do with Cookies For A Cure, the gifting also serves a great cause and makes it doubly special.

Take Action!
Recommended actions:

___ Schedule time in your planner to implement each one of these strategies.

___ Print off the marketing checklist and review your existing marketing, and keep it in a place so you can review all marketing going forward.

__ Start putting together a customer packet to give out. Even if you don't have the budget for one as robust or full-color as the one I use, start with what you can and grow from there.

Add your own actions:

__ Stop doing actions (Actions you currently do now but should stop doing)

_____

_____

__ Keep doing actions (Actions you currently do now and should keep doing)

_____

_____

__ Start doing actions (Actions you don't do now but should start doing)

_____

_____

__ Who will do new actions? (Assign the action to yourself or someone else)

_____

_____

__ By when? (When will these actions be complete?)

_____

_____

Serving Customers: Magic? Mystery? Or Just Knowing What To Say?

I'm going to make an assumption here: I'm going to assume that you didn't get into the service industry because you absolutely loved sales. Chances are, you got into the service industry because you were interested in or particularly good at one of the service trades—such as plumbing, electrical, HVAC, pest control, painting, appliance repair, or whatever business or trade you're in.

And as you worked for someone else, you didn't have to think much about sales. But now that you are working for yourself you're facing the reality that you have to make sales.

Selling can sometimes have a bad rapport because of the many, many bad examples that we encounter every day in every industry. For that reason, I put my emphasis on serving instead of selling. Selling tends to focus on the exchange of money from the customer in a one-time transaction, while serving tends to focus on what you can give the customer to build a lifetime value customer. Good service will pour more money into your business than you ever thought possible.

So, forget what you think you know about sales. I believe that good selling is about serving first. I'm not even going to talk about selling anymore. I'm going to talk about serving. It's time to reprogram your mind, and that's what I'm going to do here.

What is serving? I'll answer that question by putting it into a larger context: your marketing has captured a prospect's interest and established a sense of trust in you. Now, you serving them will solve their problem, they'll pay you, and you'll build a relationship with that customer for life. That's all serving is: Helping customers to solve their problems over and over again, and building a relationship with them.

If that's the only thing you get out of this chapter, and you implement that new way of thinking into your business today, you'll fast track your business past any competition that is purely focused on transactional selling.

So, how do you serve your customers? How do you build on that interest and trust to help them? Since I like to teach by example, I'll give you the framework for service that my team uses in my business. It's been tested and refined and updated over the years, and the emphasis on each interaction is to serve the customer. This is something that all of my experts are trained to do. You'll notice how serving first is woven throughout the conversation, and you'll also notice that the conventional misconception of transactional (one-time-only) selling is totally missing.

Framework For Service

Marketing: our marketing has already captured some interest and built some trust and the prospective customer has booked an appointment to have one of my experts come to their house. The prospective customer's response has launched the rest of this Framework For Service...

Pre-rapport Formula: about 15 to 20 minutes before the scheduled visit, my expert will call the customer and say, "I'll be there in about 15 to 20 minutes. I understand you're having problem with your water heater, tell me about it." And they'll listen to the customer. And then they'll offer something friendly like, "Hey, I'm passing a coffee shop, can I get you a coffee?"

This step prepares the customer, and the expert, and it builds additional rapport with a friendly offer of coffee

Say hello: when my expert arrives at the prospective customer's house, they greet the customer. "Hi, I'm Mike from Gold Medal Service. Nice to meet you. Is it okay where my vehicle is parked? Do you have any dogs or cats I should be aware of? Do you have any time constraints that might impact how much time we have to work? Is there anyone else that should be involved in this?"

This step is friendly and very service-oriented. And, it tells the expert a lot: like if the person had a time constraint, perhaps the expert needs to move a little more quickly through the visit. Or if someone else should be involved in the process, perhaps the expert needs to arrange a different time to visit so that the spouse (for example) is also at home.

Discovery: during this step, the expert learns all they can about the situation. They're asking questions—not just about the specific problem but about the larger picture. (You'll see in a moment why this is important.) For example, the expert might ask, "How old is the water heater?" And, "Has it given you any problems in the past?" And, "Has anyone worked on it before?" And, "Does it give you enough water?"

These questions are key because anyone can go in and fix the immediate problem but by asking more questions about the broader situation, the expert might be able to recommend a completely different solution—one that fits the customer even better. In this example, perhaps the hot water heater is broken and the prospective customer called for a repair. But by asking questions, the expert might discover that it never really gave enough hot water for the entire family anyway. Remember, we're not trying to solve a one-time problem for a one-time customer; we're building a relationship because we want to serve this customer for their lifetime. This is a very different approach and it helps us to provide solutions that are of a higher, longer-lasting value to the customer (and to our business).

The answers to the questions in the discovery step will help in the recommendation, next...

Recommendation: in this step, the expert makes a few recommendations based on the best solutions for the prospective customer's problems.

- First, the expert would say: "Let me tell you about myself and the company" and then briefly talk about how the company helps other customers.
- Then the expert would say, "Let me tell you what I heard you say," and they'd repeat back what the customer said. This kind of confirmation is helpful to ensure that the expert has correctly heard the customer's concerns, and it gives the customer another opportunity to add any other problems they are facing.
- Then the expert would say: "Here are six options. Let's see what fits for you and your family." And with that, the expert lays out a few options that they believe the customer would benefit from.
- And last, the expert asks the customer which solution they would prefer.

The customer will choose something that they are comfortable with, that fits their budget, and that solves their problem. This is not some sales technique. This is a serving-first communication tool and system to help people think through the process of what they should consider. While other businesses might call this a "closing technique" as part of a sales pitch, we think of this very differently: We're always serving and this recommendation comes from a service mindset. We don't have to sell or close the customer because the WOW service we provide closes itself.

Get it done: now it's time to get the job done. This is important because the customer is watching to see what the expert is doing! Are they doing what they promised? Are they respectful of the customer's house? Are they communicating what they are doing? That's what the customer is watching for, so the expert will use a tarp, keep the area clean, keep the customer informed of what they are doing and what the timeline is like. And when the expert is done, they'll clean up and vacuum the area. The expert's service and attentiveness and ability to solve the problem will confirm for the customer that the customer made a great decision.

Finish it up: in this step, the expert will explain what they did and how they did it, and then they'll talk about the existing things the company also does for its customers. Then the expert will talk about referrals—how referrals from the customer are appreciated and encouraged. Finally, the expert will make sure the customer is happy with the work and they'll complete the payment and close out the job.

Neighborhood impact: the expert will complete some simple marketing activities in the neighborhood. For example, the expert will put out door hangers, yard signs, and even say hello to the neighbors.

You'll notice that the expert started serving the customer long before they arrived (by calling, listening, and offering coffee) and that they served the customer all the way through the visit. Even when it was time to make a recommendation, it didn't feel like a so-called "hard sell," did it? It might take some work to break your mindset of selling and put the focus on service.

This Framework For Service is a powerful tool and I recommend that you build something like it into your business. (You don't have to build it exactly the same, as long as you have good reasons for building the steps that you do choose to build.)

One more thing to mention about this Framework For Service: There is a lot more you can do with this framework. I've only listed the first layer but it goes much, much deeper. In my Warrior Fast Track Academy I demonstrate how to use techniques like agenda mapping and I show specific strategies and tactics, and even specific phrases to say when interacting with the customer to build trust and rapport and to serve.

While serving, make sure you always do the following:

- Focus on benefits: remember that the customer wants to hear about how you're going to solve their problem; they don't want to hear about the nitty-gritty details.

- Answer questions: customers will sometimes have questions about the process or price or timeline. Equip your experts to answer these questions upfront and to be very transparent. Honesty goes a long way in an industry that has the stigma of not being honest.

- Ask for the order: after you have presented a valuable solution to the customer, ask for the commitment from the customer. Too often, business owners present a recommendation, talk about different options, but never ask for the customer to choose one.

- Supersize strategy: this is one that fast food businesses nailed by not only asking, "Would you like an apple pie with that" but also, "Do you want to supersize your meal?" In our service business industry, after a customer agrees to buy, ask yourself what you might be able to offer to supersize their purchase. (But remember: It always needs be valuable to them. Always offer it with a mindset of service.)

- Follow-up: follow-up is one of the most profound ways to serve the customer. Following-up with prospective customers can help you sell more because they might not have committed to you one day but circumstances change and they might suddenly need to buy from you later.

And, following-up with previous customers can help you to sell more because they already know and trust you and they've seen you successfully help them with one problem so they'll likely hire you again to help them with another problem.

Train all of your employees to serve. Help them to feel comfortable throughout the entire Framework For Service I've described above. Demolish their old misconceptions about selling, if they have any (and a lot of people do), and replace those misconceptions with easy service scripts that they can use.

Here are some best practices to help you as you serve the customer:

- Ask questions. Ask lots of questions and get the customer's answers. Those answers will help you to formulate recommendations that will solve the customer's problem.

- Maintain the "alpha dog" status during the visit with the customer. Customers want a confident expert helping them—not someone who is quiet and shy and uncertain. Take control of the visit (but do so professionally and courteously) and be commanding. For example, you might want to say to a customer: "Did you have an agenda set for today's visit or would you like to hear mine?"

- Keep things clear. A confused mind says no. Be a confident expert and explain things clearly and in language that your customers understand. Remember that your customers do not have the industry experience and training that you have, so be respectful of them but explain things simply and clearly.

- Remember that you are not your customer. For example, you might prefer to buy the cheapest product for your own needs but just because you do doesn't mean your customer does. The fact you like to ask for a savings every time does not mean your customer wants to. Don't create offers and price your products for the way you buy but for the way your customers buy.

- Always serve people (whether they are prospective customers or actual buyers) and you will increase how many people become customers and how happy and loyal your customers are.

Take Action!
Recommended actions:

__ Take a clear, honest look at your existing service call. How much service happens? Do you have a serving first mentality?

__ Script out an ideal service call based on the Framework For Service example I gave above. Then try it out the next time you visit a customer. (Note: I'm not advising that you write a script and memorize. Rather, your script should give you a general guideline to follow; and when you realize you've strayed from it, you can try to get the call back on track.)

Add your own actions:

__ Stop doing actions (Actions you currently do now but should stop doing)
_____
_____

__ Keep doing actions (Actions you currently do now and should keep doing)
_____
_____

__ Start doing actions (Actions you don't do now but should start doing)
_____
_____

__ Who will do new actions? (Assign the action to yourself or someone else)
_____
_____

___ By when? (When will these actions be complete?)

_____

_____

Serving On The Phone

Service doesn't start when the expert arrives at the customer's house and it doesn't end when the expert leaves. If you are in the service business, you should always be serving your customers because you are helping them own a worry-free home. Serve them regularly and you will always have as much work as you can handle.

All of your staff should be trained to serve, even those who do not go to the customer's house. For example, the people who take calls and make calls should be trained to have a serve first mindset (even if you're a really small company and it's just your child or your spouse on the phone). Teach them to serve on the phone and you'll never have downtime in your business.

I'll show you how to serve in two types of phone situations—inbound calls and outbound calls.

Inbound calls: when a customer calls in that their furnace is broken, here's what I've trained our customer service staff to say: "That's too bad. That's frustrating. Let me tell you about our company." By saying this, they build rapport and a connection by empathizing with the customer's frustration and then they build further rapport and trust by positioning my company as the company to help the customer end their frustration. You always want to make this personal emotional connection on the front end of every interaction.

But here's how my staff takes it one level higher: we use a concept I call "one plus one". What that means is, whenever someone calls in with one particular problem they often have another problem as well that they just might not realize or be thinking about at this time.

For example, if a customer calls in about a water heater problem, there's a good chance that they might also have a sump pump problem, too, so we offer to take a look at that as well. You always need to lead with specific example of what other customers have experienced when they have a similar problem. (Compare this to what most service businesses do: after setting the appointment, they ask: "Is there anything else I can help you with?" hoping that the customer remembers some other problem in their house.) Lead the conversation with typical examples.

And we're also mindful that the customer may want our services in the future so my staff is trained to capture the customer's email address so we can market to them in the future. We usually ask for the customer's email address like this: "By the way, let me get your email from you. I'll put your email in our system and you'll have a thousand dollars of coupons waiting in your inbox, and one of those coupons might work for this service call." This is one of the most powerful lead captures.

Outbound calls: the inbound calls I talked about above are great because they're often from people who are facing an immediate, specific home-related pain that we can help them with right away. They're often very motivated to buy. But that's not the only way we serve our customers. We use outbound calls as well.

I want to minimize staff downtime in my company so we run a three day gap board to keep my field experts busy. A three day gap board is a three calendar with all of our existing service calls mapped out. This reveals where we have service call gaps that need to be filled—periods in which my experts would not be on call. When we have availability over the next three days, my staff starts making calls to previous customers and prospective customers until each of the next three days is filled. When the next three days are full, we stop.

(We use three days because one or two days is too short and you have no time to fill the board, while anything longer is sometimes harder to schedule for. We have found that three days is the magic number for our gap board. And we also use this same concept for other areas of the business, which I talk about in the Warrior Fast Track Academy).

When we're calling prospective customers and past customers, here are a couple of reasons we give for calling:

- We make follow-up calls to customers who have purchased from us in the past. We'll ask how their new furnace is working and we'll make some recommendations about other work they may want to consider.
- We also always have a couple of specials we'll run as well. For example, we might have a special on generators and we'll call people and say, "A lot of customers in your area are experiencing power outages, so they're getting generators. Is that a problem for you?"

Both of these types of calls allow us to say hello to our customers on a regular basis.

As you can see, both our inbound calls and our outbound calls are about serving. By serving, we position ourselves as value-builders and value-adders and it gives us the credibility to make recommendations. We gain the customer's respect and show them that we have their best interests at heart and then we make a recommendation that we think will help them.

Take Action!
Recommended actions:

___ Sit down with your telephone team and talk to them about serving. Help them see how a serving first mentality is good for everyone, including them, the customer, and the business. Script out some words to say and a flow chart of how a call should go, role-play a few calls, and then motivate your team to get back on the phone and start serving.

___ If you don't have an outbound call strategy, create one right away and start calling previous customers for follow-up service. (What if you got married and then never spoke to your wife again? If you're not speaking to your customer, someone else is.) Implement a three day gap board into your business to minimize downtime.

Add your own actions:

___ Stop doing actions (Actions you currently do now but should stop doing)

_____

_____

___ Keep doing actions (Actions you currently do now and should keep doing)

_____

_____

___ Start doing actions (Actions you don't do now but should start doing)

_____

_____

___ Who will do new actions? (Assign the action to yourself or someone else)

_____

_____

___ By when? (When will these actions be complete?)

_____

_____

Conclusion

This was a huge chapter that covered two of the most critical functions of your business: marketing and serving (remember: stop thinking about selling; think serving instead). Marketing and serving are essential to your business' survival and to your business' success because marketing brings in new customers and serving generates revenue and turns those customers into lifetime value customers.

Unfortunately, most business owners do it wrong and they survive (instead of thrive) based on the few customers they get rather than proactively getting more customers.

In this chapter you learned how to create your ideal customer avatar—the perfect customer that you should be focusing on. Then you learned to use stackable marketing, even if it means only marketing to just one street in a neighborhood at first, and then to put your marketing on steroids to increase its effectiveness.

And you learned one of the easiest and fastest ways to build a long-lasting relationship with customers was to serve them. Do this in person with a Framework For Service, and on inbound and outbound calls, and you'll see your business grow in surprising new ways.

Master Action List For Chapter 7

At the end of each section of this chapter you had actions to perform as well as Start Doing/Keep Doing/Stop Doing lists. Gather those actions together into a Master Action List, add any new actions that you think of, and then go through the questions below to think about how these actions can transform your life and your business:

___ **Is it going to make me money?** Are the actions you've listed going to help you generate more income? (If they are, great. Think about how they might be able to help you generate even more income. If they aren't making you more money then are those actions really as important as you thought they were?)

___ **Is it going save me money?** Reducing how much you spend will help you increase your profit. Are the actions you're thinking of doing going to help you cut back on your expenses without sacrificing the quality of your service? (If they save you money, great. If they aren't saving you money then are those actions really as important as you thought they were?)

___ **Is it going to save time?** Your time is precious and scarce. So the actions you take should help you to save time. Keep the big picture in mind because some actions may take a few extra minutes in the short term but will ultimately help you save time in the long term. (For example, training an employee might be an action that will take a few extra minutes now but will save you a lot of time in the future).

___ **Is it going to help me achieve market domination?** Your business needs to own the market it works in. Whenever someone thinks of the service you provide, they should only think of you. Do the actions you've listed in this chapter support that market domination? What can you change about them to help you dominate the market even further?

___ **How do I start fast to get the low-hanging fruit?** It's easy to say you're going to take action but it's much harder to actually do it. One way to take

action and push through to its successful completion is to go for the quick wins—the low-hanging fruit. From the actions you've listed, what low-hanging fruit can you immediately pick?

__ **What's the leverage?** Leverage has a few different meanings but, in this context, I'm talking about how you can motivate yourself. For example, if you commit to complete an action within a certain period of time you can leverage that commitment by saying, "If I don't make that commitment, I'll donate $10,000 to a charity." Since you may not have $10,000, and you'll probably feel some pain donating that much money, you are leveraging your commitment and compelling yourself to complete the actions you said you'd complete.

__ **What's the reward?** For each action, list what you expect to get out of it. If you can't think of a reward for the action, seriously consider whether it is as valuable as you thought. Spend more of your time on actions that have rewards. Two of the best rewards for your actions are below (although there are other rewards you may choose to take action for)…

__ **Is it going to help me achieve wealth?** One of the best rewards you can take action for is to achieve wealth. For each action ask whether that particular action will help you make more money to give you the sense of safety and achievement and allow you to buy whatever you want whenever you want it. If possible, develop the action even further if a stronger, clearer, bigger action will help you achieve more wealth.

__ **Is it going to help me get more freedom?** Another one of the best rewards you can take action for is to get more freedom—the time and financial capacity to do whatever you want whenever you want to (without sacrificing your business). For each action ask whether that particular action will help you get more freedom. If possible, develop the action even further if a stronger, clearer, bigger action will help you get more freedom.

CHAPTER 8

MASTER YOUR MONEY

Money is essential for our businesses and lives. It puts food on the table, rewards employees for their effort, pays vendors for supplies, and can be used to grow your business. For many business owners, money can feel like a scarce resource that is gone too quickly. In this chapter you'll learn how to maximize this resource and put it to best use so you can create more of it.

Introduction

You work for money. Not only is your business built around earning money but your life is built around using money (to put food on the table and a roof over your head). Money is a basic need—not money itself but the value it gives to the Core 5 Dimensions of Life and Business Mastery. Money helps you contribute to your relationships and your health and your wealth and your freedom.

Money is often used to measure your success, as you compare one quarter to another or one year to another. An increase in money usually indicates that your business is growing. Money is the "tool" that helps your business to grow—by paying vendors and employees and by investing in different parts of your business.

Money is important but it's rarely the end-target of your business. Rather, your personal vision and your business vision are your end-targets. The money you earn can help you to achieve that personal vision and business vision.

Money flows into your business and it flows out again and the true money master does the following: they get more to flow in, they manage the money while it's in the business, they reduce the money that flows out (and carefully manage how it flows out), and they use the remaining amount strategically. That describes money mastery.

Unfortunately, few service business owners are truly masters of their money. All too often they are mastered by money—working hard for less than they deserve, then giving up more than they should, and wasting the rest. Those are strong words but this is a serious subject and it's a subject that is too easy to screw up. It's not a surprise that money mastery is one of the most popular topics in my Warrior Fast Track Academy.

In this chapter I want to transform what you think about money—how you perceive it, how you get it, how you keep it, and how you use it. And, I want you to end this chapter with a powerful game plan to master your money rather than be mastered by it.

Money Attitudes

Just like mastering anything else, you need to work on your inner game before you can master the outer game. When most people think of martial arts, they think of the powerful kicks and strikes. But as a martial artist I can tell you that kicking, striking, blocking, and any other move is only the outer mastery on display for everyone to see. What few people realize is the inner mastery required first before you can become proficient in the outer mastery. When you see a Black Belt martial artist performing powerful moves, it's a demonstration of years of inner discipline.

To a larger degree, that's what's going on in this book—you worked on your inner mastery first in Part 1 of this book and then in Part 2 you are working on the outer mastery of your business. But I'm going to revisit the inner mastery for a moment on the specific topic of money. And before I get into the actual money-making and money-management aspects of money mastery, I want to talk about the *inner* mental mastery of money.

First, you need to revisit your relationship with money. As children, we're often told by parents and teachers that "money isn't everything" or "money doesn't grow on trees."

We're told that money isn't everything because we were encouraged not to make money the primary focus of our lives. Our parents and teachers didn't want us to become greedy; they wanted us to pursue our talents and to look for enjoyment in life rather than enjoyment in money. This sounds good at first but it often did us a disservice by damaging our attitude toward money.

Money *is* important; it's more important than a lot of things. And when you have money (I'm speaking here of wealth, not just income) you have the freedom to do whatever you want.

And, we were told by our parents and teachers that money doesn't grow on trees because money is scarce. However, this is wrong, too. Money isn't as scarce as people think. Sure, money doesn't grow on trees—but wait, maybe it does in a manner of speaking! If you have an orange tree, you could sell those oranges and make money. And that's a metaphor for so many other aspects of life. When you see an opportunity and turn that opportunity into a financial transaction, you are plucking a money tree. For example, if you're a talented electrician then you can turn that talent into money (by selling your services) whenever you want money. In that case, money does grow on trees!

We also have incorrect attitudes toward money as we get older: We develop limiting beliefs about money in adulthood, just as we did when we were children. For example, someone might say "My credit is bad, so I can't get funding." That is a limiting belief that they develop in adulthood. That limiting belief can prevent you from pursuing opportunities because you think your bad credit prohibits you from moving forward. However, a more positive, accurate statement would be, "My credit is bad, so I cannot get funding at the best price." See the difference? The fact is the same (bad credit) but the limiting belief is replaced with a more accurate, positive statement about the fact, specifically that bad credit only increases the cost of funding.

Our attitudes about money are very limited. We often think of money as something scarce that trickles to us if we work hard. That limited view impacts how we think of the Wealth Dimension of the Core 5 Dimensions of Life and Business Mastery. But a better view would be to broaden our definition from that limited trickle of money and instead to start thinking about the bigger concept of wealth.

I define wealth as **the amount of money you own or are making that creates a sense of safety and accomplishment and allows you to buy whatever you want whenever you want it.**

Note the important concepts embedded in this definition:

- Money: we're still talking about money but we're looking at it from a completely different perspective—a wealth perspective.
- Money you own or are making: this definition includes money you have saved but also your cash flow and your ability to earn more money. You don't need to measure wealth only by what you have saved in your bank account but also by what you can earn.
- A sense of safety: wealth lets you sleep at night instead of lying awake restless with anxiety about how you'll pay the bills.
- A sense of accomplishment: wealth gives you a sense of accomplishment. I don't necessarily mean that you'll feel rich but rather that you can point to the money you own or the money you can earn as a symbol and a measurement that your business is growing.
- Allows you to buy whatever you want whenever you want it: wealth leads to freedom so that you are free to buy anything you want without worrying about whether you should save the money instead.

This wealth can be daily wealth, if you have enough money to get through the day; but this wealth can also be lifetime wealth, which is enough money to help you live the life you want for your whole life. You might start by working toward daily wealth but as you master your money, you'll master lifetime wealth.

Your business is a wealth-building machine. (There are several other wealth-building machines, including stocks, real estate, and affiliate programs. This book is just focused on your business as a wealth-building machine.)

Wealth should support all 5 of the Core 5—not just the Wealth Dimension (which is the obvious one) but also each of the other ones: money helps you contribute to your Belief, it helps you afford a healthy lifestyle (Health), it helps you support your family (Relationships), and it contributes to your ultimate Freedom.

As you think about your business as a wealth-building machine, it changes how you make money, how you view money, and how you use that money. You use money more strategically to build a longer-lasting business that ultimately gives you more than just money—it gives you freedom and supports your life.

Take Action!
Recommended actions:

__ Think about your attitudes toward money. What were you told as a child about money? What have you grown to believe about money? For example: do you find money to be scarce? Are you working for an income or for wealth? How did you feel when I talked about money growing on trees?

__ Think about how money can contribute to all areas of your Core 5 Dimensions of Life and Business Mastery. List out each of the 5 areas—Belief, Relationships, Health, Wealth, and Freedom—and then write down how money can help to grow those areas. (For example, money can help you buy healthy food so that you eat better.)

__ Create a stop-doing list of limiting beliefs about money. Every time you encounter a limiting belief such as "I don't have enough money" or "I can't do that because it's not in the budget" write it down on your list of limiting beliefs. Replace these beliefs with a positive, accurate statement about money.

Add your own actions:

__ Stop doing actions (Actions you currently do now but should stop doing)

_____

_____

__ Keep doing actions (Actions you currently do now and should keep doing)

_____

_____

__ Start doing actions (Actions you don't do now but should start doing)

_____

_____

__ Who will do new actions? (Assign the action to yourself or someone else)

_____

_____

__ By when? (When will these actions be complete?)

_____

_____

The Basic Money Equation

The basic money equation is:

$$Revenues - Expenses = Profit$$

Maybe you looked at this equation and thought, "Well 'duh,' of course that's the basic equation. Why are you telling me this?"

The basic equation of money in your business is so simple that you might be tempted to skip this part of the chapter, but don't! When it comes to money, it never hurts to go back to basics and review the fundamentals one more time. Other things in life and business can become more complicated but in finances there is beauty in simplicity.

It also reminds me of martial arts: the most skilled, highest achieving martial artists didn't attain their Black Belt by learning more moves than anyone else. You don't get a Black Belt based on the number of moves you know. Rather, these Black Belt martial artists became more skilled at the same moves that everyone else knows—the fundamentals. They may still be doing the same katas as a beginner but they've done those katas hundreds of thousands of times and they execute those moves to perfection.

Or think of it like driving a car. There are many bad drivers out there on the roads and there are many good drivers out there on the roads. The bad drivers and the good drivers each learned the same moves and they drive on the same roads in the same kind of cars and follow the same laws. But the bad drivers execute poorly while the good drivers execute flawlessly.

Likewise, **you'll master money by stripping away the complexity and going back to the most basic "financial kata" of them all—the basic financial equation:**

Revenues – Expenses = Profit

It can get more complicated than that (which is why we have accountants) but that is the basic equation you should understand and master in your business. And if I were to ask you what your revenue numbers, expense numbers, and profit numbers for the last day, week, month, quarter, and year were, you should be able to tell me from memory.

If you put a bunch of people into a room and I ask them for those numbers—revenue, expenses, and profit from the last day, week, month, quarter, and year—you would notice something quite profound: even though everyone would agree that this is the most basic equation, there would be a very small group of people who actually knew their numbers from heart while a much larger group had no clue or who just guessed. And then if you determined which of the two groups were more successful, 100% of the time the greatest success stories would come from the group that knew their numbers—no question. It always happens that way.

Of course, knowing your numbers in and of itself won't make you successful but it's a start. The old adage is true, "What gets measured gets managed." So if you know your numbers then you have a starting point—a baseline—that you can manage from.

There are two more aspects to this equation that I need to address here before we move on in the chapter:

First, you might be asking yourself the question, "Should I raise the ceiling or lower the floor?" (meaning, should you increase income or decrease expenses?)—but what if you do both? What if you used the strategies in this book to increase your income *and* decrease expenses?!? By just making a ten percent improvement to increase income in the next 12 months and a ten percent improvement to decrease expenses, you'll combine those improvements to increase profit far more than 20 percent. Combined, it will have a dramatic impact on your business that has the potential to be life-changing.

With that in mind, that leads me to the second aspect I need to address about this simple equation: your business' ability to earn profit is entirely under your control. Forget your CFO, COO, and accountants (if you have them in your business). Your business' ability to earn profit is up to you. You're the one to decide how much is coming in and how much is going out and what you do with it all. And if your business hasn't been earning enough profit in the past, I have a cold, hard truth for you that you might not want to hear: it's your own choice that your business hasn't been earning enough profit.

Fortunately, you can change it. In the next section I'll show you how.

Take Action!
Recommended actions:

___ Create a spreadsheet that lists revenues, expenses, and profit, for the last days, weeks, months, quarters, and years. Start by trying to write them in from memory and then go find the real numbers and see how close you were.

__ Schedule time regularly in your planner to update this spreadsheet with accurate numbers. For example, add the daily number every day. Yes, you should do this daily at first (although once you become very practiced at it, perhaps you can update the daily numbers weekly). I would also suggest that you don't get your CFO or accountant to do this right now. At first, do it yourself, since it's your responsibility and choice to know and manage these numbers. In the future, as your business grows, you can of course get someone else to do this (and to report these numbers to you regularly) but at first you should know these numbers well. As you grow in your familiarity with these numbers, use them to take action (because information without action is never going to create change or results in your business).

__ Forecast what you think the next set of numbers will be. Try to estimate the next day's, week's month's, quarter's, and year's numbers for revenues, expenses, and profits. At first, your estimates will probably be way off but you'll get better at understanding your numbers and you'll eventually become very good at forecasting your numbers.

Add your own actions:

__ Stop doing actions (Actions you currently do now but should stop doing)

_____

_____

__ Keep doing actions (Actions you currently do now and should keep doing)

_____

_____

__ Start doing actions (Actions you don't do now but should start doing)

_____

_____

__ Who will do new actions? (Assign the action to yourself or someone else)

_____

_____

__ By when? (When will these actions be complete?)

_____

_____

Money: Make More, Save More, Spend More

In this section, I want to address three things that will influence the basic equation in your business—making more money, saving more money, and spending more money. Yes, you read that correctly: I'm recommending that you probably need to spend more money!

Make more money: you need to build your business so that you have more customers coming into your business in a constant stream. And you need to build your business so that those customers see you as an expert. You'll increase the number of prospects who turn into customers, and you'll also position yourself to earn the kind of income that an expert earns.

Side note: **experts always earn more.** If a customer doesn't see a difference between you and the other dozen service providers who offer a similar service, then they won't want to pay you more. But if you position yourself as an expert—as someone who is more knowledgeable and provides a superior overall service than anyone else—your customers will happily pay you more. And if you're thinking, "Maybe that's true for your ideal customers but not my ideal customers" then I would challenge your thinking: you can be an expert compared to the other service providers for your ideal customer... Or perhaps you should consider changing who your ideal customer is. After all, your ideal customer should be only too glad to pay you what you're worth!

As you sell to more customers and make more money from them, you should also sell more products and services to each customer.

So, create a business that commands respect from your customers and then charge accordingly. This is really what a lot of this entire book is about, so let's move on to some of the other pieces of money mastery.

Save money: I'm an advocate of strategically spending (on the right things) in your business and I'll discuss that in detail in the next section of this chapter. However, I want to first talk about saving money. We all like to save money when we can, although you need to spend on the right things and save on the right things.

Saving money makes a lot of financial sense because it frees up dollars that would have been otherwise committed, allowing you to use them on other things. For example, when you switch from a higher-priced vendor to a lower-priced vendor, money that was previously thought to be committed is suddenly freed up. You still get the supplies or services that you need from the vendor but now you have more money to invest in other aspects of your business, allowing you to grow. Be careful not to sacrifice quality or relationships for money, but look at it from all angles.

I want to be clear: I'm not suggesting that you pay as little as possible for everything and that you grind down your vendors and never give your employees raises. If you grind down your vendors, you'll eventually run out of vendors to work with, or you'll start getting shoddy, low-quality supplies or services. And if you pay your employees as little as possible, you won't attract and retain them. I hope you can see that paying the absolute cheapest all the time is actually a higher cost alternative over the long run. However, I am recommending that you look at every single expense to ask yourself whether you are getting all the value you can out of it and whether you can get the same thing or better for less.

You should constantly investigate where you are spending money and explore whether or not it's an opportunity to save money. Commit time in your monthly schedule to ask yourself, "Where are we paying too much for something?" Investigate everything. Leave no stone unturned in your business. When you see a cost or expense, ask yourself the following question: "Can I get an equivalent or better result by spending less?" This might come from making a larger order to get a bulk discount or it might come from asking for a competitive bid on some supply or service.

With vendors, you should go out for competitive bids twice a year at least. Not only will you find lower-priced alternatives for the supplies and services your business uses, there's another (non-financial) benefit: your vendors know that they need to work extra hard to serve you and they'll step up to the plate and not take you and your business for granted.

Another way to save money is to make purchases without using money. For example, when purchases are made on a corporate credit card, that card might earn points that can be used toward additional purchases. Take a look at your corporate credit card and see if you are earning points. If you are, and you haven't done anything with them, then you might have quite a few banked up to spend. If your corporate credit card doesn't accumulate points with every purchase, look at some alternatives and find a card that will accumulate points and reward you for your spending. Or if you have several loans and are going for another loan, talk to your bank about pulling them altogether as one blanket loan so you can get a lower interest rate.

Buying power is another way to save money. That's when you can use volume of purchases to negotiate a lower price with your vendors. You can create internal buying power by looking at what your purchase patterns are like and perhaps rearranging when and how much you order at one time. (For example, a weekly purchase of supplies might actually be cheaper if you purchase a larger quantity once a month—assuming that your storage costs won't rise by storing those supplies.) Buying power can also be obtained by partnering with another company to purchase products. Find another company that needs the same supplies you need and go in together to make your purchase.

Sometimes it is just asking your vendors this age-old question, "If I could save money from you how could I do it?" Asking this question is very effective and much more professional than, "Can you give me a discount on this because I'm such a regular customer?"

Once you start saving money, what are you going to do with all that new-found money? Put it into your marketing. That's the best investment to make on any free dollars. Put that money into marketing to generate more customers and, ultimately, more money.

Spend money: *saving* money is a favorite topic for a lot of people… But *spending* money? Not so much. Most people are wired to spend less and save more but that mentality is not always the best approach when you want to master your money.

Yes, I did just finish telling you in the previous section that saving money is good, and critical for your business. But you have to spend money—it's necessary to spend money in your business. As you focus on saving money, you should also give just as much thought to how you are spending the money you need to spend.

Part of money mastery is rewiring how your brain thinks about money. While many business owners are reluctant to spend money, a money master is willing to spend money—even a lot of money—as long as it fits the following parameter:

Think of every dollar you spend in your business as an investment into your business. That's how I want you to think about all of the money that is coming into your business and is about to flow out to cover expenses. Every single dollar is an investment.

If you invest a dollar and get back $1.25, $1.50, or better yet, $2.00, would you say that dollar was wisely invested? Of course you would.

And if you invest a dollar and get back 75 cents or even 50 cents, would you say that dollar was poorly invested? You probably would.

So think of every dollar you spend as an investment and think about what it will return to your business. For example, if you had $25,000 in your bank account and you had the opportunity to spend that money on some marketing, would you do it? $25,000 might seem like a lot… unless you had a pretty good idea that the $25,000 investment would return $50,000. Then you might readily spend it. In fact, you would probably try to pull together $50,000 that you could spend to get back $100,000, right?

Think of every dollar spent as an investment. Before you spend it, decide what kind of return you will get. To connect this back to something I said earlier, that's why you shouldn't try to pay your employees the lowest amount of money possible. Because when you pay them fairly, and invest in their training, you'll earn back far more than you spent.

Money masters willingly spend money on the right things, and they decide what those best expenses are based on what they believe the return will be to their business.

Take Action!
Recommended actions:

___ Create a list of ways you can make more money in your business.

___ Create a list of ways you can save more money in your business.

___ Create a list of ways you can spend more money (wisely) in your business.

___ Keep these lists and refer to them regularly, adding to them often and using the ideas you've listed to master your business' basic financial equation.

Add your own actions:

___ Stop doing actions (Actions you currently do now but should stop doing)
_____
_____

___ Keep doing actions (Actions you currently do now and should keep doing)
_____
_____

___ Start doing actions (Actions you don't do now but should start doing)
_____
_____

__ Who will do new actions? (Assign the action to yourself or someone else)

_____

_____

__ By when? (When will these actions be complete?)

_____

_____

Financial Management

Financial management is the last piece of the money mastery puzzle. You're making money, you're saving money, you're wisely spending (investing) money, and in this section I want to talk about how you manage the money while it's in your business and what you do with the money left over (profit).

Develop a decision-making criteria. The first thing you need to do is to be ready to use that profit. Develop a decision-making criteria to make better business and financial decisions: whenever you are faced with a choice, review all options and select the one that will deliver the greatest return on investment and the longest return on investment. Here's what is on my decision-making criteria, which I use to determine how I'll spend every dollar of profit (bonus: I also use this for other decisions, too):

- The greatest return on investment is usually the return that delivers the higher dollar value (or equivalent).
- The longest return on investment is the one that will provide the greatest ongoing return. To illustrate what I mean, I like to use the example of a slot machine versus a company bond. A slot machine could give you $1000 but that benefit ends as soon as it pays out, compared to a bond, which pays interest on a regular basis over the lifetime of the bond.

Make it a habit to think through this decision-making criteria every time you are faced with any decision, especially how you'll spend your profit.

Leverage an accountant. If you don't have an accountant in your business, get one. If you do have an accountant, make sure you're working with someone who is an expert at saving money and making money. There are many accountants out there and, unfortunately, some of them are only experts at just writing checks. They have the credentials but they don't have the motivation to go looking for financial strategies that can help your business.

Here's an example of what I mean. We put up 120 foot flags at our head office location. It was going to cost $28,000. Many accountants would look at that and get ready to cut the check for us. But our accountant knew that there was a 35% tax credit for the purchase of flags for your business, so we were able to save some money because our accountant knew his stuff. Make sure your accountant will become an asset, not an expense!

Find hidden money: a lot of times there's hidden money in your business—money you don't even realize is there. The easiest example that you can immediately implement into your business is to find out what else your customers are buying that they can buy from you instead of someone else. But that's just the beginning.

In the service industry, there's a lot of scrap left over—can you do something with that? Perhaps you can sell scrap steel, for example.

And here's an example from my business: we realized that we were losing a bunch of time (and therefore money) as our team drove to the gas station to fill up their vehicles. So we had a gas tank installed on our property. Problem solved. Suddenly, our team was instantly more productive because they could fill up on our property and head out to the customers' house.

Similarly, we have our material delivered to our property. This also cuts down on time that our team used to spend going to get supplies.

Profit buckets: this is a lesson I learned from Mike Michalowicz, author of the book *Profit First*. I've implemented it in my business and it is a powerful way to master your money. He advises that you set up separate bank accounts for all different types of money that flows into your business.

Not all your money should go to one checking accounting. Instead it should be first allocated to different purposes, like Taxes, Payroll, Owner's Pay, Profit, etc. For example, set up one bank account for payroll. Set up another bank account for taxes. Set up another bank account for ordinary expenses. You should also set up a separate account for profit and immediately take the money as it comes in and put some of it into the profit bucket (don't wait to do that with whatever is leftover). As the money comes in, break it up into these separate buckets. You'll gain a better idea of where each dollar goes and how much you are spending on each part of your business.

Take Action!
Recommended actions:

___ In this chapter I've given you several powerful ways to improve your financial management and start achieving financial mastery. Pick one that you can implement right away and do it immediately. Then schedule the others into your planner and get to them as soon as possible.

Add your own actions:

___ Stop doing actions (Actions you currently do now but should stop doing)

_____

_____

___ Keep doing actions (Actions you currently do now and should keep doing)

_____

_____

___ Start doing actions (Actions you don't do now but should start doing)

_____

_____

__ Who will do new actions? (Assign the action to yourself or someone else)

_____

_____

__ By when? (When will these actions be complete?)

_____

_____

Conclusion

Money is so important in life. It allows us to do all the things we need to do and all the things we want to do. Unfortunately, most of us were raised with severely limiting beliefs about money, shared by well-meaning but misguided influencers. You need to break these limiting beliefs so you can start on your journey toward money mastery.

Then, go back to basics and become like a martial artist. You don't need to learn thousands of new ways to grow your financials; you need to start with the basics and master those basics. Just like a Black Belt martial artist, you need to learn to do the basics really, really well.

And then adopt the attitude of "more." Learn to make more money using the strategies in this book, learn to save more and even spend more (wisely, of course) by applying the strategies in this chapter.

Mastering your financials will transform your business and your life. And if you've been struggling with not having enough money at the end of each month then re-read this chapter immediately and put into practice all the money mastery strategies I've explained.

Master Action List For Chapter 8

At the end of each section of this chapter you had actions to perform as well as Start Doing/Keep Doing/Stop Doing lists. Gather those actions together into a Master Action List, add any new actions that you think of, and then go through the questions below to think about how these actions can transform your life and your business:

__ **Is it going to make me money?** Are the actions you've listed going to help you generate more income? (If they are, great. Think about how they might be able to help you generate even more income. If they aren't making you more money then are those actions really as important as you thought they were?)

__ **Is it going save me money?** Reducing how much you spend will help you increase your profit. Are the actions you're thinking of doing going to help you cut back on your expenses without sacrificing the quality of your service? (If they save you money, great. If they aren't saving you money then are those actions really as important as you thought they were?)

__ **Is it going to save time?** Your time is precious and scarce. So the actions you take should help you to save time. Keep the big picture in mind because some actions may take a few extra minutes in the short term but will ultimately help you save time in the long term. (For example, training an employee might be an action that will take a few extra minutes now but will save you a lot of time in the future).

__ **Is it going to help me achieve market domination?** Your business needs to own the market it works in. Whenever someone thinks of the service you provide, they should only think of you. Do the actions you've listed in this chapter support that market domination? What can you change about them to help you dominate the market even further?

__ **How do I start fast to get the low-hanging fruit?** It's easy to say you're going to take action but it's much harder to actually do it. One way to take

action and push through to its successful completion is to go for the quick wins—the low-hanging fruit. From the actions you've listed, what low-hanging fruit can you immediately pick?

___ **What's the leverage?** Leverage has a few different meanings but, in this context, I'm talking about how you can motivate yourself. For example, if you commit to complete an action within a certain period of time you can leverage that commitment by saying, "If I don't make that commitment, I'll donate $10,000 to a charity." Since you may not have $10,000, and you'll probably feel some pain donating that much money, you are leveraging your commitment and compelling yourself to complete the actions you said you'd complete.

___ **What's the reward?** For each action, list what you expect to get out of it. If you can't think of a reward for the action, seriously consider whether it is as valuable as you thought. Spend more of your time on actions that have rewards. Two of the best rewards for your actions are below (although there are other rewards you may choose to take action for)...

___ **Is it going to help me achieve wealth?** One of the best rewards you can take action for is to achieve wealth. For each action ask whether that particular action will help you make more money to give you the sense of safety and achievement and allow you to buy whatever you want whenever you want it. If possible, develop the action even further if a stronger, clearer, bigger action will help you achieve more wealth.

___ **Is it going to help me get more freedom?** Another one of the best rewards you can take action for is to get more freedom—the time and financial capacity to do whatever you want whenever you want to (without sacrificing your business). For each action ask whether that particular action will help you get more freedom. If possible, develop the action even further if a stronger, clearer, bigger action will help you get more freedom.

CHAPTER 9

MASTER YOUR CULTURE AND TEAM

One of the biggest struggles that service business owners face is the attraction and retention of good employees. And even beyond your employees, your team is also made up of other people as well. In this chapter I'll explain how you can build a culture that empowers your team and expects the best from them, and I'll show you how to create a long-lasting team that will stick with you through thick and thin.

Introduction

When I say "team" you probably immediately think of employees. And if you're working on your own right now, your temptation might be to skip this chapter because you don't think you have a team. But a team is much more than your employees. It includes your vendors, too. And even if you are a business of one, the decisions and structures you put in place right now will help to influence the culture of your team (your employees and vendors) as your business grows.

So, in this chapter I want to talk about mastering your team, which includes your employees and your vendors. I'll talk about adding people to your team and building up a culture where everyone works together for the same target.

A boat with many rowers is a great picture of what I'll talk about in this chapter. Rowers are usually facing the opposite direction of where they want to go and they rely on the leader to point them in the right

direction. The leader ensures that the team heads where they need to go and makes sure everyone is doing their job at the right time. That's a healthy team. A boat where rowers are paddling out of sync or where the leader is not focused are two illustrations of an unhealthy team.

Whether you have a team right now or you will in the future, this chapter will help you become the master of your culture and team.

One more key item to mention: Avoid the temptation to think of your employees as an entirely separate group from the rest of your life, as if they're "only" the people you direct during the day while you're at work. Instead, think of them as a key part of your Core 5 Dimensions of Life and Business Mastery. They're part of your Relationship Dimension, plus their work contributes to your Wealth Dimension and Freedom Dimension. And, you're part of their Core 5, too: you are one of their Relationships and the money you pay them contributes to their Wealth.

A Good Team Starts With A Good Leader—You

Most people are followers. I don't mean that disrespectfully—that's just the way it is. Most people are followers and that's okay because leaders need followers. If you want to run a business, you need to realize that you are no longer among the followers; you are a leader. It's time to step up and lead.

This book is a toolkit for leaders. Implementing each of the chapters in this book will help to accelerate you into the leadership position and solidify your ability lead your team.

But a good leader realizes that they can't do it alone. They need help.

At first, your business might start out with just you (plus a couple of vendors as part of your team). Then, it will grow and you'll have a couple of employees. Then it will grow even more and you'll need to add some additional leaders to help you manage your team.

Each of those stages of leadership requires different qualities but one thing is common among all of those stages of growth I listed above: good teams are built either by default or design. That means, if you don't work hard to design a great team then your team will be built by default and it won't be what you want.

As your business grows, you need to continue to be intentional about building your team. Don't settle! Right from day one start building something I call a "warrior team"—which is a team that is willing to fight together for a common target. Adopt this mentality as you hire and train your team.

As your team grows, you'll need to put additional leaders into place to help you manage your team. These should be selected from your top-line warriors, the ones who motivate others to move the needle in your business.

Take Action!
Recommended actions:

__ Make a list of people on your team (employees and vendors) and think about how you can lead your team. What do they need to know about you and your business to make sure that they are headed in the direction you want them to go? What do you need to say and do? What expectations should you have of them? How can you hold them accountable? How can you lead by example?

__ Once you realize that you're a leader, it means others are watching you and doing what you do and what you say. Create a start-doing list and a stop-doing list of all the things you need to start doing and stop doing to ensure that you are leading ethically and responsibly and congruently (i.e. what you say and what you do are the same).

Add your own actions:

__ Stop doing actions (Actions you currently do now but should stop doing)

_____

_____

__ Keep doing actions (Actions you currently do now and should keep doing)

_____

_____

__ Start doing actions (Actions you don't do now but should start doing)

_____

_____

__ Who will do new actions? (Assign the action to yourself or someone else)

_____

_____

__ By when? (When will these actions be complete?)

_____

_____

Vending Machine Hiring

A lot of service business owners who are adding to their team make this critical mistake: they hire only when they need to fill a role. Perhaps they need a field expert so they put an ad in the paper and they collect resumes and then try to pick from among those resumes.

But that is a huge mistake. It solves an immediate problem yet it doesn't necessarily solve it in the best way possible. You'll have to go through the whole process again when you need another role filled, and you aren't always filling the role with the best person—just the best person who responded to your ad at the time.

I want you to rethink hiring. Start with this: **adopt the mentality that you are *always* hiring. Don't wait until you have a role to fill; maintain a "we're always hiring" policy and collect prospective team members.** It's okay if you don't hire them right away but always be on the lookout for more people to add to your prospective hires list, just as you would add people to a prospective customers list. By making this one change, you gain two advantages…

First, when a role does open up, you have a much broader selection of better people to choose from (compared to a smaller list of only those who answered your help wanted ad). Second, if you find a superstar who you know will be a huge asset to your company, you may want to think about creating a role for them because you know that adding them to your team will help your business grow.

It's kind of like a vending machine. When you want a drink, you just press the button and a cold drink is delivered to you. In the same way, if you're always hiring, you've got a list of prospective employees at the ready when you need one.

Actually, **having slightly more employees than you think you need might be a good thing.** That sounds like a funny concept when you first read it but here's what I mean: if you want to take on more work, you need the people to do the work. Besides, if have one employee and they break their leg, what are you going to do? You're in a hostage situation. (Of course, you don't want a company that is bloated with employees who are sitting around doing nothing. You'll need to put them all to work. But having slightly more employees than you think you need will force you to go out and find more work for them and will keep your business flexible).

To hire effectively, start with a hiring avatar. This is a very similar concept to the marketing avatar you created for your target prospect in the marketing chapter. With a hiring avatar, you create a picture of the ideal person who you want to work for you. Describe them in detail, including:

- What educational background do they have?
- What experience do they have?
- What are their interests?
- How do they like to spend their non-working time?
- Do they have a family?
- What drives them?
- Where do they live?

Again, just like the marketing avatar, this hiring avatar should be detailed and should give you a very clear picture of the perfect employee.

When hiring, don't rely on a single help wanted ad to fill a role. Instead, get out there and actively look for people all the time. A great place to get new employees is to ask your existing employees and new hires about who else they know who might want a job. These people know other people and can refer them if they're happy working for you.

And here's something I do when hiring in my company: I don't want to waste time interviewing 25 people individually for a single job, especially since everyone's resume basically looks the same and everyone puts their best foot forward during a one-on-one interview. Instead, my company holds a hiring night. This is when we interview 10 to 40 people (sometimes more) all at the same time in one hour. It's a fun experience and a great way to sift through a lot of people and to spot the cream rising to the top really fast.

Here's how a hiring night works: we bring as many people in as we can for an hour. We have a big room, with some snacks and drinks, and then we give a presentation about the company, our core values and vision, and what we're looking for and what we're not looking for in an employee. Then, we ask them to tell us if they're the right person. We go around the room and ask questions like, "Why should I hire you?" and, "If you were a vehicle, what kind of vehicle would be?" (Hint: we're looking for someone who says they're a Porsche; we're not looking for someone who says they're dependable like a Kia). In this format, we also get to see how they interact in an unusual setting and with each other.

Not only is this process a lot of fun (and a huge time-saver) for us, it's also a lot of fun for the participants. It changes the perception of what your business is. When someone comes to this experience, they become automatic recruiters. And when you compare how much time would normally be spent on one-on-one interviews, this format saves time and money and it allows you to see these prospective employees on so many levels at once.

There are a lot of details to this vending machine hiring concept and I've only scratched the surface to get you thinking about it and to get you started. I go deeper into this in my Warrior Fast Track Academy, and those who attend a Warrior Fast Track Academy leave with a powerful plan to hire the very best employees for their business.

Take Action!

Recommended actions:

__ Develop your hiring avatar—the description of the ideal employee.

__ Assess your existing employees to determine which of them already match with the hiring avatar and which do not. Then, put together a plan to improve all employees—and for those who do not match the hiring avatar, either bring them up to the level you need them at, or find them a different position to work in, or let them go.

__ Create a file for resumes. If you already have such a file, go through the resumes and keep the best ones and get rid of the ones who do not match your hiring avatar.

Add your own actions:

__ Stop doing actions (Actions you currently do now but should stop doing)

_____

_____

__ Keep doing actions (Actions you currently do now and should keep doing)

_____

_____

__ Start doing actions (Actions you don't do now but should start doing)

_____

_____

__ Who will do new actions? (Assign the action to yourself or someone else)

_____

_____

__ By when? (When will these actions be complete?)

_____

_____

Onboarding and Training

Your team represents your business to customers. A good employee can keep a customers for life and a bad employee can repulse a customer and send them running to your competition.

When you add people to your team, it's your job as a leader to set expectations as early as possible and as clearly as possible. You need to make sure they know what's expected of them, and you need to make sure they are up to the task.

For my employees I have an onboarding experience, which is something we offer them as soon as they join. And on an ongoing basis we continually train our employees in the skills we want them to possess while they're out serving customers.

Onboarding experience: our onboarding experience is a total immersion experience for new employees. It's a one day "welcome to the company" experience when they learn about our core values and core purpose, and when they get to meet everyone. We want them to quickly learn who we are and ideally get excited about working with our team.

Training: we use a four-step training method whenever we want to teach our team anything. All of our leadership is trained in this four-step method, which keeps it consistent throughout our company. Here's how it works: when we want to train a team member in a skill, we follow these steps:

1. Explain—the trainer explains to the team member what they want them to do.
2. Demonstrate—the trainer shows the team member what they want them to do.

3. You demonstrate to me—the team member demonstrates back to the trainer what they have learned, and they demonstrate it until they are confident.
4. You teach me—the team member teaches the trainer. (If they can teach it, they will do it consistently.)

Along with this four-step training method, we also use video and role-play to train our team. We use video to show how something is done and we frequently use roleplay to help employees practice something in a safe, structured, no risk environment before they implement it on the job in front of a customer.

Take Action!
Recommended actions:

__ Compare my onboard process with yours and see how you can model elements from my process to increase the immediate effectiveness of your new employees.

__ Schedule times regularly to bring together your team in small groups or as a large group to practice new techniques. Create videos of how you want your employees to work in a specific situation and then roleplay with your employees so they get some experience.

Add your own actions:

__ Stop doing actions (Actions you currently do now but should stop doing)
_____
_____

__ Keep doing actions (Actions you currently do now and should keep doing)
_____
_____

__ Start doing actions (Actions you don't do now but should start doing)

_____

_____

__ Who will do new actions? (Assign the action to yourself or someone else)

_____

_____

__ By when? (When will these actions be complete?)

_____

_____

Working Together

Your team is growing. How do you, as a leader, keep them on track? To borrow the rowboat analogy from earlier, how do you make sure everyone is pulling together? Communication is the key and the best way to communicate with each other is with brief meetings where everyone connects.

Meetings are a great way for leaders to communicate with their team. Unfortunately, many businesses just have meetings for the sake having meetings. These meetings turn into social gatherings, they often have no agenda (or no firm agenda), and an equal importance is given to low-priority items and to high-priority items. I believe that meetings are for action items and to make decisions. That's it. If you're not doing those, it's a social gathering.

Here are the types of meetings I recommend:

Daily huddle: you don't have to have these every day but you should have them regularly. Increase frequency during key times (i.e. a new marketing promotion). This is a 5-10 minute check-in for all team members to see what each person needs to do today. During this brief huddle, everyone shares what is good, what is not good, and the day's outcomes should be. (If you have a big team, as we do, it might not be practical for everyone to meet in one huddle. Therefore, you might want to huddle by departments—so your customer service people huddle, and your field experts huddle, and so on.) Make them stand-up meetings only—no sitting because when you're sitting then you're tempted to prolong the discussion. These meetings are quick for rapid-fire communication.

Level 10 meetings. I have these twice a month. They are meetings where I want people to bring a higher level of motivation to move things forward. That's what the "Level 10" is all about—that's the level of energy people need to bring to them.

Alignment meetings: these are as-needed meetings. For example, if management goes through the building and notices that something is not aligned with the corporate guidelines then they can hold an alignment meeting to bring all the relevant people together to make adjustments.

Weekly meetings: these are held at the end of each week. My team goes into a room and we go through our numbers and what we have to do next week.

Financial meeting: these are held between the 10th and 15th of the month. Management, leaders of departments, and accountants all get together and talk about the budget and whether we're on-track or off track, and this is the time to discuss any other financially-impacting topic.

All company gathering: these are quarterly meetings. Everyone comes together. We talk about big things in the future such as culture, marketing, leadership, and sales. We make sure we're all rowing in the same direction. For each of these meetings, we create a theme. Some of our recent things included: "212 degrees," "Above the line, below the line," and "Customer service." Whatever theme we choose for the company gathering will become the quarterly mantra to keep everyone aligned and to reinforce the lessons discussed.

Note: you do not need to do all of these meetings all the time. Choose the ones that work for you. Also, you do not always need to attend these meetings in person; you can use webinar programs for meetings that allow you or your team to attend a meeting from a different location.

When you create your meetings, make sure you set healthy guidelines. For example, no one is allowed to use their cell phone or laptop during the meeting; make sure everyone has a pen and paper to take notes; assign a timekeeper to keep the meeting on track; and never go over the time you've set for the meeting to end.

Take Action!
Recommended actions:

___ Time for some honest reflection: how many meetings do you and your staff have? How productive have they been?

___ Schedule regular meetings and review who you think should show up at these meetings (you don't need everyone at every meeting).

___ Develop agendas for every meeting and stick to them.

Add your own actions:

___ Stop doing actions (Actions you currently do now but should stop doing)
_____
_____

___ Keep doing actions (Actions you currently do now and should keep doing)
_____
_____

__ Start doing actions (Actions you don't do now but should start doing)

__ Who will do new actions? (Assign the action to yourself or someone else)

__ By when? (When will these actions be complete?)

Developing Your Company's Culture

The culture of your business sets the boundaries for how your team members will think, act, and speak—whether they are in front of you or in front of a customer or working on their own.

A lax culture that hasn't set any ground rules and demonstrates that no one really cares will create exactly the kind of team you'd expect—a lazy employee that doesn't rise to the occasion and doesn't feel that there are consequences.

On the other hand, **a professional culture that expects the best from everyone and clearly establishes ground rules and targets that everyone can work on will create exactly the kind of team you'd expect—hard working employees who know what is expected of them and will often rise to the occasion.**

Your culture is established by you. And if you're running your business by yourself, your company's culture is established by you right now—long before you add your first employee. If the culture of your business isn't exactly what you'd want an employee to work in, now is the time to make the change!

To establish a great culture in your business, start with your business vision and blueprint and make sure everyone is on the same page. Create a 52 week culture plan that includes events, special days, and memorable occasions that employees will enjoy.

Culture is everything in your business—from the quality and cleanliness of your uniforms to expectations about the kind of language that employees use during work time... even down to the pictures you have on your walls. Walk around your office with a critical eye and ask whether or not each part of your business adds to or takes away from the culture you want to establish.

Take Action!
Recommended actions:

__ What kind of culture does your business have? (Every business has a culture but it's not always articulated or intentional).

__ What kind of culture would you like your business to have? Even if you were somewhat happy with your culture from the above activity, there will probably be some improvements that need to be made.

__ No matter what kind of culture your business has, it is determined by you. What changes do you need to make in your actions, speech, and habits that will model your preferred culture for your employees?

Add your own actions:

__ Stop doing actions (Actions you currently do now but should stop doing)
_____
_____

__ Keep doing actions (Actions you currently do now and should keep doing)
_____
_____

__ Start doing actions (Actions you don't do now but should start doing)
_____
_____

__ Who will do new actions? (Assign the action to yourself or someone else)

_____

_____

__ By when? (When will these actions be complete?)

_____

_____

Turn Your Vendors Into Team Players

A team is not just made up of employees. As I've said throughout this chapter, a team is also made up of your vendors as well. Sure, they might not be employed by you and they don't wear your uniforms, but they are still an integral part of your team. Therefore, you should view your vendors just as you would view your team of employees—you want to create a warrior vendor team.

Develop a relationship with your vendors where they are excited for your success. Help them see how your success will make them more successful, too, and figure out ways that they can contribute to helping you grow. Don't think of your vendors as a group of companies you contact once in a while whenever you need something from them. Rather, figure out how to empower your vendors to help you build your business.

In my business, for example, my vendors have a monthly meeting—without me present—about how to build my business. That's the kind of mindset you want your vendors to have about your business. If your vendors don't have that mindset right now, revisit your relationship with them and try to develop that mindset in them or find new vendors who will think that way about you.

Take Action!

Recommended actions:

__ Make a list of your vendors. Beside each vendor, assess how aligned they are with your business. Do they even know what your goals are? What are they doing to help further those goals?

__ Schedule time in your planner to meet with each vendor and to discuss your business with them and to see how they can help you.

__ Evaluate how you have been treating your vendors. Are they partners or just someone you're giving money to so they perform a service?

Add your own actions:

__ Stop doing actions (Actions you currently do now but should stop doing)

_____

_____

__ Keep doing actions (Actions you currently do now and should keep doing)

_____

_____

__ Start doing actions (Actions you don't do now but should start doing)

_____

_____

__ Who will do new actions? (Assign the action to yourself or someone else)

_____

_____

__ By when? (When will these actions be complete?)

_____

_____

Delegation And Accountability

As a leader, you have followers. It's an intrinsic aspect of leadership. Unfortunately, many leaders fall short in delegating and they struggle to hold their team accountable. It's so easy for leaders to keep tasks to themselves because they want those tasks done a certain way, plus it seems easier to just do it yourself instead of spending the time training someone else and then reprimanding them if they do it wrong.

At least, that's how a lot of leaders view delegation and accountability.

But if you want to master your team and your culture, and if you want to be the kind of leader that inspires your team to give their best work always, then you'll need to learn to delegate and hold your team accountable.

I realize that it can be tempting to do a task yourself because training someone will take more time. However, here's how I want you to think about your time from now on: **always ask yourself how much your time is worth. And keep that in mind when looking at the tasks you need to do.** Although it might seem like training someone will take extra time, it will ultimately save you time in the long run as you hand off that task to someone else, allowing you to free up your time to do other things. Remember: as the leader of your business your time is worth far more than that of any other employee so it makes sense to hand off many other of the "lower value" tasks to them so you can remain focused on the bigger picture.

To help you know what to delegate here is a powerful tool we use; I use this for both my team and for vendors. I list all of my team members (or vendors) and I score each team member based on who "gets" our core values, who truly wants to achieve them, and who has the capacity to do more. By using this tool, I can make sure that I delegate increasingly important tasks to the people who get what we're doing and have the ability to do it. It's a powerful tool.

To help keep your team on track, create an accountability chart that lists each position in your company and the three to five things that they do. This gives you and your team a very transparent list of expectations that you can use to check in with employees to see if they are on track and to easily make small corrections if they are not. From this chart, you can build out a scorecard based on those three to five things that each team member does and you can use that scorecard to evaluate your team regularly.

When you hire right, and you lead well, most of your employees rise to the occasion and work with everyone else toward the same targets. However, not all employees fit 100% of the time and there are times when your accountability reveals that you must take disciplinary action against an employee. It's not pleasant but you shouldn't avoid it because letting disciplinary issues fester will destroy your culture. Worse yet, your customers will notice that something is broken in your business and you'll start to notice a sick culture in your bottom line.

So, when disciplinary action is necessary, here are the steps I recommend:

1. Verbalize the situation and make a note of it in the employee's file.
2. If it happens again, document the situation and have them sign it.
3. If it happens a third time, the employee gets a week off, unpaid.
4. If it happens a fourth time, they are relocated out of the business.

Don't think of these steps as harsh punishment. Instead, think of these steps like you're working to get the employee back on track by giving them multiple chances to fix their mistake and make sure they don't repeat it.

And remember: accountability is a two way street. You have certain expectations of your employees. But guess what; they have certain expectations of you (as a leader) and the business. You should be surveying your staff regularly—at least once a year but you could do it as often as each quarter. Survey your team on different areas of the business and culture to determine what changes are needed. Invite them to make recommendations. Although you cannot do every recommendation, their feedback will help you gain a view of what your employees collectively think of the business.

Take Action!
Recommended actions:

___ Assess your ability to delegate and hold people accountable. Create a start doing list to increase how much you delegate—and don't forget to hold them accountable. And, create a stop-doing list of actions and behaviors that you need to stop doing in order to do a better job of delegating and holding people accountable. (Hint: often, it will start with your mindset.)

Add your own actions:

___ Stop doing actions (Actions you currently do now but should stop doing)

_____

_____

___ Keep doing actions (Actions you currently do now and should keep doing)

_____

_____

___ Start doing actions (Actions you don't do now but should start doing)

_____

_____

___ Who will do new actions? (Assign the action to yourself or someone else)

_____

_____

___ By when? (When will these actions be complete?)

_____

_____

Conclusion

Your business runs as a team made up of vendors and employees, and they are all led by you. Even if you don't have very many vendors or employees now, you have a few and that's your team; and, as your business grows, your team will grow.

Therefore, it is imperative that you master your team by taking charge of the hiring and onboarding practices. Do this now so that you are staffed with the right people now (instead of "putting up with" the people on your staff now and hoping that your business grows in spite of them).

Take your meetings up a level with the strategies I've outlined for you—make sure all of your meetings are productive. You'll be amazed at the benefits: you'll have fewer (but better!) meetings and you'll see greater results from those meetings.

Work with vendors by making sure they are aligned with you. Invest time in the relationship and you'll suddenly find an entirely new group of people who are working at improving your business even without you being there!

Master Action List For Chapter 9

At the end of each section of this chapter you had actions to perform as well as Start Doing/Keep Doing/Stop Doing lists. Gather those actions together into a Master Action List, add any new actions that you think of, and then go through the questions below to think about how these actions can transform your life and your business:

__ **Is it going to make me money?** Are the actions you've listed going to help you generate more income? (If they are, great. Think about how they might be able to help you generate even more income. If they aren't making you more money then are those actions really as important as you thought they were?)

__ **Is it going save me money?** Reducing how much you spend will help you increase your profit. Are the actions you're thinking of doing going to help you cut back on your expenses without sacrificing the quality of your service? (If they save you money, great. If they aren't saving you money then are those actions really as important as you thought they were?)

__ **Is it going to save time?** Your time is precious and scarce. So the actions you take should help you to save time. Keep the big picture in mind because some actions may take a few extra minutes in the short term but will ultimately help you save time in the long term. (For example, training an employee might be an action that will take a few extra minutes now but will save you a lot of time in the future).

__ **Is it going to help me achieve market domination?** Your business needs to own the market it works in. Whenever someone thinks of the service you provide, they should only think of you. Do the actions you've listed in this chapter support that market domination? What can you change about them to help you dominate the market even further?

__ **How do I start fast to get the low-hanging fruit?** It's easy to say you're going to take action but it's much harder to actually do it. One way to take action and push through to its successful completion is to go for the quick wins—the low-hanging fruit. From the actions you've listed, what low-hanging fruit can you immediately pick?

__ **What's the leverage?** Leverage has a few different meanings but, in this context, I'm talking about how you can motivate yourself. For example, if you commit to complete an action within a certain period of time you can leverage that commitment by saying, "If I don't make that commitment, I'll donate $10,000 to a charity." Since you may not have $10,000, and you'll probably feel some pain donating that much money, you are leveraging your commitment and compelling yourself to complete the actions you said you'd complete.

__ **What's the reward?** For each action, list what you expect to get out of it. If you can't think of a reward for the action, seriously consider whether it is as valuable as you thought. Spend more of your time on actions that have rewards. Two of the best rewards for your actions are below (although there are other rewards you may choose to take action for)…

__ **Is it going to help me achieve wealth?** One of the best rewards you can take action for is to achieve wealth. For each action ask whether that particular action will help you make more money to give you the sense of safety and achievement and allow you to buy whatever you want whenever you want it. If possible, develop the action even further if a stronger, clearer, bigger action will help you achieve more wealth.

__ **Is it going to help me get more freedom?** Another one of the best rewards you can take action for is to get more freedom—the time and financial capacity to do whatever you want whenever you want to (without sacrificing your business). For each action ask whether that particular action will help you get more freedom. If possible, develop the action even further if a stronger, clearer, bigger action will help you get more freedom.

CHAPTER 10

MASTER YOUR SERVICE

How do you treat your customers? Many business owners would say they treat their customers well but in this chapter I'll reveal some of the biggest mistakes that business owners make to actually drive customers away. I'll show you how you can transform your business to deliver the level of service that will keep customers coming back for years to come.

Introduction

In this chapter I'm going to talk about service. In a previous chapter about mastering your marketing and sales I redefined selling as serving so that you will put the emphasis not on the one-time transaction but on the lifetime value of the customer.

There's more to say about service, and in this chapter I want to explore it further. In some ways, you might think of this as "customer service"—how you treat your prospects and customers. It's not really different than the serving I talked about in the previous chapter but in that earlier chapter I was talking about serving within the context of marketing and helping customers. Now I want to talk about serving customers at a deeper level.

Service is one of the most misunderstood aspects of business. Therefore it's one of the easiest to screw up.

If you think you already offer good service, it might be tempting to skip this chapter and continue on to the next chapter. However, I'm going to show you how you can really take your business to the next level using simple strategies that cost little or no money but have a massive, long-lasting impact on your business.

213

First I want to talk about what I mean when I say "service"...

What Is Service?

Service is how you treat your prospects and customers. It's what the customer experiences when they interact with you—in all the different ways that they interact.

Your customer's perception of service they receive from you doesn't start when you show up at the door to do the work. It starts much earlier—during marketing campaigns and sales efforts. And although first impressions are the most important and longest lasting, the customer's view of your service changes and solidifies when you show up to do the work and after the work is complete.

Therefore, service is made up of the following...

- What your marketing says about you
- What other people say about you (family, friends, neighbors, and online)
- What it's like to interact with you by phone
- What it's like to interact with you by website
- What it's like to interact with you by email
- What the sales presentation or quotation process is like
- How prompt you are with your commitments
- The things you say
- The tone you use
- Your word choice
- How you look (i.e. your uniform; how clean it is, etc.)
- The expression on your face
- How prepared you are
- Where you park your vehicle
- How proactive you are
- How much you listen
- How thoroughly you address the problem or situation that the customer initially called about
- How much or how little work you do to meet their needs

- How you treat others (your customers, your coworkers, your customers' pets, your customers' neighbors)
- How you treat your customers' stuff
- How helpful you seem
- How quickly you finish
- How clean you leave the project area
- How professional you are with finalizing the invoice and processing payment
- How much you follow-up afterward

… that might seem like a long list but I'm just scratching the surface! Service includes far more than the few I've listed above!

When I say service I mean absolutely everything that the customer sees, hears, feels, and perceives starting from the moment they first learn about you (i.e. through marketing or word-of-mouth) and continuing on forever afterward—long after you've sold to them the first time, the second time, even the hundredth time!

Every single component listed above (plus the countless other components I don't have the space to talk about here) contributes to the level of service you provide.

Now, a lot of readers will read the service components I've just listed and think, "Yeah, I give pretty good service." Unfortunately, that exact mindset contributes to the downfall of many businesses.

Stop giving good service. Yes, you read that correctly. I want you to immediately put a stop to giving good service.

Here's what I mean: **service is always a degree worse than you think. Good service is actually bad service.** If you are proud that you give good service, I'm sorry to tell you that you've been giving bad service—service that won't provide the benefits to your business that you were hoping for.

To illustrate, I want you to imagine you are eating at a restaurant and one of these three scenarios takes place when you arrive at the restaurant:

1. You were seated late, you were served cold food, and the waiter was rude.
2. You were seated promptly, you were served decent food on time, and the waiter as polite.
3. You were warmly welcomed into the restaurant by a waiter who seemed genuinely thrilled that you were there, you were given delicious food faster than you expected, a violist walked up to your table and played you a song, and the manager came by to personally thank you for your patronage, and then dessert was unexpectedly delivered free at the very end.

It's easy to see how scenario #1 was bad. And it's easy to see the level of service excellence in scenario #3.

But scenario #2 is the deadliest form of service because the restaurant thinks that they're giving "good service" by seating you promptly, serving decent food on time, and having polite waiters. But is that really "good" service? No, it's actually just the baseline. It's the bare minimum that any customer should expect at any restaurant. You will generally find that the majority of average restaurants you eat at will offer this type of service. It's average… And guess what: average is forgettable!

Compare that to the top level experience in scenario #3. That is true excellence and most people would love to eat at the restaurant that delivered that flawless experience every time.

Now take it beyond just the restaurant and think about other industries and activities where this is also evident: people love experiences where multiple layers of great things happen all at the same time—a memorable Cirque de Soleil experience, a trip to a Las Vegas resort and casino, a dinner at a high end restaurant, a family vacation at Disney World. These all share the same qualities of being truly excellent because so many pieces work together to contribute at a higher level to your experience.

These experiences are the ones that people talk about; the ones they spend more money on; the ones they tell their friends about.

And by comparison, all the places and experiences and restaurants that are merely good (like the average restaurant example of #2, above)—they just pale in comparison and are momentarily enjoyed and then immediately forgotten.

Unfortunately, many businesses define their mediocre base-level of service as "good" and they are proud of it… yet they don't realize that all they are doing is giving the bare minimum that you can get from anywhere.

The restaurant that will do predictably better than all others is the restaurant described in scenario #3 because they go out of their way to make each customer feel special—to surprise and delight and WOW customers. Their service achieves a level of excellence because it is memorable and very clearly great.

I gave the restaurant example for a reason—because you probably spend all day in your service business and think you offer good service so I wanted to use a different but familiar industry to illustrate the difference between bad, good, and great service.

So now let's bring these concepts back to the service industry. If you are giving good service to your customers, I want you to stop. When you go to a prospect's house, you give them a quote on some service, you perform what you promised, you collect your money and you leave. Along the way you were polite and smelled half decent and didn't swear. You completed the job as promised and charged what you agreed to up-front. The customer got what they wanted and said "Thank you" at the end. Some might say that this was "good" service. I think that service sucked because it's exactly the same level of service that nearly every other company provides. You did nothing to stand out and make the customer feel special; you only gave the customer the bare minimum that they'd expect from any other company they called.

Good service is really just bad service and you're only fooling yourself into thinking that customers love what you've been delivering. The only service that customers will actually remember, appreciate, and tell their friends about is excellent service (like restaurant #3, above) —when you've delighted and surprised them.

I would venture to say that the above paragraphs hit a lot of readers between the eyes. Good service is really just bad service.

If you want to actually deliver the kind of service you can be proud of and the kind of service that can make a significant bottom line financial difference in your business, you need to deliver great service.

I'll talk about great service in a minute but first I need to talk about this…

Why service is important: I want to talk about this because I suspect that some readers will read what I've read so far and although they may agree that great service is better than good (baseline) service, they may wonder about the cost and effort required to implement great service.

So I'll talk about what service excellence looks like but first I want to talk about why it is so important.

When you achieve excellence with your service, you don't *just* end up with happier customers. That's just one piece of the puzzle. When you give this level of service, you ultimately end up with a significant bottom line financial impact to your business. And I can't think of a better reason to give excellent service:

- Service excellence **improves competitiveness**, which lowers your marketing costs, reduces sales efforts, increases customer attraction, and increases cash flow, revenue, and profitability.
- Service excellence **leads to more prospects**, which increases your sales, which increases your cash flow and revenue.
- Service excellence **leads to a higher level of trust**, which increases the amount of business you get from each customer, as well as the amount of money you can charge for services, which leads to higher revenues and profitability.
- Service excellence **leads to a lifetime value customer** and not a one-time value customer, which lowers your marketing costs, reduces sales effort and time, and increases cash flow, revenue, and profitability.
- Service excellence **leads to more referral business**, which lowers your marketing costs, reduces sales effort and time, and increases cash flow, revenue, and profitability.

See? Excellent service isn't just about leaving a customer happy with having hired you. There is a direct connection between the level of service you give and the financial impact on your business. And by now your mind should be making the automatic connection to your Core 5 Dimensions of Life and Business Mastery: good service leads to long-lasting customers who pay you more, thus contributing directly to your Relationship, Wealth, and Freedom dimensions but also indirectly to the other dimensions as well.

Now let's talk about some obstacles you face: first, the reputation of service in the service industry is not good. Every friend or relative has a horror story about terrible service they've received from other service businesses—perhaps for paid work that was never completed or shoddy workmanship. Or, turn on the television and you'll always see those hidden camera shows when they catch contractors who lie about what's broken.

Second, you should know that a prospect's or customer's earliest impression of your business' service will color their opinion of your level of service for every interaction to come. It's said that first impressions are the hardest to break, and this saying is so true for the service industry. It's extremely difficult to improve on a service perception once it has been formed. It's harder to improve someone's perception of the service you provide and it's far too easy to diminish someone's perception of the service you provide.

Third, the service industry is a very technical service. That means people hire you because they don't understand how something works or how to fix it. It's easy for an expert to go in and assess the problem but it's much harder for that expert to help a client understand what needs to be done in a way that isn't condescending or confusing.

Fourth, people are very proud of their homes (no matter how modest and private they are). You are an outsider who is coming into their home at a time when they are most vulnerable (they need something fixed and they don't really understand what the problem is). They are on their guard and worried that you might judge them and they are confused about the problem and concerned about the expense.

With these obstacles, and with the misunderstanding that good service isn't that good at all, it's not a surprise that many service businesses have become notorious for giving really bad service and then struggling financially as a result.

But, to the business who understands these obstacles as well as the financial motivation to give great service, the opportunity to improve your business is amazing.

Take Action!
Recommended actions:

__ Assess your level of service. This could be one of the most painful exercises you do, if you're honest, because most businesses believe they give good service when, in fact, it's mediocre at best.

__ Think about the biggest, best, most memorable experience you had (for example, if you went to Disney World). Write down what made that experience so memorable. What was it that was so excellent? Now think about how the same concepts can be modeled and implemented into your business (obviously in a different way).

__ Make a list of the things that your customers would consider to be shocking, jaw-dropping levels of service that they would not believe they are receiving from a service business. Put aside your inner critic that says you can't afford it because that's not what this exercise is about. Instead, just brainstorm the most amazing level of service you can possibly imagine—so stunning that you would earn a spot on the evening news because it's so excellent. Keep this list handy because you'll add to it in the next section of the chapter.

__ Using the list you've just created, figure out how you can bring a lot of those elements into the service you deliver every day.

___ Create standards in your business that you and your employees measure yourself against to ensure that you are delivering service excellence at all times.

Add your own actions:

___ Stop doing actions (Actions you currently do now but should stop doing)

_____

_____

___ Keep doing actions (Actions you currently do now and should keep doing)

_____

_____

___ Start doing actions (Actions you don't do now but should start doing)

_____

_____

___ Who will do new actions? (Assign the action to yourself or someone else)

_____

_____

___ By when? (When will these actions be complete?)

_____

_____

Turning Your Service Into WOW Service

So far you've learned the painful truth that good service is really bad service, and what **businesses should be striving for is a level of service excellence** that few ever achieve.

When I say "service excellence" I mean jaw-dropping service that WOWs customer. Service that is so shockingly better than any other business out there that a customer wouldn't even consider calling anyone else. Service that a customer receives and then immediately calls their

friend and says, "You won't believe what just happened when a service company came to my house today…"

Remember, this kind of service has a significant bottom line financial impact on your business so why wouldn't you offer it?

In this section, I want to help you figure out how to offer this level of service to your prospects and customers.

First, you need to identify all the different times that the customer could interact with you. List them out in a numbered list from the very first time they receive your marketing right up to the point where you have completed the service, and beyond (don't forget to list out any follow-up you do).

List every one of these potential interactions (whether or not you currently do anything with them today).

Chances are, your interactions probably look something like this:

1. Marketing
2. Customer calls the office and an appointment is scheduled
3. Service expert arrives to give the customer a quote
4. Customer hires you to do the work
5. Installation expert arrives and does the work
6. Customer follow-up

Perhaps you have more steps or perhaps your process looks a little different, but I'll use this as an example.

Now that you have this list, think about what the customer should see, hear, think, and feel at every step. Put yourself in your customers' shoes and think about what they are thinking. They probably have questions, are confused; maybe they're frantic because water is spilling all over their basement; maybe they are angry that they have to spend this money on their house because they were saving up for a vacation; maybe they are embarrassed to mention that their toilet is plugged; maybe they are wary because their brother-in-law had a very bad experience with someone in the service business. And most important, they just want their problem solved as quickly and painlessly as possible.

So that's the customer situation you're working with. Now it's time to shock and delight them because of how helpful you are and how different you are from any and every other service business they've ever met.

For example, here are some WOW service standards that you might use in your business (I've filled out a few of these to illustrate although I haven't filled them all out—I'm just using this to highlight some key points):

1. **Marketing**
   a. Customer sees unified branding
   b. Customer is assured that we have helped many people facing similar problems
   c. Customer is educated to make the best decision
2. **Customer calls the office and an appointment is scheduled**
   a. Customer gets an expert who answers the phone by the second ring
   b. Customer has all questions answered by a knowledgeable rep
   c. Customer is assured within 30 seconds of the call that they have made the right decision to act now and call us
   d. Customer has an appointment booked by the end of the call
3. **Expert arrives to give the customer a quote**
4. **Customer hires us to do the work**
5. **Expert arrives and does the work**
   a. Customer receives a call before the expert arrives to confirm customer is there and to introduce themselves
   b. Customer sees that the expert arrives on time
   c. Customer sees that the expert looks clean and neat
   d. Customer is greeted by name
   e. Customer is asked if the expert parked in the right location
   f. Customer sees the expert use floor protectors
   g. Customer gets a time-frame to complete the work and is asked if that is okay
6. **Customer follow-up**

224 | The Secrets of Business Mastery

I've just started, of course, but you would end up with a long list of standards for each step. This list may look familiar: you're building the Framework For Service I showed you in an earlier chapter. You're building levels of service excellence into this framework and you'll use it to WOW your customers every time you serve them. (And if you attend my Warrior Fast Track Academy, we go through this exercise.)

Continue building this out for your business. Be as detailed as possible. Think of it as a conveyor belt. It starts at one end and keeps moving until it reaches the next step (and then the next and the next and the next). The quality of the first step will determine the quality of the second step.

Think of this as an experience—a surprising and delightful experience for the customer at every step. If you're not sure whether you've done enough, here's my recommendation: think about whether any of your competitors do this. If you are doing the same level of service that your competitors are doing then there is nothing surprising about it. If you want to stand out you have to be better—massively better!

When you're done, you have a list of changes you may need to make in your business, which may include changes to your marketing, improvements to your staff training, the development of service-related systems and processes, and an investment into better tools, uniforms, etc.

I cannot stress this enough: be thorough! Every aspect of your business that the customer sees or hears will play a part in what they experience. Even the little things make a difference. Here are some examples:

- The hours that your business operates
- Whether you use eco-friendly cleaning products
- How knowledgeable your telephone representatives are
- Whether your uniforms are clean
- The condition of your tools
- How clean you leave the work area when you're done

Everything! Even the little things!

Another way to develop WOW service is to ask yourself whether you are delivering everything your customer needs. You should try to be a one-stop shop for your customers. This doesn't mean that if you are a plumber you need to also become an electrician. But it does mean that if your customers ask you for a recommendation, you should know the name of an electrician who would deliver the same level of service that you provide.

If someone asks for anything, we want to be the one to facilitate that, even if we don't deliver that service ourselves. Even in the unlikely event that a customer calls and asks for a dentist, we want to be able to recommend someone who meets our standards of service! Think about the services that you are frequently asked for and consider whether you can add these services or work out an arrangement with another company. For example, if you are a maid service but you are asked for carpet shampoo cleaning. Or if you are a landscaper, you might be asked to do gutter cleaning and power washing. When we don't choose to offer the services ourselves, we set up an affiliate or joint venture or referral program where a set fee or percentage of a sale is kicked back to us.

As you commit to providing amazing service to your customers, be very careful what you say. It's okay that you say you give great service but make sure that you do! (Remember how many people say they give good service but really don't.) Make sure you do. Better yet, adopt an "under-promise and over-deliver" mindset with every customer interaction. That way, your actions speak far louder than your words.

Follow-up: we often think of providing service excellence while interacting on the phone or face to face with a customer before and during the repair. But as I've said earlier, you also provide great service in your marketing. And, you also provide great service in your follow-up.

Follow-up regularly with your customers. Immediately after you've done the work, ask them how the experience was. But don't stop there. From time to time, reach out to them and let them know that you are thinking about them and how you can help them. Create offers; send out direct mail.

As your business grows, you may not have enough time to call each client individually. We do try to call many of our customers in person but sometimes we also use automated technology to keep in touch: one way that we provide great service during the follow-up stage is to use a voice shot, which I described earlier in the marketing chapter. This is a pre-recorded phone broadcast. We record a call and then broadcast it out through an automated calling software. (Make sure that this is legal to do in your area.)

Follow-up is easy: just find a reason to reconnect with your customers that provides them with some value.

Take Action!
Recommended actions:

___ Review all of the steps that a customer goes through when they encounter and interact with your business. Identify ways that you can provide a higher level of service and achieve service excellence at every stage. Don't settle for good service—push beyond your comfort zone and service habits to provide a level of excellent service that will shock your customers.

Add your own actions:

___ Stop doing actions (Actions you currently do now but should stop doing)

_____

_____

___ Keep doing actions (Actions you currently do now and should keep doing)

_____

_____

___ Start doing actions (Actions you don't do now but should start doing)

_____

_____

__ Who will do new actions? (Assign the action to yourself or someone else)

_____

_____

__ By when? (When will these actions be complete?)

_____

_____

How To Embed A WOW Service Mindset In Your Business

You've developed the level of service you want for your business, now it's time to make sure everyone is delivering it. Remember, your word is only as good as your actions; and if you run a business, your word is only as good as the actions of the lowest performer that your customers will encounter.

Therefore, you should ensure that absolutely everyone in the company knows and is committed to the level of service you want to provide. Here are some ways to provide that level of service in your business:

Training: we're always training our staff—both formally and informally —to give great service to all customers. If you want to deliver good service, you need to start here. And push beyond your concept of formal training about the job. We're always helping our staff grow professionally and personally, as this creates a rich, rewarding culture and helps retain great team members.

Set the bar high: at Gold Medal Service, we say that we want to give our customers a Zappos level of service with a Disney level of experience. That is a very high standard but it's easy for our staff to understand what we mean and it's also exciting to strive for. Everyone in the business can imagine what that level of service is like and they are motivated to work toward it.

Use a simple standard for all interactions: we use a simple happy face, medium face, and frowning face as a standard for our experts to keep in mind as they interact with customers. We have these three faces hanging on the walls for our phone experts and we give our field experts on the road a reminder of it as well. Their target is to assess which of the three faces the customer is and then to do whatever they can to help the customer ascend to the happy face level. This strategy is simple but very effective. It's easy to remember and visualize so our experts—whether on the phone or in the customer's home—can instantly assess the situation and rely on the training and ideas we've given them to help them move the customer toward happy.

Another standard we use is this: "Treat every home like you're working in your grandmother's home." This is another simple way for our experts to fully understand exactly how they should act and treat every aspect of their time in the customer's house. For example, you would be respectful and polite; you wouldn't swear; you'd make as little mess as possible and you'd always clean up after you were done.

Develop a checklist: develop a checklist from the list you created earlier in the chapter and use it to constantly review every aspect of your business to ensure that it contributes to the WOW service level you want to provide. Each expert should get their own checklist for the type of interactions they do (in our marketing or on the phone or when visiting the customer's home). Here are some of the things I have on the checklists in my business:

- Does the marketing portray the service that the customer will get?
- Incoming call or online chat, the customer needs to think that they're talking to the right person.
- Online or on the phone, does the expert give the customer the total feeling that you've got their back?
- Is the expert doing the pre-visit call?
- When the expert gets to the home, do they have an amazing introduction? (i.e. "Is there a dog or cat who will run out of the house?" "Is now a good time?")
- Did the expert leave the place cleaner than when they got there? (For example, if the expert had to move something, it needs to be put back better than it was before.)

- When the expert is cleaning up, ask the customer if they want orange scent, mint scent, or no scent. The expert should use their own vacuum or broom and not borrow the customer's.
- Did the expert wear floor protectors?

Empowerment: this is another place where service businesses fall short in the service they provide. They simply don't empower their experts to provide amazing service up-front, and worse yet, they don't empower them to fix problems when a customer doesn't have an amazing experience. Train your staff and give them tools and ideas to know what to do when a customer is not happy and how to fix it.

Evaluate service: of course you can keep an eye on your staff and, perhaps, shadow your experts or listen in on their phone calls. But if they know you're doing that, they tend to follow the script a little more closely. And what really counts is not what you hear but what the customer perceives. For that reason, here are two ways that you can evaluate your service effectively: surveys and referrals.

Surveys: survey the customer as soon as the service is complete. As soon as the expert leaves, we have an automated machine call the customer. (The reason why we use a machine instead of a person is because we've found that people are completely honest with a machine and are more likely to be dishonest with a human.) And we ask a few questions during the survey but the last question is always, "Would you refer us to family and friends?"

If the customer responds with less than an 80% then a team leader or a manager calls them immediately and asks how to make it right. They have an open, honest conversation by saying, "You ranked us below 80% and we're curious why. We want to change that. What happened and how can we change that today?" Most of the time, that follow-up call changes the perception.

Referrals: the survey method above hints at another way to measure your service. The number of referrals you receive is a direct result of how good your service is. If you don't get any referrals, that's a sign that your service is not as good as you may think it is. The more referrals you get, the better.

Take Action!

Recommended actions:

___ There was a lot in this section of the chapter. Create a start-doing list to outline all of the things you need to implement into your business immediately to raise the level of service you provide to customers. And, create a stop-doing list to outline the bad habits that you and your staff are doing right now that keeps you from providing service excellence to your customers.

Add your own actions:

___ Stop doing actions (Actions you currently do now but should stop doing)

_____

_____

___ Keep doing actions (Actions you currently do now and should keep doing)

_____

_____

___ Start doing actions (Actions you don't do now but should start doing)

_____

_____

___ Who will do new actions? (Assign the action to yourself or someone else)

_____

_____

___ By when? (When will these actions be complete?)

_____

_____

Conclusion

Marketing brings prospects into your business. But it's serving that turns those prospects to lifetime value customers. As you serve, you transform the customer's situation (often negative—such as a leaky pipe or a furnace that doesn't work) into a positive one.

Unfortunately, service is tragically misunderstood and too many businesses (in the service industry and outside of it) mistakenly believe that their "good" level of service is good enough. It's not. If you believe you give good service, you can be sure that it's really barely acceptable, and your customers will barely remember you when they need your services again.

But here's the good news: you can elevate your level of service and start delivering service excellence. If you create a level of service that rivals Disney's level of service, you'll surprise and delight and WOW your customers. They'll remember you, they'll call you back when they need more service, and they'll tell their friends to call you too.

Master Action List For Chapter 10

At the end of each section of this chapter you had actions to perform as well as Start Doing/Keep Doing/Stop Doing lists. Gather those actions together into a Master Action List, add any new actions that you think of, and then go through the questions below to think about how these actions can transform your life and your business:

___ **Is it going to make me money?** Are the actions you've listed going to help you generate more income? (If they are, great. Think about how they might be able to help you generate even more income. If they aren't making you more money then are those actions really as important as you thought they were?)

___ **Is it going save me money?** Reducing how much you spend will help you increase your profit. Are the actions you're thinking of doing going to help you cut back on your expenses without sacrificing the quality of your service? (If they save you money, great. If they aren't saving you money then are those actions really as important as you thought they were?)

___ **Is it going to save time?** Your time is precious and scarce. So the actions you take should help you to save time. Keep the big picture in mind because some actions may take a few extra minutes in the short term but will ultimately help you save time in the long term. (For example, training an employee might be an action that will take a few extra minutes now but will save you a lot of time in the future).

___ **Is it going to help me achieve market domination?** Your business needs to own the market it works in. Whenever someone thinks of the service you provide, they should only think of you. Do the actions you've listed in this chapter support that market domination? What can you change about them to help you dominate the market even further?

___ **How do I start fast to get the low-hanging fruit?** It's easy to say you're going to take action but it's much harder to actually do it. One way to take

action and push through to its successful completion is to go for the quick wins—the low-hanging fruit. From the actions you've listed, what low-hanging fruit can you immediately pick?

___ **What's the leverage?** Leverage has a few different meanings but, in this context, I'm talking about how you can motivate yourself. For example, if you commit to complete an action within a certain period of time you can leverage that commitment by saying, "If I don't make that commitment, I'll donate $10,000 to a charity." Since you may not have $10,000, and you'll probably feel some pain donating that much money, you are leveraging your commitment and compelling yourself to complete the actions you said you'd complete.

___ **What's the reward?** For each action, list what you expect to get out of it. If you can't think of a reward for the action, seriously consider whether it is as valuable as you thought. Spend more of your time on actions that have rewards. Two of the best rewards for your actions are below (although there are other rewards you may choose to take action for)…

___ **Is it going to help me achieve wealth?** One of the best rewards you can take action for is to achieve wealth. For each action ask whether that particular action will help you make more money to give you the sense of safety and achievement and allow you to buy whatever you want whenever you want it. If possible, develop the action even further if a stronger, clearer, bigger action will help you achieve more wealth.

___ **Is it going to help me get more freedom?** Another one of the best rewards you can take action for is to get more freedom—the time and financial capacity to do whatever you want whenever you want to (without sacrificing your business). For each action ask whether that particular action will help you get more freedom. If possible, develop the action even further if a stronger, clearer, bigger action will help you get more freedom.

CHAPTER 11

MASTER YOUR SYSTEMS

You have an opportunity every day to accelerate your business by serving customers with excellence. But there's a lot to do to run a business and sometimes it doesn't seem like you have the time or manpower to get it all done. In this chapter I'll show you how systems are the affordable, efficient, and effective way to get more done in less time—and to avoid reinventing the wheel.

Introduction

Throughout this book, I've given you many action steps to help you master various aspects of your business. By now you might be saying: "Mike! When will I have time to implement all of these changes?" It can feel like you already have a lot to do and there are now even more things to do to grow your business. That's why one of my biggest recommendations is to build systems in your business.

Each day in your business you perform literally tens of thousands of activities—from simple, unconscious stuff like turning on a light switch when you come into the office in the morning to more complex stuff like repairing your customer's air conditioner.

Tens of thousands of activities! Fortunately, not every activity requires the same amount of thought, does it? (For example, you probably switch on the light switch almost automatically without thinking about it.) If every activity required the same amount of thought, you'd never get anything done.

The reason why you can do so many things in the day is because you're doing a lot of it without thinking. You have unconsciously developed a pattern to do it. For example, maybe you arrive at the office, unlock the door, turn on the light, turn on your computer, and make the coffee. And then your day starts. You don't think about these things because you have a pattern, a habit, a routine. Without realizing it, you have developed a system—it's the steps you take and the order you take them in.

If even one thing got mixed up, your system slows down a bit as you think about it. For example, if the light burned out, you have to rummage around in the dark to find a new light bulb before you can return to the pattern of your morning. But when everything is the way it should be in the morning, you go through this system without thinking about it.

Systems give you an advantage: you don't have to give a lot of physical or mental attention to the activities. You can think about other things. You perform these things quickly and efficiently as you also think about your day or listen to voicemails or think about a scheduling challenge you know you'll face today. In other words, systems give you freedom. Systems contribute to your Freedom Dimension by taking your mind off of a specific, repetitive task and allowing you to work on other parts of your business or to take time off and enjoy the time for yourself.

Most business owners have a couple of basic systems in place, like the morning routine I described above. But if you examine the most successful businesses in the world, you'll discover that they are run almost entirely by systems.

Consider the fast food restaurant McDonald's. That business is a whole bunch of systems that have been perfected over time. If you took a couple dozen untrained high school students and gave them all the ingredients and equipment to serve burgers and fries to hundreds of customers during a lunch hour, you would see a total failure. However, if you add systems into the equation, this is the exact model that runs successfully at the every McDonald's restaurants all around the world every single day.

McDonald's is just one example. Every successful business uses systems—FedEx, Amazon, Walmart, Google—just to name a few really recognizable businesses. Each of these businesses has created systems to help them run.

Systems help to make all of your work faster and simpler and better. And, when you share your systems with others, it allows you to hand off parts of your business to others so that the work is done to your expectations. Systems are the greatest opportunity for business owners to build their business because systems give you more time and bandwidth to work on other things. Systems make the job easier for your employees. Systems make your customer experience more positive and consistent. Systems ultimately deliver more profit.

Your business may have a couple of systems now—perhaps ones you have unconsciously created, like the morning routine I mentioned earlier, or you may have ones that you have consciously created, like a way to answer the phone when someone calls. But there are so many different areas in your business to create systems and I want to show you in this chapter the full opportunity that systems provide for your business.

What Do I Mean When I Say "Systems"?

I've used the word "system" above as a general label but there are actually two things you can create:

- **System**: a system is a sequence of steps to complete a task. For example, your morning routine that I described earlier in the chapter is a system you use to start your day. Another system might be the automated process of collecting financial information from various spreadsheets to feed into a main financial dashboard used by you and the CFO.

- **Process**: a process is a sequence of many little systems that apply to different people. For example, the money-handling process in your business, which may start when the customer hands a check to the installation expert and then follows that check as it is delivered to the finance department, is processed and applied to the customer's invoice, and then is sent with other checks to the bank at the end of the day. Hopefully you can see that each of those steps are their own system (the system of what the installation expert does with the check when he receives it from the customer; the system of what the finance department does when they receive the check and process it, etc.) And those systems come together to create a process.

Your business needs systems and processes. Your systems and processes might be as simple as a checklist that someone needs to do or they might be more complex and involve automated software to perform part of the work. There are many different ways to build systems and processes and I want to be clear about this point—that a system or process could be as simple as a checklist—so you know that you can start building systems and processes into your business immediately.

Systems and processes are sometimes thought of as being "set it and forget it" opportunities that you build once and then ignore. And, because of this misconception, many business owners don't build systems for the things they know they shouldn't ignore.

I take a different approach: I think "set it and forget it" is a mistake. You should never build a system or process and then ignore it. You have to build it then implement it, and also build in measurement mechanisms to make sure it still applies and is still valid the way it works. You need to check in on each system regularly. In fact, I would suggest that the key to successful management is about building great systems and then checking on them regularly.

Consider one of those plate spinners you might see performing at a fair or circus. They have a system for keeping the plates spinning and it includes regularly flicking the plate to keep it in the air. Likewise, in your business, each system is spinning on its own and you have to always check in on each one to make sure it's running. It takes about 15 minutes to create a system and then it takes a lifetime of checking it to get results.

One important note here: your systems and processes will be unique to you. You may read about some of my systems and processes, and perhaps you've read about the systems and processes that other businesses use. But whatever you decide to do, you should make sure it's developed by you. It's impossible to take any generic system or process and apply it exactly as-is to your business; you need to modify them.

And here's another reason to create your own systems: my company once belonged to an association and we used their proprietary systems but when we left the association we could no longer use their systems and suddenly had to figure out our own. Figure out the systems and processes that work for you and develop them yourself to meet your unique needs.

To use the McDonald's example again, every McDonald's has multiple systems and processes and they look similar from one restaurant to the next (and certainly they are successful at creating similar-tasting burgers and fries no matter which restaurant you go to) but each McDonald's will have slightly customized their systems and processes because the street and parking lot look different or the state food handling laws are different.

It doesn't matter if you are a one-person business or a huge business operating in many jurisdictions—systems and processes are critical. Your one-person business will benefit from building systems and processes because it will help you do your work faster, easier, more efficiently, and more proficiently—resulting in more time, more money, and happier customers.

For the rest of the chapter I'll use the generic label "system" when I mean system or process (although occasionally I'll mention "process" when I'm referring only to processes).

Take Action!
Recommended actions:

___ What systems and processes do you have in your business right now? This may be a challenging exercise since some of your systems and processes—such as the one you do first thing in the morning when you open up the office—are totally unconscious.

___ What systems and processes should you have in your business? You'll probably need to start doing several. Keep this list handy because you'll be working on it in the next section of the chapter as well.

Add your own actions:

___ Stop doing actions (Actions you currently do now but should stop doing)

_____

_____

___ Keep doing actions (Actions you currently do now and should keep doing)

_____

_____

___ Start doing actions (Actions you don't do now but should start doing)

_____

_____

___ Who will do new actions? (Assign the action to yourself or someone else)

_____

_____

___ By when? (When will these actions be complete?)

_____

_____

Which Systems And Processes Should You Build In Your Business?

Now I'll discuss which systems to build but I would remind you that I am offering only a general overview of systems that I think you should build based on my own experience. Your business is different and you should take my ideas but customize them for your needs.

So, which systems and processes to build? I recommend that you build systems for everything in your business. Look at every aspect of your business and create a system or a process for it. Remember, the most successful businesses have systems and processes for everything.

Recommended systems to build for your business:
- How to take a customer service call
- Start of your day system
- Lock-down/shut down for the end-of-the-night procedure
- Parts replenishment system

Recommended processes to build for your business:
- What happens through the lifetime of the customer—from first call to follow-up survey
- Money collection process
- Accident process—who to call, who gets notified, how does it get fixed
- Hiring process—interview to training/onboarding
- Customer care process—from their complaint and how you get them back to WOW

How do you know that you need a system or a process? It's simple: when you do the same thing different ways each time, or when you have to tell someone the same thing more than twice. Doing the same thing differently, or repeating yourself more than twice should set off a warning light in your mind to tell you, "Hey, I need a system or process for this!" At my Warrior Fast Track Academy, we go into greater detail and I'll give you even more systems you can build.

Good systems are built around KPIs that contribute to specific targets that feed into your business vision. If you've built the systems and processes listed above and you want to keep going, you should think about the things you measure in your business and identify how you can turn them into systems.

And, don't forget to get your team to help you identify and build systems. Many of them are doing the work each day and may have some ideas about how to save time and make their jobs a little easier by implementing a system. (Plus, when your team helps identify and build a system, they are more likely to follow it than when you build a system and tell them to follow it.)

Bonus tip: create a systems and process whiteboard. Put it up in your office and whenever anyone in your company sees a situation and thinks "we need a system for this," they can write it on the whiteboard. This allows one place for everyone to add things in real time.

Take Action!
Recommended actions:

___ Using the list you started in the last section of the chapter, add more systems and processes that you discovered in this section.

___ Talk to your employees and ask them what systems and processes they have. It doesn't matter how small or insignificant those systems might seem. Even something like where they keep a certain tool in their work truck may benefit all of your staff as a system that can be shared to cut down on time spent looking for a tool.

___ Put up a systems whiteboard in your office immediately and let everyone know that it is to be used to add systems and processes ideas to.

Add your own actions:

___ Stop doing actions (Actions you currently do now but should stop doing)

_____

_____

___ Keep doing actions (Actions you currently do now and should keep doing)

_____

_____

___ Start doing actions (Actions you don't do now but should start doing)

_____

_____

__ Who will do new actions? (Assign the action to yourself or someone else)

_____

_____

__ By when? (When will these actions be complete?)

_____

_____

How To Build A System That Makes Your Business Better

Building a system or a process is so easy and although it does take a few minutes up-front, it saves you hours upon hours later. It's an amazing investment of your time and energy.

Include your team in this exercise—they're the ones who will be implementing it and they may have ideas you didn't consider. And once this is completed, they'll be more likely to adopt it if they were included in its creation.

Give your team the situation or scenario that you want to build a system around and instruct your team with the following: "What is the best way that we want this scenario to get done? If someone walked in and we gave them a piece of paper with the system written down, we want them to be able to do it as good as we would do it ourselves."

Start by using sticky notes to write down all the steps (tasks, activities, events, and even people) that are required during the situation that you're building a system for. Think about all the things that happen before, then the things that happen during the activity that you're building a system for, and then the things that happen after. (Thinking about what happens before and after is helpful because it can identify more opportunities to build systems or it might show you where the system needs to start and finish and what might trigger the system to begin).

Outline all these steps (and tasks and activities and events and people), each on its own sticky note and then put them into a logical order. Map out the entire scenario before it starts and well past when it finishes.

From this flowchart of sticky notes, you'll have many different steps to the system or process. Now, think very specifically about how you want each of those activities or tasks to be performed in the same way over and over. For example, if you are creating a money-handling process, one of your steps is "the installation expert accepts the check from the customer and confirms that the date and amount are correct," and another one of your steps might be "the installation expert uses a paperclip to attach the check to the office copy of the invoice and then puts it back on the clipboard."

These might seem overly detailed but consider how many times an installation expert might have accepted a misdated check or shuffled a check in among other paperwork accidentally. The two steps I listed in the example above will now "automatically" ensure that the checks received are correct and don't need to be re-written, and will always show up to the finance office with the invoice attached. These two steps save hours of time searching for checks or going back to the customer to have them correct the amount written on the check.

As you identify each step and then outline the best way it should be performed, think about how that can happen. There are many different ways that you can ensure that a step is performed the same way over and over. Here are some examples:

- **Checklists**: checklists are great ways to ensure that something is done the same way over and over, and they are so simple to create. If all you do in your business is create checklists for everything and then follow-up periodically to ensure that every expert is checking off every box every time, you will see a huge change in your business.
- **Tools**: tools are resources and templates that you provide to your team that they can use as part of their system. For example, in a previous chapter I mentioned that we use the happy face, medium face, and frowning face. That's a tool we use to help us in our service process. But tools can be much more complex than that: our team uses cameras to take pictures before they do their work and then after, and these pictures provide a way to ensure that the work is done and it's of high quality. Another tool we use is collaboration software—where everyone logs in and can instantly chat with multiple people all at the same time.

- **Measurement**: measuring the system with a KPI allows you to track the system and ensure that it is being completed. You can use a simple whiteboard and write measurements in green, yellow, and red as each step is measured. This can provide you with a simple at-a-glance look at how your systems are running.

As you build your systems, it's important to address today's issues but you should always build your systems like you're a one-million dollar business... even if you're not. That way, you can grow your business and your system will have capacity built in to handle the growth.

You'll never stop building systems: when you solve a problem with a system you create a new problem. For example, when you create systems and processes to deliver great service, you've got one problem solved but you'll get more customers than you can handle, so you've created a new problem... one that requires a system.

Building a system is never done. You just solve the next thing.

Take Action!
Recommended actions:

___ Schedule a meeting with your team as soon as possible to start brainstorming systems and processes you can build in your business, and work together to build one or two during that first meeting. This will get people understanding why you do it and how to do it and when they put the new systems or processes into practice, it will get them even more excited about the benefits.

Add your own actions:

___ Stop doing actions (Actions you currently do now but should stop doing)

_____

_____

__ Keep doing actions (Actions you currently do now and should keep doing)

_____

_____

__ Start doing actions (Actions you don't do now but should start doing)

_____

_____

__ Who will do new actions? (Assign the action to yourself or someone else)

_____

_____

__ By when? (When will these actions be complete?)

_____

_____

Conclusion

You have systems and processes in your business right now and you do them without realizing it. From the time you come into the office in the morning to the time you leave at night, you use systems sometimes.

Many of your existing systems are developed without any thought given to them. But you do them because they tend to make things faster and easier.

Now imagine if the rest of your business was as simple as the unconscious system you follow every morning to open up the office. Systems and processes automate your business but they don't take the thinking part away. Rather, they automate the parts that don't require thinking so you can devote your attention to more important issues.

Every employee who was trained to work this way would be able to complete all of their work in an excellent, consistent manner and, because they didn't have to think about the little things, they could give more attention to serving the customer.

Systems and processes take a few minutes of work up-front to think about (and maybe they require some habit-changing) but the long-term benefit to your business is that everyone works in the same consistent way and your customers are served at a higher level.

Master Action List For Chapter 11

At the end of each section of this chapter you had actions to perform as well as Start Doing/Keep Doing/Stop Doing lists. Gather those actions together into a Master Action List, add any new actions that you think of, and then go through the questions below to think about how these actions can transform your life and your business:

___ **Is it going to make me money?** Are the actions you've listed going to help you generate more income? (If they are, great. Think about how they might be able to help you generate even more income. If they aren't making you more money then are those actions really as important as you thought they were?)

___ **Is it going save me money?** Reducing how much you spend will help you increase your profit. Are the actions you're thinking of doing going to help you cut back on your expenses without sacrificing the quality of your service? (If they save you money, great. If they aren't saving you money then are those actions really as important as you thought they were?)

___ **Is it going to save time?** Your time is precious and scarce. So the actions you take should help you to save time. Keep the big picture in mind because some actions may take a few extra minutes in the short term but will ultimately help you save time in the long term. (For example, training an employee might be an action that will take a few extra minutes now but will save you a lot of time in the future).

___ **Is it going to help me achieve market domination?** Your business needs to own the market it works in. Whenever someone thinks of the service you provide, they should only think of you. Do the actions you've listed in this chapter support that market domination? What can you change about them to help you dominate the market even further?

___ **How do I start fast to get the low-hanging fruit?** It's easy to say you're going to take action but it's much harder to actually do it. One way to take

action and push through to its successful completion is to go for the quick wins—the low-hanging fruit. From the actions you've listed, what low-hanging fruit can you immediately pick?

__ **What's the leverage?** Leverage has a few different meanings but, in this context, I'm talking about how you can motivate yourself. For example, if you commit to complete an action within a certain period of time you can leverage that commitment by saying, "If I don't make that commitment, I'll donate $10,000 to a charity." Since you may not have $10,000, and you'll probably feel some pain donating that much money, you are leveraging your commitment and compelling yourself to complete the actions you said you'd complete.

__ **What's the reward?** For each action, list what you expect to get out of it. If you can't think of a reward for the action, seriously consider whether it is as valuable as you thought. Spend more of your time on actions that have rewards. Two of the best rewards for your actions are below (although there are other rewards you may choose to take action for)…

__ **Is it going to help me achieve wealth?** One of the best rewards you can take action for is to achieve wealth. For each action ask whether that particular action will help you make more money to give you the sense of safety and achievement and allow you to buy whatever you want whenever you want it. If possible, develop the action even further if a stronger, clearer, bigger action will help you achieve more wealth.

__ **Is it going to help me get more freedom?** Another one of the best rewards you can take action for is to get more freedom—the time and financial capacity to do whatever you want whenever you want to (without sacrificing your business). For each action ask whether that particular action will help you get more freedom. If possible, develop the action even further if a stronger, clearer, bigger action will help you get more freedom.

CHAPTER 12

MASTER THE FUTURE

It's tempting to think of the future as a blank page that is yet to be written. But who writes that page? And when? I believe that you determine your own future, and the best time to determine it is right now. Don't let the future unfold without your direction. In this chapter I'll show you how you can guide your life and business toward the best future you can achieve.

Introduction

Business owners are so busy, and it's easy for them to become overwhelmed by the day-to-day challenges that constantly arise. From unique customer situations to a shortage of supplies to a scheduling problem to a flat tire to managing the income and expenses, there are so many things vying for the service business owner's attention. There's usually enough to do today to fill more than 24 hours… and that's the same for tomorrow and the day after and the day after that!

So, it's no surprise that many businesses run with the owners, managers, and staff simply trying to keep up with the demands each day. If they're lucky, they'll have some idea of what the rest of the week might look like, and only a few rare businesses will have a clear idea of what the rest of the month will look like.

The work of the business owner, though, isn't to just master today, or the week, or the month. **The work of the business owner is to master the entire future of the business.** Many of the topics you've read about in this book will help you do just that. Mastering systems enables you to take care of

251

the present so you can master the future. Mastering service ensures that you have enough business coming in now and in the future. Mastering finances enriches your business so you can survive into the future. Mastery of each of the topics you've read about in this book will turn you from trying to keep your head above water today to rising above the day-to-day challenges and seeing far into the future.

Here's an analogy about seeing into the future: When you step into the kitchen and decide what you're going to cook, the first step is to have a recipe. That's what it means to master the future for your business—you know what you want to cook and you have a recipe. (Meanwhile many people are trying to cook but they don't know what they want to cook!)

Why Think About The Future?

Have you ever driven down a winding road only to come around the bend and suddenly see an obstacle ahead on the road? You stomp on the brakes and the car screeches to a halt, and hopefully you stop in time. That's what running a business is often like: driving around a winding road without seeing what's just around the bend. When something unexpected happens, the whole business grinds to a halt briefly to deal with the situation before moving forward.

Now compare the above situation with driving on a straight, flat road—like in the desert where you can see for miles ahead. That kind of drive is so much safer because there are no surprises just around the bend. And for businesses, having a longer view into the future allows you to see challenges long before they become serious show-stoppers.

Master the future to solve more problems faster and easier: when you focus on the day-to-day, you end up spending more money and time to deal with each crisis as it arises. When you see into the future, you see the crisis and solve it before it becomes big.

Master the future because it's cheaper and more profitable: the future is telling you the trends. When you master the future, you know what will happen in the industry and in your business long before it happens, allowing you to create a business that is ready for it. I like the Disney story as an example: Walt Disney wasn't just building one amusement park. He saw the larger vision he wanted of a global brand, a family destination, a memorable experience unlike any other. Not surprisingly, Disney is massive—with amusement parks, cruises, stores, movies, and so much more. For you, thinking about the future is knowing the destination you're going for, looking at the all the pieces, and then making sure you're laying a strong foundation.

Master the future because other people are relying on you: you need to see into the future. Everyone is relying on you to do so. Your employees are relying on you to see into the future, to handle problems before they become problems, so that the business succeeds and they get paid and can feed their families. Your customers are relying on you to see into the future so that you are fully prepared to help them in whatever way they need to be helped. Your vendors and suppliers are relying on you to see into the future so that they can provide you with the supplies you need so they get paid and can feed their families. Your family is relying on you to see into the future so that you can make money to give them food and shelter, and so you can plan appropriately to spend more time with them.

In spite of these excellent reasons to master the future, most business owners do not see very far into the future—so it's not a surprise that employee turnover is high, customers go elsewhere when their problems aren't solved, vendors fail to deliver and shut down, and a business owner's family life sucks.

Think about what's at stake in your business—the Core 5 Dimensions of your Belief, Relationships, Health, Wealth, and Freedom—and not just yours but for everyone who relies on you, from your employees to your vendors to your customers, as well as their families. Wouldn't you rather wake up each day with a clear vision of the road ahead so that you can confidently work through the day without surprises and disasters? That will help you run a better business, lead a better life, and contribute more effectively to your employees, vendors, and customers.

In the rest of the chapter, I'll show you how to master the future.

Take Action!
Recommended actions:

__ Think about what's at stake in your business. Who is relying on you? Name each person who is relying on you. Guess what… they're hoping that you can see far enough down the road in your business to keep your business from crashing.

__ Create a start-doing list and a stop-doing list based on this section of the chapter. Think about all the ways that you've been reactively running your business instead of proactively running your business. What challenges, obstacles, and disasters have halted your progress and what could you have done ahead of time if you knew about them? (Note: the purpose of this exercise isn't to get you to wallow in the struggles you've had but rather to think about a few times when you could have benefited from glimpsing the future).

Add your own actions:

__ Stop doing actions (Actions you currently do now but should stop doing)

_____

_____

__ Keep doing actions (Actions you currently do now and should keep doing)

_____

_____

__ Start doing actions (Actions you don't do now but should start doing)

_____

_____

__ Who will do new actions? (Assign the action to yourself or someone else)

_____

_____

__ By when? (When will these actions be complete?)

_____

_____

How To Master The Future

Remember the driving analogy I used earlier? I said that mastering the future was being able to see farther down the road in your business. But how far down the road should you look? When you're driving, you probably know the answer already: you look at various distances—sometimes you look at what's immediately in front of your car, sometimes you look at what is a car-length or two ahead, sometimes you look at 5-10 seconds ahead, and sometimes you look miles down the road. You can't drive well if you only focus on just one of these points; you need information from all of these points to drive successfully.

Likewise, in your business, mastering the future means looking at various distances into the future, and thinking about different things for each of those distances. For your business, you should be looking…

- An hour from now
- A day from now
- A week from now
- A month from now
- A quarter from now
- A year from now
- A decade from now

Think about what could happen in these time periods. You need to look at these varying times because everything in your business has a time period associated with it: for example, if you are about to talk to a customer, you need to look at an hour from now; if you're going to plan your day, you need to think about day from now; if you are going to think about payroll, you need to think about a week from now. And so on.

Look at each distance in the future and then reverse engineer it. Map in reverse to identify what you need to do between now and that future point to achieve the target you are thinking about. For example, you need to ask yourself: "In order for me to get to X target in ten years, I need to do this in nine years, this in eight years, this in seven years…" (and so on) all the way down to: "… and I need to do this in one year, this in the next quarter, this in the next month, this in the next week, and this tomorrow."

By doing this exercise, you put together a game plan that gives you specific activities in the near, medium, and distant future and each of those activities contributes not just to helping your business survive today but helping your business grow and succeed in the future.

Sometimes people believe that they can achieve their future vision without pain. But every great person has experienced pain. To get to greatness— to see your future vision ultimately materialized, you have to try many different ways and you have to expect some struggle and missteps along the way. But don't think of these as failures. Thomas Edison never failed, even though he didn't invent a light bulb until his 10,000th try. When asked about all the attempts he made along the way, he said he hadn't failed; he found 9,999 ways *not* to make a light bulb. Likewise in your business: as you view the future and then attempt to grow and improve your business to achieve that future vision, you should expect to discover a few ways not to do it!

To help you master the future, here are some key questions to answer:

- What is your largest opportunity in the next year?
- What is your largest challenge right now in your company?
- What is your largest resource or capability you would like to add to your company?

By asking these questions regularly and pushing my mind to come up with the answer, I've been able to tap into massive opportunities that would normally have slipped by. You can do the same. When you do, you'll discover that there are often too many opportunities to pursue and you'll also discover that you can optimize your business to run at full capacity more often.

And here's another way that you can master your future, with a tool called the Largest Tool Sheet, which you can download from the free resources page: **CEOWARRIOR.com/masteryresources**. On the Largest Tool Sheet, you'll list the strategies you want to pursue and then assess them against their potential ability to make you money, their ability to save you money, their alignment in your life, and more. This helps you identify and prioritize strategies to pursue.

Take Action!
Recommended actions:

__ Make a note in your schedule, occurring regularly, to glimpse into the various futures (one hour from now, one day from now, one week from now, etc.)

__ Ask yourself the three questions I listed in this section.

__ Download and use the Largest Tool Sheet to help you assess and prioritize which strategies to pursue.

Add your own actions:

__ Stop doing actions (Actions you currently do now but should stop doing)
_____
_____

__ Keep doing actions (Actions you currently do now and should keep doing)
_____
_____

__ Start doing actions (Actions you don't do now but should start doing)

_____

_____

__ Who will do new actions? (Assign the action to yourself or someone else)

_____

_____

__ By when? (When will these actions be complete?)

_____

_____

Master The Future By Solving The Problems Of The Future

Imagine what it would be like for your business if you forecasted a key industry change before any of your competitors and were able to prepare for it better than anyone else. How would your business be rewarded by such a decision?

Consider the story of Apple Inc. They pushed the cellphone to new levels of excellence and forecasted a generation of highly devoted mobile device users who won't use anything else. (Sure, other companies were doing something similar first—such as Blackberry—and other companies may even do it better, but Apple saw the future more clearly to identify what their customers really wanted... And they delivered with excellence.)

This kind of advanced thinking is possible for you. It might not always feel like you can be an industry leader while you're struggling through the day-to-day busyness of your business but if you start mastering the future, you can achieve this and you'll be rewarded for it.

In my service business I've seen trends change and, because I've been paying attention to them and intentionally mastering the future, I've been able to change my business ahead of the curve. (Bigger companies are often watching for what's changing while smaller companies don't—and those smaller companies miss out on the opportunities.)

You don't have to become an industry trend expert overnight to succeed at this. Most business owners do not have a crystal ball to show them the future. But in every industry there are industry thought-leaders who are already paying attention. Find those thought-leaders and follow them. Listen to them. Learn from them.

You're either ahead of the curve or behind the curve. Build knowledge and education to learn about industry changes and stay ahead of the curve.

Take Action!
Recommended actions:

__ What are the problems your industry will face in the future? You may read this question and then be at a loss for the answer right now. That's okay. This isn't a question you can immediately answer today. But think about it anyway. Think about it today, and tomorrow, and every day (schedule time in your planner to think about it). As you think about it, inspect trends and watch how they change. Before long, you'll start to glimpse the future. At first you'll glimpse the nearer future and then you'll be able to see farther and farther.

Add your own actions:

__ Stop doing actions (Actions you currently do now but should stop doing)

_____

_____

__ Keep doing actions (Actions you currently do now and should keep doing)

_____

_____

__ Start doing actions (Actions you don't do now but should start doing)

_____

_____

__ Who will do new actions? (Assign the action to yourself or someone else)

_____

_____

__ By when? (When will these actions be complete?)

_____

_____

Master The Future By Copying Others

Many business owners who are unhappy with their existing situation and want to improve their business make the following fatal mistake: they try to figure out how to improve and then they set out to do it—but in doing so, they try to break new ground or reinvent the wheel each time. This is a lot of work and it does not always lead to the success they strive for.

That's why I like the phrase that Tony Robbins said: "Success leaves clues." Whatever you want to do in your business—it's already been done by someone else. It's being done right now by other companies, even though it's not being done by you. There already is a proven roadmap for whatever you're imagining. Stop trying to invent your future and instead find another business that is already succeeding and copy them. It's so simple—perhaps it seems too simple—but the business owners who don't do it will continue to spend too much time, money, and energy and will struggle and ultimately not attain the better business they hope for.

Building a great business is not difficult—all you need to do is find someone who is already doing it and copy them.

Of course you want to only copy what might make sense and fit your market. Too many people copy the wrong things at the wrong time and wonder why they are getting no results. There is some strategic thinking that has to happen here.

Note: I don't recommend that you directly copy a business. I don't recommend or endorse copycat businesses. Each business stands in its own unique place and time. However, **you can draw inspiration from other**

companies and model the kinds of things that they're doing but apply them uniquely to you. Only copy the concepts that work but apply them individually to your unique business.

Take Action!
Recommended actions:

___ Identify a business that is really achieving the level of excellence that you aspire to achieve in your business. Find out what they're doing that makes them successful and see how you can model a similar approach in your own business.

Add your own actions:

___ Stop doing actions (Actions you currently do now but should stop doing)

_____

_____

___ Keep doing actions (Actions you currently do now and should keep doing)

_____

_____

___ Start doing actions (Actions you don't do now but should start doing)

_____

_____

___ Who will do new actions? (Assign the action to yourself or someone else)

_____

_____

___ By when? (When will these actions be complete?)

_____

_____

Master The Future With A Transformer

When you run your business, you're so busy meeting your day-to-day challenges that it's hard to keep your eye on the future. This entire book has been about helping you get control of today and master everything about your business so you can spend more time thinking about the future.

But all that day-to-day busyness can sometimes leave you feeling alone. I don't mean lonely, I mean alone: like you're fighting a five-alarm fire by yourself with just a small bucket of water. And it's easy for business owners to start down a path of good intentions—of learning to master their business and their future—only to find that the busyness of the day tends to crowd out all of the other things they need to think about.

Worse yet, these same business owners end up adopting an insanity approach where they do the same activities over and over and expect a different result. The want their business to grow but they don't do anything to make the change.

One of the best ways to make changes is to bring in an expert to help you. That's why coaches, mentors, consultants, and transformers are so critical to your business. The right coach, mentor, consultant, or transformer is someone who has already done what you want to do and can show you how to do it.

Here's how I define each of these experts:

- A coach cheers for you and helps you discover what you want to achieve. They root for you. They guide you. They help you to discover and articulate what you already know.
- A mentor is someone you can learn from (sometimes from a book; sometimes in person; sometimes they communicate through a channel like email or webinars) who will carefully guide you step by step and show you the way you need to go.
- A consultant is someone who is often more hands-on and may step into your business and help you do the work or may provide very specific advice to get you moving in the right direction. A consultant says "let me do this for you; watch me do it."

- A transformer is all three of the above wrapped into one. They have experienced what you're experiencing and can tell you what to do on all levels, filling the space of what you need to do at each stage. Transformers are hard to find today but they're out there. I am one of them.

I'll illustrate the difference between each of these experts in the following way: You've probably heard the saying, "give a man a fish and you'll feed him for a day but teach a man to fish and you'll feed him for life." Here's how each of these experts will apply this "teach-you-to-fish" concept:

Coaches will cheer you on as you fish. Mentors will show you how they fished and perhaps answer questions while you try fishing. Consultants will fish for you for a short period of time.

But as a transformer I teach you how to fish but I try to do so much more—I'll teach you why you're going to the fishing hole, and how to fish, and then I help you go for bigger fish.

I mention this so you understand that a coach, mentor, or consultant may come in different forms or have different labels, and as a transformer I try to take it a step further than the traditional ways that coaches, mentors, and consultants serve you.

So, which one do you need in your business? I believe that all businesses need at least one and usually some combination of these all the time.

To find the right expert in your business, first ask yourself where you want to go. Be specific. There might be many areas in your business you want to grow but start by focusing on just a couple of things. Then look at how one or more of these experts can save you the learning curve and fast track you forward more quickly than you would have achieved on your own.

Then, as you look for an expert to help you, remember that you should be looking for someone who has done it before and has a proven track record of success. After all, you wouldn't go to a 500 pound guy to learn to eat healthy!

The giants in business—Warren Buffett, Steve Jobs, Bill Gates, and others—have tons of advisers and experts on their team. They have advisers help them with business and finance but they even have advisers who guide them spiritually as well.

In fact, I believe so strongly in learning from experts that I've invested more than $900,000 dollars in coaching, training, and education. And the results of that investment? I have a company that runs without my day-to-day input, and it generates more than $30 million a year... because I went to the experts to teach me.

Let me clarify a key point here: sometimes you might be tempted to skip a coach, mentor, consultant, or transformer because you view the expense as a cost instead of an investment. I've seen business owners partner with other people because they don't want to pay the up-front investment but instead feel that a partner has skin in the game and therefore might be more motivated to see the business succeed. However, I ask the following two questions to set business owners back on track: "Why would you give up a percentage of your profit to a partner when you can hire a coach, mentor, or consultant for much less?" And, "What is the likelihood of your business growing to achieve your targets when (according to Forbes) nearly 80% of business partnerships fail?" A coach, mentor, consultant, or transformer can help you do the same thing with a lower failure rate—plus you keep all of your profit!

And forget free coaching because it's worth exactly what you pay. They're not going to be devoted to you. An expert should be someone who is committed and devoted to your progress. They should encourage you, guide you, show you the best way, take you to a higher level, and hold you accountable. That's how these experts help you see the future.

Working with an expert is one of the best ways you can grow your business and compel change. **I love this quote by Sir Isaac Newton: "If I have seen further, it is by standing on the shoulders of giants". That's exactly what I'm recommending you do in your business. Find some giants—some transformers—and then stand on their shoulders to see further into the future of your business.**

Take Action!
Recommended actions:

__ Identify one person who can help you in your business—a coach, mentor, consultant, transformer—an expert who understands your business and can help you take it to the next level.

__ Get in touch with this person immediately and arrange a time to meet with them to review and assess your business and to start making changes.

__ Understand that this is a commitment—it's not an instant fix—so set aside time and budget to invest into this transformation.

Add your own actions:

__ Stop doing actions (Actions you currently do now but should stop doing)

_____

_____

__ Keep doing actions (Actions you currently do now and should keep doing)

_____

_____

__ Start doing actions (Actions you don't do now but should start doing)

_____

_____

__ Who will do new actions? (Assign the action to yourself or someone else)

_____

_____

___ By when? (When will these actions be complete?)

_____

_____

Conclusion

The future arrives every single day, whether we're ready for it or not. Unfortunately, most business owners aren't ready for it and they're taken by surprise. Their business rounds the corner, they see an obstacle, and then everything screeches to a halt to deal reactively with that issue.

That's no way to run a business! It's expensive and it creates inconsistencies and undermines your finances and your ability to serve customers.

There's a better way: you can see into the future. It takes practice and regularly scheduled times when you focus on trying to figure out what the future holds. But when you do see into the future, you can create a better business today—one that will respond to changes before they appear.

Fortunately, you don't have to do this alone. One of the fastest and most effective ways to see into the future is with the help of an expert who has walked the path that you're now walking and knows exactly what you're facing. They can help you to see farther and understand what's happening in the industry and in your business, and they can help you create fundamental changes in your business.

Master Action List For Chapter 12

At the end of each section of this chapter you had actions to perform as well as Start Doing/Keep Doing/Stop Doing lists. Gather those actions together into a Master Action List, add any new actions that you think of, and then go through the questions below to think about how these actions can transform your life and your business:

___ **Is it going to make me money?** Are the actions you've listed going to help you generate more income? (If they are, great. Think about how they might be able to help you generate even more income. If they aren't making you more money then are those actions really as important as you thought they were?)

___ **Is it going save me money?** Reducing how much you spend will help you increase your profit. Are the actions you're thinking of doing going to help you cut back on your expenses without sacrificing the quality of your service? (If they save you money, great. If they aren't saving you money then are those actions really as important as you thought they were?)

___ **Is it going to save time?** Your time is precious and scarce. So the actions you take should help you to save time. Keep the big picture in mind because some actions may take a few extra minutes in the short term but will ultimately help you save time in the long term. (For example, training an employee might be an action that will take a few extra minutes now but will save you a lot of time in the future).

___ **Is it going to help me achieve market domination?** Your business needs to own the market it works in. Whenever someone thinks of the service you provide, they should only think of you. Do the actions you've listed in this chapter support that market domination? What can you change about them to help you dominate the market even further?

___ **How do I start fast to get the low-hanging fruit?** It's easy to say you're going to take action but it's much harder to actually do it. One way to take

action and push through to its successful completion is to go for the quick wins—the low-hanging fruit. From the actions you've listed, what low-hanging fruit can you immediately pick?

__ **What's the leverage?** Leverage has a few different meanings but, in this context, I'm talking about how you can motivate yourself. For example, if you commit to complete an action within a certain period of time you can leverage that commitment by saying, "If I don't make that commitment, I'll donate $10,000 to a charity." Since you may not have $10,000, and you'll probably feel some pain donating that much money, you are leveraging your commitment and compelling yourself to complete the actions you said you'd complete.

__ **What's the reward?** For each action, list what you expect to get out of it. If you can't think of a reward for the action, seriously consider whether it is as valuable as you thought. Spend more of your time on actions that have rewards. Two of the best rewards for your actions are below (although there are other rewards you may choose to take action for)…

__ **Is it going to help me achieve wealth?** One of the best rewards you can take action for is to achieve wealth. For each action ask whether that particular action will help you make more money to give you the sense of safety and achievement and allow you to buy whatever you want whenever you want it. If possible, develop the action even further if a stronger, clearer, bigger action will help you achieve more wealth.

__ **Is it going to help me get more freedom?** Another one of the best rewards you can take action for is to get more freedom—the time and financial capacity to do whatever you want whenever you want to (without sacrificing your business). For each action ask whether that particular action will help you get more freedom. If possible, develop the action even further if a stronger, clearer, bigger action will help you get more freedom.

CONCLUSION

Transformation doesn't happen with a single magic pill. **Deep transformation that enriches your life and gives you wealth and freedom can only happen when you make substantial transformation in yourself first and then in your business.** That's why, in *The Secrets of Business Mastery*, I covered Inner Mastery first and then Outer Mastery, and I showed you how you can build the life and business to achieve your dreams.

I'm extremely fortunate to meet business owner after business owner who have attended my Warrior Fast Track Academy events or who have read my books and who are now making those changes and seeing amazing results. Suddenly, the businesses that they once felt trapped in, perhaps even drowning in, become the exciting opportunities they've always wanted. I'm privileged to be a part of that progress.

You can have that in your business, too. Whether you're just starting your business or you've been at it awhile; whether your business is struggling with finding and keeping customers and profit or your business is way too busy and you feel like you have no life; no matter what kind of service business you run and no matter where in the world you run it, the lessons in this book can start you on the path to total transformation. Simply put: **This book is the roadmap that you can use to help you achieve wealth and freedom and market domination—true success (however you define the term) in your life.**

Now that you've read this book, you have a choice: You can close this book and put it on a shelf and go back to running your business like you always have, completely ignoring the strategies and actions you read here.

Or, you can re-read this book, keep it with you as a reference, and continually push yourself to implement the strategies and complete the actions I've showed you.

If you're ready to take control of your life and your business, to start implementing positive change and to see the successful results of wealth, freedom, and market domination, here's what you need to do next:

1. **Read this book again**: always actively read the book with pen, paper, and sticky notes nearby. Every time you read this book, no matter what level your business is at, actively reading it will help you derive more solid action steps that you can implement. Schedule time to read the book from front to back annually, and schedule time each week to refer to a chapter and take action on that chapter. That way, you're always working on your business (not in your business) using this book as a guide.

2. **Complete the action steps**: this book is not just a document of information; it's a document of transformative action. Throughout this book you've made lists of action steps. Now I want you to perform those action steps in your life and business. Take action always! (And when you read the book again, you'll create more action steps that you should implement right away.)

3. **Bookmark CEOWARRIOR.com**: you'll find a wealth of resources to help you, including a blog, and videos. Become familiar with this website and refer to it often.

4. **Sign up for weekly money making tips**: this is a must-read newsletter that arrives in your email inbox weekly. Sign up for it at **CEOWAR-RIOR.com** and watch your inbox for each issue.

5. **Get the free bonuses**: If you haven't done so yet, click to **CEOWAR-RIOR.com/masteryresources** and download the free resources that accompany this book.

6. **Connect with me on social media**: Visit **CEOWARRIOR.com** to find all the social media channels we can connect on.

7. **Watch for my next Warrior Fast Track Academy**: Warrior Fast Track Academy is a 4-day event to help business owners achieve real change

and real success in their business. I'll build on the lessons in this book. I'd like to see YOU at the next event and hear how this book has helped your business. Go to **WarriorFastTrackAcademy.com** to learn more.

You have the steps right here at your fingertips. **Now it's time to take action, take control, and master your life and business for more wealth, freedom, and market domination.**

GET ON THE FAST TRACK BY CREATING POWERFUL CHANGE IN YOUR BUSINESS

You've learned a lot in this book. Now it's time to implement it. On the following pages, you'll find powerful game-changing ways that can help you take what you've learned in this book and implement it into your business.

You'll connect directly with Mike and learn from him as he walks you through these areas of mastery. You'll create a powerful blueprint for your business (and your life). You'll be amazed at the changes.

WARRIOR FAST TRACK ACADEMY

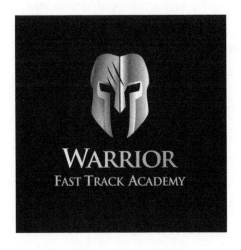

Are you tired of treading water—staying busy in your business but never really getting ahead? Are you ready to discover the most powerful strategies to create real change, growth, and market domination in your business?

Whether you're new and totally overwhelmed or you're a seasoned pro and looking to reignite, the Warrior Fast Track Academy can show you how to get to the next level.

Warrior Fast Track Academy is my 4-day hands-on event where I guide you and a group of like-minded service business owners through the exact strategies and plans that I used to build a $30+ million (and growing) business. I'll **reveal the blueprint and show you how you can implement the same blueprint into your business**, with all areas of mastery planned out and ready to be plugged in. You'll be motivated and inspired to lead positive, profitable change in your company and take your business to never-before-seen heights.

Business owners who have attended the Warrior Fast Track Academy have said it's "life changing" and gone on to build successful businesses all around the world.

If you want to take control of your business and your future, Warrior Fast Track Academy is THE event to make that happen. To see what others are saying about Warrior Fast Track Academy, to learn more about my $1 million guarantee, and to pre-register for an upcoming event, go to **WarriorFastTrackAcademy.com**

CEO WARRIOR CIRCLE

"You are the average of the 5 people you spend the most time with."
(Jim Rohn)

... Who are YOU spending time with?

Here's the fastest way to leverage the <u>power of proximity</u> by spending time with like-minded action-takers who work together—to grow your business while striving to become unstoppable.

Most industry groups and organizations take your money and give you just a few stale best practices and networking opportunities. But at CEO Warrior, we've created a powerful, exclusive "family of Warriors" who discover the best secrets and field-tested strategies, and who hold each other accountable while implementing them.

Welcome to the exclusive, invitation-only CEO Warrior Circle where business owners can join to become Warriors and inspiring leaders of a strong and growing business.

During the upcoming year we'll revolutionize your business and your life. We'll blow your wealth, freedom and personal goals out of the water by focusing on massive business building and life strategies. From weekly calls to exclusive events, from one-on-one coaching to an exclusive vault of swipe-and-deploy resources, joining the CEO Warrior Circle gives you everything you need to grow your business.

This program is designed for action-takers who are ready to make the commitment and take action to boost their business.

To learn more about the Warrior Circle, and to see if you qualify to participate in the Mastermind, get in touch at **CEOWARRIOR.com/contact**

Read The Free Magazine
Written For The Home Service Industry

Discover new information, insight, and industry-specific success stories in **Home ServiceMAX**—the free online magazine written for home service business owners.

Each issue of Home ServiceMAX is packed with practical tips and strategies that you can implement right away into your home service business. They're field-tested and written by experts and industry insiders.

Home ServiceMAX will help you improve your sales, marketing, finance, human resources and customer service. Keep it on hand as you develop best practices to meet your team's unique challenges.

Whether you're a plumber, electrician, carpenter, roofer, builder, painter or specialist in any other service industry trade, to survive you must also stand out as a business leader. We designed this magazine to help you achieve that goal.

Each easy-to-read issue is available online for free. Check out the articles and make sure you have a pen and paper in hand to write down all the actions you'll want to take when you're done each article.

Read the current issue and subscribe here: **HomeServiceMaxMag.com**

Get Mike To Speak To Your Group

Mike shares his best field-tested strategies and ideas with audiences all over the world in workshops, seminars, and keynote speeches.

From recruiting and training to marketing and service, Mike shares all of the same best practices he uses daily. He understands that real change starts within, so he's not afraid to address personal development topics like limiting beliefs and goal-setting, but he always brings it back to the practical strategies that will directly apply to his audience.

Put Mike in front of an audience and you'll have a rapt audience the entire time—begging for more by the end. Mike's engaging style and highly relevant topics will strike at the heart of your audience's most pressing problems. He'll connect with the audience by sharing his own story and then reveal powerful insights and ideas that they can apply immediately in their businesses. And, audiences love seeing Mike on webinars. Between his dynamic style and his tattoos, Mike isn't afraid of saying what needs to be said and he'll engage your audience while doing so.

Mike speaks on topics including:
- Recruiting and Training
- Culture
- Marketing
- Serving
- Limiting Beliefs
- Additional Trade Lines
- Market Domination

From Keynotes to workshops, from webinars to podcasts, Mike is comfortable speaking in many formats.

CEOWARRIOR.com/about-us/speakerskit

ABOUT THE AUTHOR

Mike Augugliaro helps his clients grow their service businesses utilizing his $30 Million Warrior Fast Track Academy blueprint, which teaches them how to achieve massive wealth, freedom, and market domination.

Two decades ago he founded Gold Medal Electric with his business partner Rob. After nearly burning out, he and Rob made a change: they developed a powerful blueprint that grew the company. Today, Gold Medal Service is now the top service industry provider in Central New Jersey. With over 190 staff and 140 trucks on the road, Gold Medal Service now earns over $30 million in revenue each year.

Mike is a transformer who helps service business owners and other entrepreneurs master themselves and their businesses, take control of their dreams and choices, and accelerate their life and business growth to new heights. Mike is the author of the popular book *The Secrets Of Business Mastery*, in which he reveals 12 areas that all service business owners need to master. He's also the author of *Secrets Of Leadership Mastery*, *Secrets Of Communication Mastery*, *The Nine Pillars Of Business Mastery*, and *Timeless Secrets Of A Warrior*.

Mike speaks and transforms around the world; his Warrior Fast Track Academy events are popular, transformational events for service business owners; he also leads a mastermind of business owners known as Warrior Circle. Mike has been featured in MSNBC, Financial Times, MoneyShow, CEO World, and more.

Mike is an avid martial artist who has studied karate, weaponry, jujitsu, and has even developed his own martial art and teaches it to others. The discipline of martial arts equips him to see and act on opportunities, create change in himself and others, and see that change through to successful completion.

Mike is a licensed electrician and electrical inspector, he is a certified Master Fire Walk Instructor, certified professional speaker, and a licensed practitioner of Neuro-Linguistic Programming (NLP).

Whether firewalking, breaking arrows on his neck, studying martial arts, transforming businesses, or running his own business, Mike Agugliaro leads by powerful example and is changing the lives and businesses of service business owners everywhere.

Mike lives in New Jersey with his wife and two children.

CONNECT WITH MIKE AGUGLIARO

Connect with Mike in the following places and find even more free resources and strategies to help you grow your business.

Website: **CEOWARRIOR.com**—Go here now to get free resources, including chapters from Mike's book and a library of resources.

Warrior App: **CEOWARRIOR.com/warriorapp**—stay up-to-date on the latest strategies and events by downloading the Warrior App for iOS and Android.

Podcast: **CEOWARRIOR.com/podcast**

Events: **CEOWARRIOR.com/events**

Social: Visit **CEOWARRIOR.com** to connect with Mike on Facebook, Twitter, LinkedIn, and elsewhere.

Home ServiceMAX Magazine: **HomeServiceMaxMag.com**

READ THESE BOOKS BY MIKE AGUGLIARO

Find these books and more at **CEOWARRIOR.com/books**

The Secrets Of Business Mastery: Build Wealth, Freedom and Market Domination For Your Service Business in 12 Months or Less. A chapter-by-chapter collection of best business practices, tools and strategies for service business owners.

Secrets of Leadership Mastery: 22 Powerful Keys To Unlock Your Team's Potential and Get Better Results. 22 powerful keys to help you create a culture where you build and lead a hardworking team of superstars, inspire them to give their very best, and generate measurable results.

Secrets of Communication Mastery: 18 Laser Focused Tactics To Communicate More Effectively. We all communicate. We can all learn to communicate more effectively. When you do, you'll see instant results in every personal and professional relationship.

Timeless Secrets of A Warrior. Discover the most powerful, time-tested Warrior secrets that will propel you toward success by revealing strategies from some of history's greatest minds.

9 Pillars Of Business Mastery Program. Discover the nine most powerful and transformative strategies that are PROVEN to completely transform your business and your life.

And, get a bundle of Mike's best strategies...

The Warrior Library. Want a free bundle of strategies, tools, and resources that I use daily in my $30+ million service business? The Warrior Library contains powerful strategies to help you achieve wealth, freedom, and market domination. Get them at: **CEOWARRIOR.com/warriorlibrary**

YOUR BUSINESS SUCKS!

(Or maybe it just feels that way!)

Perhaps your business is wearing you down every single day and you're thinking about shutting it down and going to work for someone else instead, just because it's easier.

Perhaps it's going okay (maybe it even feels successful) but you've hit a plateau and you can't quite break through—so it sucks because the higher level of success eludes you.

Here's the good news: your business doesn't have to suck. In fact, with just a few changes, you can unlock strong, rapid growth that completely changes the game for you:

- Earn more money and keep more of it as profit
- Hire A-players and build a strong culture where everyone loves to give their best
- Finally start generating real leads that turn into happy customers
- Build a business that runs on autopilot—so you have more time to spend with family

If you own a business that is not delivering more of these things to you daily then this book is for you. You'll discover the strategies and secrets you need to finally create a successful, fulfilling, meaningful business for you.

Learn more about the book at: **CEOWARRIOR.com/books/whyyourbusinesssucks**

Morgan James
Speakers Group

www.TheMorganJamesSpeakersGroup.com

We connect Morgan James published authors with live and online events and audiences whom will benefit from their expertise.

Printed in the USA
CPSIA information can be obtained
at www.ICGtesting.com
JSHW082227140824
68134JS00016B/766

9 781683 503255